BRAINDANCE

UNIVERSITY PRESS OF FLORIDA / STATE UNIVERSITY SYSTEM

Florida A&M University, Tallahassee
Florida Atlantic University, Boca Raton
Florida Gulf Coast University, Ft. Myers
Florida International University, Miami
Florida State University, Tallahassee
University of Central Florida, Orlando
University of Florida, Gainesville
University of North Florida, Jacksonville
University of South Florida, Tampa
University of West Florida, Pensacola

UNIVERSITY PRESS OF FLORIDA

Gainesville
Tallahassee
Tampa
Boca Raton
Pensacola
Orlando
Miami
Jacksonville
Ft. Myers

BRAINDANCE

Revised and Expanded Edition

New Discoveries
about Human Origins
and Brain Evolution

Dean Falk

09 08 07 06 05 04   6 5 4 3 2 1

ISBN 0-8130-2738-1
A record of cataloging-in-publication information is available from the Library
of Congress.

The University Press of Florida is the scholarly publishing agency for the State
University System of Florida, comprising Florida A&M University, Florida Atlantic
University, Florida Gulf Coast University, Florida International University, Florida
State University, University of Central Florida, University of Florida, University
of North Florida, University of South Florida, and University of West Florida.

University Press of Florida
15 Northwest 15th Street
Gainesville, FL 32611-2079
http://www.upf.com

For Helen Taverniti—pianist extraordinaire and dearest,
most-beloved aunt

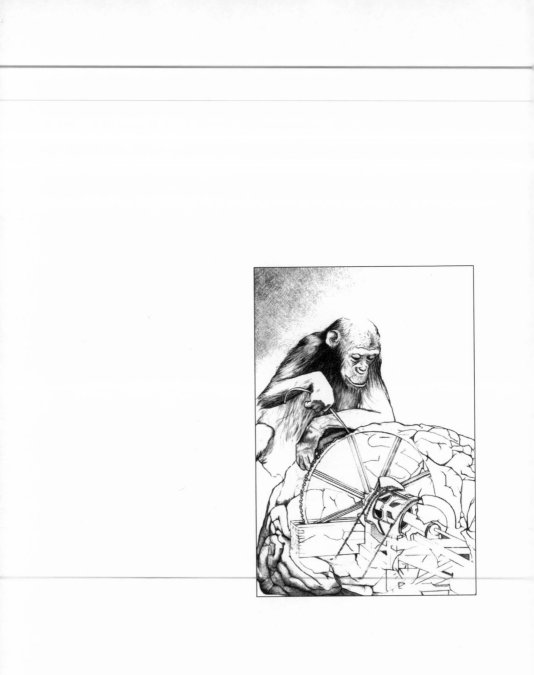

CONTENTS

ACKNOWLEDGMENTS

Because the field of paleoanthropology moves so rapidly, a good deal of updating was required in order to revise and expand *Braindance* in light of what has been learned about human evolution in the past decade. I am deeply grateful to a number of people for their help with this project. First and foremost, my wonderful editor, John Byram, is thanked for suggesting that a second edition of *Braindance* be prepared and published with the University Press of Florida. I've worked with John before (on *Primate Diversity*) and have come to regard him as a friend as well as a superb, insightful editor. Michele Fiyak-Burkley has been a great project editor, and I am also indebted to Adrienne Zihlman, not only for her great research, but for urging that this book be updated. I struggled mightily with whether to continue using the term "hominid," or to go with the more recent alternative, "hominin." I am grateful to Glenn Conroy for helping me with this dilemma. (In this edition, "hominin" is used because, unlike current use of its predecessor, everybody understands it to mean the same thing—namely, what "hominid" used to mean!) Speaking of which, I am particularly pleased to have John Reader's beautiful photographs of fossil hominins included in this edition. (For others, see his book *Missing Links: The Hunt for Earliest Man.*) Curt Busse is gratefully acknowledged for providing rare and wonderful photographs of wild chimpanzees. The introductory sketches for chapters 5 and 9 of this edition were created by Brian Worthington, and Joyce Crocker envisioned and sketched the others. Brian is also thanked for preparing a number of other illustrations for this edition, and I am grateful to Ann Powell for help with preparation of the manuscript and to Michelle Hughes-Markovics for help with the index. Last, but not least, Ray Stanyard is thanked for providing the flattering author's portrait that graces the jacket.

During the course of my education, I was extremely fortunate to have three mentors who nurtured my development as a physical anthropologist and paleoneurologist. Although they should not be held responsible for the opinions expressed in this book, were it not for the guidance and inspiration of the late Charles A. Reed, the late Leonard Radinsky, and the very extant C. Loring Brace, *Braindance* would never have been written.

NOTE ON THE REFERENCES

The references in this book follow a citation style popular in scientific journals. The superscript numbers in the text refer to the list of numbered references, divided by chapter, located at the back of the book.

INTRODUCTION

Around five to seven million years ago, a group of apelike individuals moved away from their relatives and began evolving in an independent direction that would one day allow their descendants to become human beings. This remarkable event occurred somewhere in Africa and, early on, these ancestors of ours started walking on two legs. It was at that point that these creatures with long arms, hairy skins, and large canines ceased to be apes and became the first hominins,[1] the earliest of which are generally called "australopithecines."

Charles Darwin's 1859 publication of *On the Origin of Species* sparked what would become an arduous controversy between creationists and evolutionists about the origin of human beings. Half a century later, many scientists and some of the public had reconciled their religious beliefs with the theory of natural selection and had even begun to apply that theory to the question of human origins. Yet many people still had difficulty with the notion of missing links and, in particular, the idea that we are descended from apelike ancestors. (The wife of England's Bishop Wilberforce, Darwin's unsuccessful tormentor, put it this way when she addressed the great scientist in private: "You say we are descended from monkeys? Well, I certainly trust you will not tell anyone else.") This attitude prevailed in the United States as late as 1925, when John Scopes was convicted of a crime for teaching evolutionary theory to high school students in Dayton, Tennessee.

In a now-classic paper published that same year, a South African anatomist named Raymond Dart announced the discovery of the first australopithecine, a fossilized hominin child from a place called Taung.

FIGURE I.
Genetic studies show that living people and chimpanzees share a common ancestor that lived between five and seven million years ago.

Dart's specimen seemed to reveal a mixture of apelike and humanlike features. Given the anti-intellectual climate within which Dart interpreted his find, it is perhaps not surprising that he overemphasized the humanlike attributes of his small fossil and downplayed its apelike qualities. At that time, people were probably more likely to accept a humanlike rather than an apelike ancestor, and it is possible that this fact subconsciously influenced early efforts to interpret fossil hominins.

Dart and his colleagues established what was to become a long tradition of overemphasizing and overinterpreting the *humanlike* features of Taung and the other australopithecine fossils eventually discovered nearby. A decade ago, when *Braindance* was first published, many paleoanthropologists still insisted that australopithecines were more humanlike than apelike, especially in the refinement of their bipedalism, the development of their teeth, and the morphology of their brains. Since then, the application of recently developed measurement techniques to the study of australopithecine fossils has convinced many workers—myself included—that Dart's australopithecines were far more apelike than previously believed.

This is not to say that all scientists agree with that assessment and that advocacy has been removed from the study of hominin paleontology. Far from it! Controversies rage over technical matters and scientists must decide, for example, which has greater value for evolutionary studies—direct examination of the fossil record or comparative studies of molecules of living species? Similarly, is it better to reckon the evolutionary relationships between different groups on the basis of special features whose functions may or may not be known (cladistic analysis) or by comparing the evolution of whole integrated physiological systems in these groups (functional morphology)? Yet, although evolutionary biologists may quibble mightily about such technical details, they all share a conceptual framework that is grounded in Darwinian theory. Their theoretical differences of opinion eventually get resolved by scientific means, despite the uninformed yelps of delight from creationists who assume that such differences invalidate evolutionary theory.

Clearly, there continues to be much dispute over theoretical interpretation of the hominin fossil record. Paleoanthropologists believe that bipedalism provided a major impetus for the origin of hominins, and delineation of its causes is one of the hottest topics (and biggest mysteries) in hominin paleontology. Although the assumption that males were the primary focus of selection for various good and noble human features has lost much of its earlier credibility, the debate about the relative importance of man the hunter versus woman the gatherer still simmers, and the convergence of sexual politics with paleoanthropology continues to influence discussions about our origins. However, these controversies are nothing compared with those that ensue when investigators staunchly defend their prize fossils or their published hominin family trees—no matter what the evidence. Ten years ago, this was happening in the case of a fossil called Lucy. Today's bones of contention involve newly discovered specimens nicknamed Toumai ("hope of life"), "Original Man" (*Orrorin*), "root hominin" (*Ardipithecus*), and numerous others.

Consensus has changed about several surprising issues in the last decade. When this book was first published, received wisdom held that hominins originated in East Africa's famed Rift Valley. That view was upset in 1995 with the announcement that a French team led by Michel Brunet had discovered an australopithecine jaw some fifteen hundred miles west of the Rift Valley, at a site in Chad. As discussed in this edition, older and even more exciting fossils have since been discovered in Chad, so pinpointing the country or even the general region where hominins originated in Africa has become problematical. Similarly, most workers used to believe that early hominins evolved in relatively open, savanna grasslands. This idea is currently under revision because a number of the very earliest hominins that have recently been discovered appear to be associated with forested rather than open habitats. If true, this suggestion has important implications for the origins of bipedalism that are discussed in this edition. A third major change concerns the timing of the original migration of early hominins from Africa to other parts of the world. A decade ago, this event was estimated to have occurred around one million years ago. Today, that estimate has been pushed back to approximately two million years ago—quite a change and, again, one that has important implications for understanding human evolution.

Despite the field's recognition of these major changes, hominin paleontology continues to be contentious, and one reason why this is so is because it is very much like an Old Boys' club. To study fossils, you've got to be *privy* to them. Somebody has to let you into the shop. But the shop, alas, is a fairly closed one. Just a few people in the world control access to the archaeological sites and fossils that must be studied if one is to do the research necessary to understand our origins. It is tough for independent workers whose scientific contributions conflict with the ideas of established authorities because their work is frequently dismissed out-of-hand, if not simply ignored (and I am not thinking only of myself). If an outsider *does* succeed in getting new ideas published and discussed, he or she had better have a sturdy hide. This is doubly true for individuals who obtain permits to conduct fieldwork at important archaeological sites.

Lest I sound too petulant, I am pleased to say this book is less about the politics of paleoanthropology than it is about hominin brain evolution. Early in my career, I was lucky enough to be allowed into an inner sanctum in South Africa to study casts of the interior of fossil skulls (endocasts) that reflect the brain's anatomy. To my surprise, these endocasts clearly indicated that the cerebral cortex of australopithecines was apelike, rather than humanlike, as had been believed since Dart's initial publication on the Taung fossil. Although my observations were documented and innocent of preconceived ideas, upon their publication I found myself plunged into what would become a decades-long bitter controversy. As discussed in chapter 2, this particular controversy has recently taken a surprisingly refreshing turn.

Because australopithecine brains appeared apelike, it was necessary to investigate other early hominins to learn something about the evolution of the human brain. I therefore turned my attention to the fossil record of *Homo,* which goes back just a little less than two million years. And what a record it is. Not only did humanlike cerebral cortices first appear in early *Homo,* but brain size continued to increase, so that by the time of *Homo sapiens* it was triple the volume of an australopithecine brain. Why did brain size continue to increase dramatically in *Homo?* And what about the relationship between bipedalism and brain evolution? It used to be thought that the two were linked. Mary Leakey's spectacular discovery in 1978 of fossilized footprints of early hominins that lived 3.6 million years ago showed that this was not the case. The makers of the footprints had clearly been bipedal, walking upright long before brain size increased in *Homo.* Why, then, did bipedalism precede the increase in brain size? More than a decade ago, I attempted an answer, the radiator hypothesis of brain evolution, which you will encounter in this book along with an update about its controversial reception and relevant evidence that has become available since then.

But there is more to studying brain evolution than just looking at skulls and endocasts. Much can be gleaned from comparing the brains and cognitive capacities of humans with those of our closest nonhuman relatives, the chimpanzees. Comparative psychologists show us that chimpanzees are smart. Some chimps have even been taught nonverbal language. However, unlike most children, no chimpanzee has ever looked at its human caretaker and asked the question, Where do I come from? Chimpanzees are intelligent, but they simply do not have brains that are capable of formulating abstract questions.

Although the cerebral cortex of humans is larger and more convoluted than that of chimpanzees, human and chimp brains appear superficially to have the same parts. Thus, it appears that subtle differences in the nervous systems of humans and chimpanzees, not gross anatomy, are what count. These involve, in particular, the wiring and the distribution of neurochemicals in the frontal lobes and association cortices, as well as the right/left contrasts in brain organization called lateralization.

The evolution of brain lateralization that occurred over the last two million years must have been especially important because modern humans depend on the left side of the brain for functions related to spoken language and right-handedness and on the right side of the brain for other abilities such as comprehending maps and composing music. Because these skills are unique in humans, it was believed until quite recently that humans were the only primates with lateralized brains. However, thanks to the dazzling work of investigators studying the nervous systems of rodents, birds, and nonhuman primates, it is now apparent that brain lateralization is the rule, rather than the exception, for a large variety of animals. The lateralized skills that appear to be uniquely human are actually derived from the less-lateralized calling, singing, and dexterity systems of our primate ancestors. Thus, although the extent of brain lateralization in humans is dramatic, it represents an end product on an evolutionary continuum rather than an evolutionary leap.

A second myth is that the brains of men and women are exactly the same. This misconception has now been put to rest, partly because of breakthrough research on the effects of sex hormones on the brain. This book provides an evolutionary model that attempts to elucidate the ongoing evolution of brain lateralization in hominins while taking into account gender differences in the nervous system.

During the past nearly two million years the dramatic increase in brain size in *Homo* was accompanied not only by subtle shifts in the details of the wiring and the distribution of neurochemicals, but also by an equally dramatic cultural and intellectual evolution. At the bottom of the lineage, we find clunky stone tools; at today's "top" there are skyscrapers, biotechnology, and e-mail. Other spin-offs of *Homo*'s evolved brain include language, religion, art, writing, and music. Simply put, the evolutionary package of neurological changes in *Homo* was unprecedented in the evolutionary histories of other mammals, even including earlier hominins.

I once saw Rudolph Nureyev dance. The steps he did were known to any skilled ballet dancer, but the whole performance clicked in a way I had not seen before. The timing was perfect and the choreography seemed inspired. It was breathtaking. As is true for dance, it is the overall choreography of brain evolution that is unique, not its individual parts or steps. This is why the human brain has failed to evolve new gross structures that differ from those found in the chimpanzee brain.

In conventional dance, such as tap dancing, a shift in the emphasis within certain combinations of steps completely changes the feel of a routine. Thus, the sequence of steps may be identical for two routines, but because of different emphases, the resulting dances are not the same. As evolution progressed, shifts occurred in the timing of developmental events within different parts of *Homo*'s brain. As with dance, change the timing and the resulting brain is not the same. For example, the branching of nerves appears more complex in Broca's speech area on the left side of the human frontal lobe than in the equivalent region on the right. This asymmetry seems to occur because, postnatally, the region on the left develops at a slower rate and for a longer duration than its counterpart on the right. Presumably, this shift in development between right and left hemispheres occurred in conjunction with natural selection for language.

The right hemisphere matures more rapidly than the left during prenatal development as well. Even the slightest shift in the relative maturation rates of the two hemispheres can alter the balance between the specific prenatal hormonal environment and the relative stages of development of the two growing hemispheres. Since hormonal influences differ depending on the stage of development, subtle shifts in maturation rates of the two hemispheres may have provided an underlying mechanism for increased brain lateralization in *Homo*. (Such thinking is consistent with the emerging academic field of "EvoDevo," which focuses on the genetics and evolution of developmental processes across a wide range of species.) As other have suggested, prenatal shifts in developmental events may sometimes mark a fine line between mental retardation and giftedness. For the reasons listed above, and because the human brain has yielded numerous aesthetic achievements (such as Nureyev's dance), I refer to *Homo*'s evolutionary trajectory during the past two million years as the braindance.

I believe that Einstein's theory of relativity, Mozart's horn concertos, and the enormous brain of *Homo sapiens* are all due to a fortunate set of serendipitous coincidences that led to this braindance. As discussed in conjunction with the radiator hypothesis, one coincidence is that some of the hominins who were preadapted for bipedalism happened to live in just the right thermal environment for achieving both full bipedalism and a big brain. Another happy accident is that these hominins had an impetus for refining their bipedalism because they had to travel to find their daily food and water. By shaping motor patterns, communication skills, and the cleverness needed to survive in such a harsh savanna habitat, natural selection sculpted a subtly rewired human brain.

There is, alas, a dark side to the braindance. As in chimpanzees' brains, the deep part of the human brain that processes emotions (known as the limbic system) causes humans to divide the world into friends and enemies. Consequently people, like chimpanzees, are capable of carrying out atrocious acts of violence against their own kind. The same evolved brain that is responsible for human activities such as writing poetry or composing symphonies continues to be fascinated with global military endeavors that could put an abrupt end to the braindance. Although the cortical mechanisms for controlling aggression are part of the neurological package that we inherited from our hominin ancestors, our species needs to exercise vigilantly those controls over our natural primate tendency to engage in potentially catastrophic dominance interactions. Which will ultimately win out—the braindance, or the brainwar? The choice is ours, and events that have unfolded since *Braindance* was first published suggest that we should take it very seriously.

I am sometimes asked why, given the politics of paleoanthropology, I continue to pursue research on human brain evolution. The answer is that the long-established tradition of selective interpretation and advocacy in hominin paleontology—and in other fields where politics comes into play as well—is slowly being replaced by a new spirit of scientific objectivity. As much as anything, this book celebrates the investigators whose work is changing our views of human evolution.

chapter 1

FORAGING IN THE RED CAVE

It is odd how seemingly insignificant events can influence whole fields of inquiry. For example, if a young science student at the University of Witwatersrand in Johannesburg, South Africa, had not had dinner at the home of the director of the Northern Lime Company one night in 1924, the entire direction and tenor of paleoanthropology would probably be different than it is today. But Josephine Salmons had her dinner, and in the process, she unknowingly set paleoanthropology on an irrevocable course.

At her hosts' home, Josephine admired a fossilized skull of an extinct baboon that sat on the mantel. The specimen had been blasted loose from a lime quarry at a place known then as Taungs (now shortened to Taung). Josephine knew that her anatomy professor, Dr. Raymond Dart, had a keen interest in fossils so she asked if she could show the little specimen to him. Her instincts proved right. Upon seeing the skull, Dart was so intrigued that he arranged to have other potentially interesting fossils from Taung crated and sent to his home in Johannesburg.

Dart describes what happened the day he looked out his window and saw two men in South African Railway uniforms staggering up the driveway with two large wooden boxes:

> As soon as I removed the lid a thrill of excitement shot through me. On the very top of the rock heap was what was undoubtedly an endocranial cast or mold of the interior of the skull. Had it been only the fossilized brain cast of any species of ape it would have ranked as a great discovery, for such a thing had never before been reported. But I knew at a glance that what lay in my hands was no ordinary anthropoidal brain. . . . I stood in the shade holding the brain as greedily as any miser hugs his gold, my mind racing ahead. Here, I was certain, was one of the most significant finds ever made in the history of anthropology.[1]

Dart discovered that the endocranial cast (endocast) fit perfectly into a separate hunk of limestone. Furthermore, tantalizing hints of fossilized skull, face, and jaw from the same individual could be seen protruding from the limestone. Dart carefully chiseled away the cementlike matrix that embedded the specimen—a laborious process that took more than two months. Finally, on December 23, 1924, "the rock parted" and the Taung fossil was freed from the limestone. "What emerged," wrote Dart, "was a baby's face, an infant with a full set of milk teeth and its permanent molars just in the process of erupting. I doubt if there was any parent prouder of his offspring than I was of my Taung baby on that Christmas."[2]

Dart's fossil, known as the Taung "child" (but called Taung hereafter in this text), displayed a combination of apelike and humanlike features that had never before been seen in living or fossil species. According to Dart, Taung's humanlike features included its rounded forehead, the pattern of brain convolutions reflected on the endocast, certain details of the teeth, and the location of the spinal column in a central position (associated with the ability to walk on two legs). But the specimen appeared apelike in the forward thrust of its jaws and in the small size of its brain.

Clearly, Dart had found a missing link, and he said so in a landmark paper in the February 7, 1925, issue of *Nature*. In that paper, Dart named a new genus and species to accommodate his find; instead of being as-

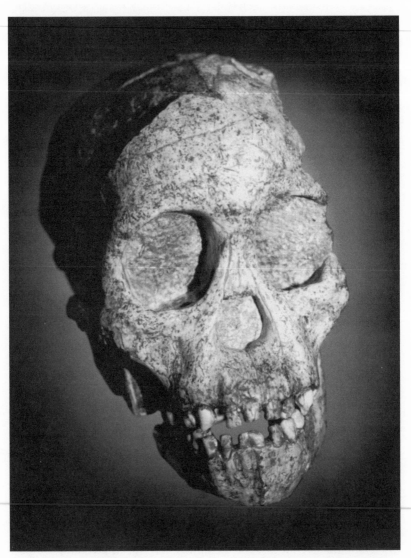

FIGURE I.I.

The first australopithecine discovered from Taung, South Africa, in 1924. Known as the Taung "child," this fossil displays a combination of apelike and humanlike features, mostly the former, that had never been seen in living or fossil species before Raymond Dart's discovery. (Photograph by John Reader, copyright 1992/Science Photo Library.)

signed to *Homo sapiens,* Taung was designated *Australopithecus africanus* ("southern man-ape from Africa"). In keeping with Dart's terminology, the common term used today for Taung and the other earliest known relatives of humans is "australopithecine."

From the outset, Dart and his colleagues overemphasized and over-interpreted the humanlike features of Taung and all other australo-pithecine fossils. This bias is reflected in Dart's reference to Taung as a "man-ape" instead of an "ape-man" in the title of his 1925 paper.[3] Hindsight suggests two reasons why Dart may have overstated the human-ness of australopithecines. The first is historical and should perhaps be viewed with some sympathy. Although Dart knew that Taung "was one of the most significant finds ever made in the history of anthropology" and was sure that Taung was truly a missing link, how was he to persuade the world of this in the anti-intellectual climate that then prevailed? His dilemma becomes apparent when one remembers that less than five months after the announcement of Taung's discovery in *Nature,* John Scopes would be convicted for teaching evolutionary theory to high school students in Dayton, Tennessee (July 21, 1925). At the time the public did not take kindly to the notion of human ancestors as ape-men. Clearly, the more humanlike it was described to be, the more palatable Taung would be as an early hominin ancestor. As mentioned in the introduction, this situation may have subsequently influenced Dart's assessment of Taung.

The second reason Taung's humanlike features were overemphasized may have been because it was a child. Like humans, other primates go through stages as they grow up. In his analysis of Taung, Dart did not fully appreciate that infant apes have not had time to develop features of the skull, such as thickened eyebrow ridges or attachment areas for heavy neck muscles, which set adult apes apart from humans. Apparently he did not carefully consider the possibility that Taung's rounded forehead or the inferred position of the spinal cord might be due to the immaturity of the apelike specimen rather than to its resemblance to humans.

These observations, made with the advantage of hindsight, are not meant to detract from the fact that Dart made a major contribution to the study of human evolution. Dart lived to be ninety-five years old and had the pleasure of seeing the essence, if not all the details, of his views vindicated. In a field fraught with contention, everyone now agrees that Dart was right about certain things: australopithecines were our earliest known ancestors, they walked on two legs (although not for the reasons Dart believed), and they manifested a combination of apelike and humanlike features. Even Dart's species designation of *Australopithecus africanus* has survived in a discipline that often sinks names shortly after they are proposed.

Much of the foregoing can be found in any introductory textbook on physical anthropology. But the story of the Taung specimen is really more complex. Fossils representing at least thirty australopithecine individuals were found during the 1930s and 1940s. Dart, along with his supporters, again emphasized the humanlike features and downplayed the apelike features of these specimens, possibly in response to early critics who dismissed the importance of these finds. Particularly vexing to these workers was the fact that the brain of Taung was about the size of that of a chimpanzee. In his 1925 article, Dart had claimed that the brain of Taung was humanlike. As it turned out, he was wrong about that.

Dart's biased analysis of Taung began what would become a long tradition of selective interpretation of evidence in paleoanthropology. Recent workers have promoted Dart's view of our earliest ancestors as humanlike because of the australopithecines' bipedalism (Owen Lovejoy of Kent State University), dentition (Alan Mann of University of Pennsylvania), or brain organization (Ralph Holloway of Columbia University). However, these previously accepted conclusions are rapidly being modified as investigators bring more advanced techniques to the study of hominin evolution. Brigitte Senut (currently of the Musée National d'Histoire Naturelle, Paris) was one of the first to challenge the traditional view, in her 1978 dissertation at the University of Paris, when she showed that the arm bones of certain australopithecines indicated that these bipeds continued to spend a good deal of time in the trees. Based on rigorous analyses of limb bones and joint surfaces, Bill Jungers and his colleagues from the State University of New York at Stony Brook have also argued convincingly that bipedalism in early hominins was not as refined as it is in modern humans. Studies of dentition by Holly Smith (University of Michigan) and Tim Bromage (Hunter College) show that the age of death for Taung is better estimated by using information about tooth development for apes than for humans. Furthermore, Glenn Conroy (Washington University School of Medicine) and Michael Vannier (University of Iowa College of Medicine) have verified this conclusion by using high-resolution computerized tomography (CT scans) to see previously hidden structures in the Taung skull. It now appears that Taung was even younger than initially believed—between three and four years of age, rather than between five and six, as Dart believed.

As Holly Smith points out, an important implication of the finding that the Taung fossil and other early hominins are more apelike than humanlike is that australopithecines matured quickly, as apes do. Based on incremental growth markings in teeth, A. D. Beynon (Dental School at Newcastle-upon-Tyne) and Christopher Dean (University College, London) concur that, unlike human children, australopithecines did not have prolonged childhoods during which they were educated and socialized by their parents. It is amazing that it took nearly sixty-five years to realize these and other important facts about what may be the world's most famous fossil. I attribute these belated realizations to a field that sometimes venerates its established authorities more that it does scientific objectivity. Because of this, the scientific method was slow to arrive at paleoanthropology's doorstep. I can't help but wonder if it wouldn't have gotten there sooner if Josephine Salmons had been invited to dinner in another decade, or if the first australopithecine had been an adult.

Two Types of Early Hominins: *Australopithecus* Big, *Australopithecus* Little

In retrospect, it is curious that it took more than ten years for scientists to find adult australopithecines that might have been Taung's "parents." That task fell primarily to Robert Broom, a Scottish physician who had a consuming interest in fossils and was one of the first to recognize the validity of Dart's claim that Taung was a missing link. Today, Broom's picture appears in many textbooks, and appropriately so, for it was he who discovered the very important fact that there was more than one kind of australopithecine.

Broom's first discovery occurred in 1936, when the manager of a lime quarry at Sterkfontein showed him an endocast from an adult hominin.

Broom soon found parts of the skull from the same young adult male. Broom was a "splitter"—that is, he tended to give each new fossil a new species name, and that's what he did in this case. Today, however, Broom's first discovery is recognized as a member of the species named by Dart in 1925, *Australopithecus africanus*. Because their skulls are generally more graceful looking than those of the second type of australopithecine (which Broom would not discover for another two years), these hominins are referred to as gracile australopithecines. (Technically, the term hominin refers to members of the tribe that includes both australopithecines and *Homo*.)

The early history of hominin paleontology is wonderfully romantic. In his book *Finding the Missing Link*, Broom tells how, in 1938, a schoolboy named Gert Terblanche "drew from the pocket of his trousers four of the most wonderful teeth ever seen in the world's history." After Gert showed Broom a site called Kromdraai where he had discovered the teeth, they found and pieced together more of the fossil. When they finished, Broom saw that they had assembled the skull of an adult male australopithecine. However, this one differed from the one found two years earlier at Sterkfontein because it was much more heavily built and had a comparatively enormous face. As was his habit, Broom gave the fossil a new name, christening his new find *Paranthropus robustus* in honor of its massiveness. This specimen and others like it are generally known today as robust australopithecines.

During the late 1930s and 1940s, numerous other australopithecine fossils were discovered in South Africa, many of them by Broom, who cheerfully went about assigning them new names. It was not until the 1950s that another worker, John Robinson, sorted out the confusion of these many hypothetical species. Sorting through the mishmash of australopithecine fossils, he discovered that certain features separated australopithecines into just two groups. Early South African hominins were either gracile (*Australopithecus africanus*) or robust (*Paranthropus robustus*) australopithecines. Robust australopithecines were characterized by enormous back teeth and huge, flat faces that provided anchorage for massive chewing muscles that operated jaws that can only be described as humongous. Still other chewing muscles were anchored to a bony crest that was located from front to back, along the middle of the top of

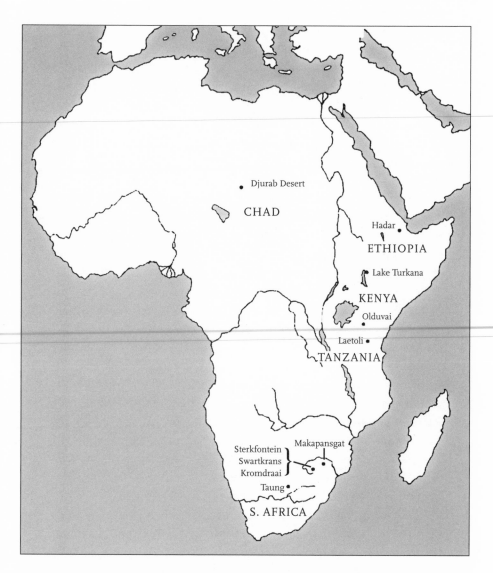

FIGURE I.2.
Approximate locations of important hominin discoveries in Africa.

the skull. (As is the case for gorillas, this crest, the sagittal crest, is more pronounced in males than in females.) Although robust australopithecines appeared apelike in these features, the markings on their skulls for neck muscles indicated to Robinson that their posture was erect and that they therefore walked on two legs. *Paranthropus robustus,* in short, was a bipedal chewing machine.

Gracile australopithecines were different. They had larger anterior teeth and much smaller back teeth than those found in robust hominins. This caused their lower face to protrude more. Their upper face and cheeks were built less massively, however. This combination of features resulted in faces that were dish-shaped rather than flat and, in general, less rugged than faces of *Paranthropus.* Gracile australopithecine skulls also appeared to have higher foreheads and to be more rounded than the skulls of robust australopithecines, partly because the former lacked the midline crest of bone that decorated the latter.

Robinson went on to interpret the physical differences of the two types of australopithecines in functional terms. Because most of the distinctions between gracile and robust australopithecines had to do with teeth or chewing muscles, Robinson proposed his now-famous dietary hypothesis: robust australopithecines used their enormous back teeth to crush and grind tough roots, bulbs, and other gritty vegetable matter. As vegetarians, these early hominins had lost the large front teeth for tearing meat or processing nonvegetable foods. Gracile australopithecines, on the other hand, retained their ancestors' large front dentition, which was useful for processing all kinds of food, including meat. In other words, while robust australopithecines specialized in a limited menu, gracile australopithecines ate what they could get.

And getting food could be difficult for gracile australopithecines, who, according to Robinson, were dealing "with the stresses of a somewhat hostile environment."[4] Nevertheless, Robinson conceded, "implements for digging will have made possible greater exploitation of . . . bulbs. . . . Implements for bashing, hitting, or throwing . . . will have made capture and consumption of small animals much easier. Improved tool-using will thus have been favored." Clearly, Robinson thought that *Australopithecus* walked on two legs and carried a big stick, and that meat-eating was crucial for the evolution of this early hominin. Although *Paranthropus* probably used tools, wrote Robinson, the "activity may have been much more poorly developed in this vegetarian." And, since tool-using was at a premium among gracile australopithecines, so too was improved intelligence. In short, Robinson thought that gracile australopithecines were less primitive and smarter than robust australopithecines and that they alone gave rise to *Homo*.

In the Transvaal Museum in Pretoria, South Africa, there is a narrow open box that contains what appear to be ordinary rocks. Careful scrutiny, however, shows that the rocks have been modified by early hominins. These rocks are therefore known as pebble tools, or Olduwan pebble tools, in honor of Olduvai Gorge, where such artifacts were first recognized. The oldest pebble tools yet discovered are around 2.5 million years old. Ideally, one would like to find a pebble tool held in the hand bones of a complete hominin skeleton. That hasn't happened yet and, at the moment, we cannot be sure if early stone tools were made by gracile australopithecines, robust australopithecines, or both.

More than sixty-five years have passed since the discovery of robust australopithecines, and Robinson's early ideas about the relationship between the two types of australopithecines sparkle in comparison with the tendency to "not see the forest for the trees" of many recent workers. For example, a robust australopithecine skull discovered in 1986 in Kenya (WT 17000, dubbed the Black Skull) caused workers to become "splitters" again; that is, to recognize more rather than fewer lineages of robust australopithecines. (Such efforts may be motivated by attempts to preserve as much as possible of previously published family trees.) It should also be noted that the term "gracile" is no longer used just to refer to *Australopithecus africanus* from South Africa, but also to other non-robust australopithecines that have been discovered (and frequently attributed to new species) in East and Central Africa. Although unnecessary splitting serves only to confuse our understanding of the past, Robinson's consolidation of early hominins into two groups and his determination to understand the differences between those two groups in *functional terms* stands as an eloquent example of how to do good science.

It is enthralling to contemplate Dart's discovery of the Taung fossil, about which he wrote, "No diamond cutter ever worked more lovingly or with such care on a priceless jewel," or to imagine Broom, the avid collector of scientific specimens, as described in his biography:

During the collecting campaign Mary Broom, always a self-effacing lady, had to drive in the back-seat of the car next to a recently collected polecat . . . and Broom in front. Says Mary Broom: "Robert, the wee beastie is smelling." Broom: "Impossible! It's still alive."[5]

Robinson's ideas about gracile and robust australopithecines were more than enthralling; they were visionary.

There is a delicious irony associated with the fact that Taung was the type specimen designated by Dart in conjunction with establishing *Australopithecus africanus*. (The type specimen is the ideal against which all other candidates for this taxon will, forever after, be compared.) As noted above, ape and human youngsters go through different stages as they are growing up. It is hard enough to decipher trends in the evolution of adult hominins from those bits of bones and teeth that happen to arrive at museums as fossils, but it is nearly impossible to learn much from those same fossils about the growth of the children of our earliest ancestors. And Taung was a child—a young child. Because of this, we cannot really be sure whether Taung was a gracile or a robust australopithecine.

In 1976, Phillip Tobias suggested that Taung might be a juvenile robust australopithecine, instead of a juvenile gracile australopithecine. That suggestion fell on deaf ears. Since then, several robustlike features have been described in the Taung specimen. These features include the structure of the sinuses in the face and features related to the brain's blood flow. Wouldn't it be ironic if the type specimen for gracile australopithecines turned out really to be a robust australopithecine?

In conclusion, the anti-intellectual climate of the 1920s and the fact that the first australopithecine discovered happened to be a child probably contributed to Dart's incorrect interpretation of australopithecines as more humanlike than apelike. Unfortunately, Dart's biased analysis of Taung established a long tradition of selective interpretation of the hominin fossil record. Today, when new fossil hominins are discovered, there are still some paleoanthropologists who would rather add extraneous branches to their previously published family trees than switch to simpler and more logical branching patterns. When it comes to australopithecines, hominin paleoanthropologists seem to agree on only one point: they came in two basic forms—robust and gracile.

Putting Flesh on the Bones

So fossilized teeth and bones tell us that there were two types of australopithecines. That is all fine and good, but the next important issue is how these early hominins lived. How did they get along with each other? And how are they related to us? Although some guesswork is required to put flesh on australopithecine bones, our ideas about the lives of early hominins are not based on mere speculation. Instead, paleontologists look to living primates for good guesses about how our earliest ancestors behaved.

The two great apes that live in Africa today—the chimpanzee and the gorilla—are genetically close to us, and it is therefore instructive for us to study their distinctive lifestyles when attempting to reconstruct the behavior of early hominins. Actually, because the chimpanzee shares a more recent common ancestor with humans than the gorilla does, it is believed to be our closest nonhuman cousin. Like the gracile and robust

FIGURE I.3.
The chimpanzees from Gombe live in the fast lane. Unprotected by mountains or tropical forests, they inhabit the more varied and dangerous lowland grasslands and woodlands. (Photograph courtesy of Curt Busse.)

ape-men, chimpanzees and gorillas have different lifestyles (that is, occupy different environmental niches).

Take the eastern highland gorilla. This largest of living primates has been terribly misunderstood. The Hollywood notion of gorillas as ferocious, charging, chest-beating bullies has been overemphasized. Most of the time, gorillas are peaceful souls. They frequently live in harems ruled by a single confident, dominant silverback male. Although younger blackback males may also reside in a harem, it is the silverback that mates with the harem's adult females and consequently fathers all of their infants. His authority is seldom challenged. Younger males eventually leave the group and join other bachelors. One day they may woo females away from other harems (*then* there might be a little chest beating), settle down, and start their own harems. Nevertheless, harems are not generally hostile to each other. And they do not normally compete for food or females.

Life in a gorilla harem is not nearly as sexy as it sounds. In fact, it's relatively boring compared with the more lively goings-on of promiscuous chimpanzees. Gorilla watchers describe the harem as a relatively stable social unit in which sexual encounters are predictable, dull, and infrequent. In keeping with this, the sexual swellings that advertise receptivity in females are not as pronounced as those of the more sexually active chimpanzees. Staid gorillas also engage in little mutual grooming or touching. (Chimpanzees are much more "touchy-feely.")

The day-to-day life of a gorilla seems rather placid. Sunbathing is a favorite pastime. So is eating. Gorillas spend up to eight hours a day consuming tough vegetation such as bamboo, vines, stalks, bark, roots, and other high-cellulose food. The bulky vegetarian diet of gorillas is reflected in the size of their skulls and teeth. Large canines are used to strip vegetation; huge chewing muscles are anchored to an enormous face and to the sagittal crest that runs along the middle of the skull. Oddly enough, the vegetarian diet of gorillas may help explain their harem social life!

Harem organizations are rare among ground-dwelling, Old World primates. However, patas monkeys, hamadryas baboons, and gelada baboons live in harems. In each case, associating in small harems instead of larger mixed or multimale groups appears to be a way of coping with food limitations imposed by harsh or uneven environments. Gorillas are strict vegetarians who live in pockets of tropical rain forests. Consequently, their food is dispersed in relatively small patches and it simply will not stretch to feed larger groups.

Because they are so big, adult gorillas spend a good deal of time moving on all fours on the ground (they are terrestrial). They share with chimpanzees a peculiar way of moving across the ground, called knuckle-walking, in which the hands are folded so that the weight of the body is distributed across the knuckles. The shoulders of gorillas are built for climbing and moving in trees, however, and this activity is frequently enjoyed by the lighter-weight infants and females. Males are much, much larger than females. Such sexual dimorphism (markedly different appearance of males and females) is associated with male defense of the group (if pressed, a male gorilla *will* defend his harem) and is fairly common among ground-living primates.

Compared with gorillas, the two species of chimpanzees (common chimpanzees and bonobos) live in the fast lane. They inhabit more varied and dangerous grassland and (in some cases) forested woodland areas. And they eat a wide variety of foods, including vegetables, fruits, nuts, insects, and even meat. Since these foods are not scarce or limited to small pockets in the environment, chimpanzees have forsaken the harem way of life for a much looser form of raucous group living. Their so-called fission-fusion society is completely open, and adults of both sexes come and go as they wish.

Promiscuous mating behavior is the norm among chimpanzees. When females become sexually receptive, they enter a hormonal state known as estrus. The genitals of estrous females become very swollen (much more so than those of less adventuresome gorilla females), and this condition is a powerful mating stimulus for both sexes. An estrous chimpanzee may mate with a series of males on one day, and go off to be alone with one particular male on another. Paternity is therefore difficult to determine for chimpanzees.

Although males are somewhat larger than females, sex differences in body sizes of chimpanzees are not as marked as those seen in harem primates. Further, the extraordinary large faces and crests of bones associated with chewing muscles in strictly vegetarian gorillas are greatly reduced or missing in the more omnivorous chimpanzees. Chimpanzees are just plain smaller than gorillas.

But what most endears chimpanzees to us are their similarities to humans. They are outgoing and expressive in their social interactions. They greet each other with hugs, kisses, and joyful vocalizations. They like to touch and to clean each other's coats. Chimpanzees are affectionate and imitative in their interactions with humans; their body language is very much like our own.

As Jane Goodall has documented at the Gombe National Park in Tanzania, chimps are also clever. In the wild, they make tools to fish for insects, collect drinking water, and (in the rain forest of the Ivory Coast) use hammerstones to crack open nuts. Chimpanzees also recognize themselves in mirrors. This has been demonstrated by Gordon Gallup of the State University of New York at Albany, who believes that chimpanzees are self-aware and have a sense of "I" or "me," much as humans do. Finally, our closest cousins have a certain appeal even in their looks—with big, humanlike ears and frequent premature baldness.

Thanks to Jane Goodall's monumental work, we now know that there is also a darker side to chimpanzee nature. I believe that understanding the Mr. Hyde in chimpanzees is very important for understanding human origins. Unlike gorillas, common chimpanzee males form groups to patrol the boundaries of their territory. Groups of males also hunt and eat small mammals, including monkeys and an occasional chimpanzee infant. And these activities are undertaken with a bloodlust that is rarely seen in other primates—except for *Homo sapiens* (but more about that later).

From Apes to Ape-men

The fieldwork that has been carried out on certain groups of chimpanzees and gorillas provides clues about how the two types of australopithecines may have lived: it is possible that robust australopithecines occupied a niche that in some ways resembled that of living highland gorillas. Gracile australopithecines, on the other hand, may have had a lifestyle more like that of chimpanzees. It is important to note, however, that the similarities between ape-men and apes would have been channeled by environmental variables such as availability of preferred food, and not by the existence of different apelike ancestors for the two kinds of hominin. Indeed, based on molecular and fossil evidence, paleontologists firmly believe that both types of australopithecines shared one apelike common ancestor.

What evidence is there for this? Recall that the two ape-men are physically distinct in the dental and facial features because of their different diets. Paleontologists agree that robust australopithecines were vegetarians who specialized in hard foods; gracile australopithecines were not. This alone shows that the two ape-men occupied distinct niches. But what is there to suggest that robust australopithecines behaved like gorillas? Or that gracile hominins acted more like chimpanzees?

All robust australopithecines have a circulatory system for the brain that appears to have been associated with living in cooler rather than hotter habitats. Furthermore, the finger and toe bones of the probable ancestors of robust australopithecines are curved. This indicates that these hominins, although basically bipedal, nevertheless retained the general apelike habit of spending some time in trees (and therefore in treed habitats). Like gorillas, the skulls of robust australopithecines are characterized by marked sexual dimorphism. And, of course, like that of gorillas, the diet of robust australopithecines was extremely specialized and highly vegetarian. (It is important to note, however, that the teeth of australopithecines differ in various ways from those of apes.)

But can we infer anything about the actual behavior of robust australopithecines? We probably can. The combination of vegetarian diet, marked sexual dimorphism, and basic ground living suggests that these early hominins lived in harems.[6] As with contemporary harem primates, males probably defended their harems as was necessary. However, interharem relationships would have been primarily peaceful, with harems joining to form larger groups for defense—as food and circumstances warranted.

That is not to say that robust australopithecines were *exactly* like gorillas. Although males were markedly larger than females, very recent findings suggest that neither sex of robust hominins may have been so robust after all![7] Robustness may have been confined to structures related to chewing, while the rest of the body remained relatively slight. This is obviously not the case for gorillas. Nor are gorillas known for tool use, or for being particularly intelligent. However, the degree to which robust australopithecines used tools, as well as the extent of their general intelligence, are questions that remain tantalizingly open.[8]

And what about gracile australopithecines? Is there evidence to suggest that they lived more like grassland and woodland chimpanzees than like gorillas? As a matter of fact, there is. Several workers have seconded Robinson by noting that some of the more recent species of gracile australopithecines (at least) lived in open savanna grasslands and therefore were subject to more solar radiation than their forest-dwelling cousins. This suggestion also receives tentative support from fossilized scraps of non-robust australopithecines from Laetoli, Tanzania, that are much older: about 3.6 million years old. One of these older specimens, a portion of the skull, shows that these early hominins did *not* have the kind of circulatory system for the brain that seems to be associated with cooler habitats and is found in all robust australopithecines. Moreover, the famous footprints that Mary Leakey discovered at Laetoli appear to have been made by feet that lacked the curved tree-clinging toes of the probable ancestors of robust australopithecines that lived at Hadar. It seems, indeed, that at least some gracile australopithecines were out in the open. Out in the open and getting hot in the sun. (Later it will be shown that this has important consequences for how brain temperature is regulated.)

Male and female gracile australopithecines may not have differed as dramatically in the forms of their skulls as robust australopithecines did. And their teeth tell us that they ate softer fruits and foliage than did their robust cousins. The combination of these features, along with woodland or savanna living, are found in the chimpanzees from Gombe and seem to go with a multimale social organization. Gracile australopithecines may have had a taste for meat that they would satisfy, catch-as-catch-can, by various means, including scavenging the kills of other animals. I also think they probably had a taste for salt.

So much for speculation about the day-to-day lives of gracile and robust australopithecines. What we would really like to know is what they were like cognitively. And how intelligent they were. Although this may sound like an impossible goal, South Africa has produced a dazzling record of natural endocasts from both kinds of australopithecines that have revealed details about the cerebral cortex of our earliest hominin relatives. I have been very fortunate to be involved in the investigation of these and other hominin fossils. My research, which can best be described as stormy, began a quarter of a century ago in a room known as the Red Cave.

Into the Cave

I first visited the basement of the Transvaal Museum in Pretoria, South Africa, during the summer of 1978 to study their collection of fossil monkeys. Although important in their own right, these fossils were in my naive view (I was fresh out of graduate school) relatively humdrum compared to the more glamorous hominins that I really wanted to study. At that time, one of the museum's walls was fronted by an exceedingly thick bank-vault door. Behind this door was the Red Cave—a small room that contained a priceless collection of fossils from our earliest ape-men ancestors. Each time I passed by the locked vault, I longed to enter the Red Cave. As a newcomer to the museum, however, I thought my wish to study these spectacular fossils of our earliest ancestors was too much to hope for. After all, from my recent graduate-school perspective, the

FIGURE I.4.
The author studies the braincase of Mrs. Ples in the Red Cave, 1978; other natural hominin endocasts await inspection on the table.

field of hominin paleontology seemed dominated by just a few privileged workers and this inner circle was notorious for being difficult to penetrate.[9] I kept to my monkey fossils. And the door to the hominin vault remained closed.

Near the end of my stay in Pretoria, I decided to examine some unidentified fossils that were kept in boxes in an out-of-the-way storage room. In one dusty, forgotten box marked "unidentified monkeys," I found a small fossil that was *not* monkey. It was hominin! But would I be able to convince museum officials that it was? I spent two days poring over reference books and monkey fossils in order to prepare my case. Carefully, I arranged the specimen, numerous illustrations, and some monkey fossils on a table. After rehearsing my arguments several times, I was ready. I sought out the director of the museum at that time, Bob Brain, and asked somewhat hesitantly, "Excuse me, Dr. Brain. I wonder if I could show you something for a moment?"

"Why of course, Dean," he said, accompanying me to my display. As he looked at the specimen, I took a deep breath in preparation for my arduous explanation. Before I could say one word, Dr. Brain said with obvious delight, "Why, you've found a hominid, haven't you!" Subsequently, Brain and another official at the museum, Elisabeth Vrba (now at Yale), encouraged me to compare the fossil with the other hominins and to publish my findings. So the door to the Red Cave was opened to me after all. When I first entered that room, I had no idea of the secrets it would reveal.

The hominin vault at the Transvaal Museum was the most amazing room I'd ever been in. It was small, rectangular, and the color scheme was blood red. (Vrba selected the color; she said it was that or purple.) The walls were lined with antique glass cabinets containing red velvet boxes—boxes that held treasures. Imagine entering this room and finding yourself face-to-face (so to speak) with an array of fossil skulls (such as the gracile australopithecine nicknamed "Mrs. Ples" and the original robust *Paranthropus*) that were pictured in most paleoanthropology textbooks! Photographs of paleontologists who did pioneering work on early hominins decorated the walls and there was a small worktable. Someone on the staff brought a space heater (it's winter there in June); then you were left to ponder the fossils. Your only interruption was the sound of a bell tinkling as an employee walked through the museum calling the staff to tea.[10]

Ever since I was rescued from undergraduate doldrums by an inspiring teacher, the late Charles Reed, I have been interested in the evolution of the human brain. Thanks to Charles, a zoologist (and one of those rare scholar/teachers), my initial interest was in the volume of the braincase, a feature known as cranial capacity and measured in cubic centimeters (cm³). Cranial capacities of our ancestors reveal a startling fact. Brain size in living humans is about three times as large as it was in our hominin relatives who lived more than three million years ago. Even when we consider that body size has also increased dramatically, this increase in brain size is unprecedented in mammals. Nothing like it has been seen before. Why did the brains of our ancestors enlarge as they did? When I first stepped into the Red Cave, I had no idea. Twenty-five years later, I have an inkling—and it's presented in this book.

The little fossil that I disinterred from the dusty box was not part of the skull or, for that matter, any other part of the skeleton. What I had found was a cast of the interior of the braincase of an individual who had lived between 2.5 and 3 million years ago. Like the Taung endocast, this naturally occurring endocast revealed details of the brain that had been imprinted on the inside of the braincase. Although endocasts may be prepared artificially from skulls (using latex), the occurrence of natural endocasts is a rare event that depends on highly favorable geological conditions. Unfortunately for paleontologists, these conditions exist in few places in the world. South Africa is one. The result is a remarkable record of natural endocasts for the animals that lived there, and it is fortunate that our earliest ancestors were among those who unwittingly took advantage of this geological opportunity. What beginner's luck I had in finding one of these hominin endocasts (only the seventh found at that time) while rummaging in a museum box!

For all practical purposes, I carried in my hand a small portion of the cerebral cortex of an ape-man when I first entered the Red Cave. Imagine the feeling! Six other hominin natural endocasts awaited inspection, and they were more complete than the little specimen I had found. (The Taung specimen, arguably the most important early hominin endocast, was located in the Department of Anatomy at the University of Wit-

FIGURE I.5.

The natural endocasts of South African australopithecines. Early hominin skulls
filled up with fine, lime-rich sediments that then became fossilized. Each endocast
preserves in unusual detail the external brain convolutions and blood vessels that
left their imprint inside the cranium. (Photograph by John Reader, copyright 1992/
Science Photo Library.)

watersrand in Johannesburg, rather than in the Red Cave. The head of that department, Professor Phillip Tobias, kindly allowed me to study that specimen.) Although brain size in these early hominins was as small as that of chimpanzees, Dart's notion that australopithecine endocasts looked like miniature versions of modern human brains had nearly achieved the status of a received truth by the time I set foot in the Red Cave. Indeed, no other view existed in the contemporary paleontological literature. That is why, in 1978, I fully expected to see humanlike sulcal patterns on early hominin endocasts. However, as I examined the hominin endocasts, I found, to my astonishment, that this was not the case. The folds of gray matter reproduced on the endocasts were not humanlike. Instead, they appeared completely apelike. At least to me they did.

The Beginnings of Controversy

In 1979, the late Leonard Radinsky published observations questioning the humanlike affinities of the Taung endocast. I followed suit in 1980 and published findings that all seven early hominin natural endocasts (including Taung) appeared apelike rather than humanlike. After all, the early hominins of South Africa had brains that were roughly the size of those of chimpanzees. So it should not have been surprising to find that the pattern of convolutions on the Red Cave endocasts appeared similar to those on chimpanzee brains. Right? Wrong. It amuses me now to recall my belief that findings that flew in the face of conventional wisdom would be accepted by the field, as long as the supporting evidence from chimpanzee, gorilla, and human brains was published with the conclusions.

In my 1980 paper, I unwittingly reopened a controversy that had lain dormant for fifty-five years by pointing out that when Dart first described the Taung endocast, he mistook the lambdoid suture of the skull for the lunate sulcus of the brain. The lambdoid suture is an irregular edge on the skull that is formed by the fusion of the occipital and parietal bones. A sulcus is a narrow valley that separates convolutions of the brain, and the lunate sulcus is a crescent-shaped groove (hence its name) that is located at the front end of the occipital lobe, which processes visual information in monkeys, apes, and humans. However, when one compares brains representing these three groups of primates, one discovers that the lunate sulcus is located much farther back in the human brain than on the others. Because he misidentified the lambdoid suture as the lunate sulcus, Dart claimed that the lunate sulcus was located in a humanlike position, far back on the Taung endocast. In other words, it was an unfortunate error that caused Dart to suggest that australopithecine brains were humanlike.[11] Oh, the poor beleaguered lunate sulcus! Its significance for hominin brain evolution was doomed to be misunderstood from the word *go*.

If the feature that Dart identified wasn't Taung's lunate sulcus, then where was it? As an alternative, I suggested that a small dimple near the top of the Taung endocast might represent one end of the lunate sulcus. (The whole lunate sulcus did not show up on Taung or on any of the other six australopithecine endocasts.) This dimple was in a relatively forward location that was consistent with an apelike position for the lunate sulcus. To me, such an interpretation seemed logical because of the overall apelike sulcal patterns on these specimens. (If the dimple did not represent the end of the lunate sulcus, then any trace of the lunate sulcus simply did not appear on the South African specimens, and nothing more could then be said about that sulcus on these endocasts.)

Ralph Holloway of Columbia University had long championed Dart's view that the brains of our earliest ancestors appeared to be humanlike. It is safe to say that he was not happy with my observations. Since my 1980 article on the australopithecine natural endocasts, Holloway and I have engaged in an exchange of more than twenty publications that can most kindly be described as lively. That I was able to publish my viewpoint at all in such a contentious field was remarkable and due in large part to the concern shown by my mentor, Len Radinsky, and his intercession with editors.

The Emperor Has No Clothes!

Politics of the field aside, what were Holloway and I arguing about? Holloway objected to my identification of Taung's dimple as a possible marker for the lunate sulcus. In true the-emperor-has-a-beautiful-suit-of-clothes fashion, Holloway took a new investigator to task for having the temerity to question Dart's authority.[12]

> It is reasonable to remind readers of this paper of . . . important histori-cal facts: . . . Raymond Dart was a protégé of G. E. Smith, who devoted a very considerable portion of his professional career to the study of the lunate sulcus. Dart's early publications were in comparative neu-roanatomy. These points are only mentioned to indicate that those who did study the original specimens were well-versed regarding com-parative neuroanatomy, and the lunate sulcus in particular.[13]

Of course, the fact that Smith and Dart were renowned scientists had nothing to do with the actual location of the lunate sulcus on the Taung endocast. Dart had misidentified the lambdoid suture as the lunate sul-cus—period. Furthermore, by the time of his 1981 response to my pa-per, Holloway had quietly shifted away from his 1975 statement that "only a few hominin endocasts [particularly the original Taung (1924) endocast] show the sulcus clearly."[14] Indeed, Holloway's 1981 view of Taung's lunate sulcus was that "*we cannot prove where the lunate sulcus is located, but only demonstrate where it is not.*"[15]

Would the lunate sulcus finally be allowed to rest in peace? No way. In a series of papers, Holloway continued his offense against Taung's poor little dimple. According to him, my identification was incorrect because the dimple was too far forward to be the lunate suclus, even of an ape. At times I just wanted to let the whole thing drop, but prodded and encour-aged by my colleagues, I met each offense with a statistical or theoretical defense. Round and round we went. Points of methodology became bones of contention. For example, we debated which methods were bet-ter for studying early hominin endocasts: measuring projection and profile indices from photographs or using a stereoplotter to measure detail of sulcal patterns. We were getting nowhere slowly (and probably nauseating more than a few readers in the process).

In 1985, I wrote:

> I hope that one year from now I will not be writing the seventh paper in this series. Obviously, neither Holloway nor I are changing our opinions about the cortical morphology of australopithecines. . . . It is

time that other workers examine the evidence and contribute to this discussion. My laboratory and endocast collection are available to other researchers (or their students) who are interested in the problem.[16]

Unfortunately, there were no takers, and only four years later, in 1989, I found myself publishing the thirteenth article in the lunate sulcus series. (I wanted to title it "Lunate Sulcus Paper 13," but the editor would not permit that.) And the subject of this paper? Again, the dimple. Would this controversy ever be put to rest? Would other workers ever stick their necks out and take a position? As it turns out, the answer to both questions was yes.

The problem with the lunate sulcus is that it simply was not reproduced on the South African australopithecine natural endocasts with any clarity. If a clear lunate sulcus had appeared on the Taung or other endocasts, it would have been a good indicator of the extent to which early hominin brains had evolved toward a humanlike condition. A forward position of the lunate sulcus would have suggested an apelike brain. If the lunate sulcus were located in a posterior position, on the other hand, the brain would have appeared humanlike. The dimple on the Taung endocast that I identified as a possible marker for the lunate sulcus was in an apelike position, but Ralph Holloway would have none of that. Since there were no other potential lunate sulci on the South African endocasts, clearly what was needed were other endocasts of early hominins.

In 1985, I had the chance to study the sulcal pattern on another australopithecine endocast, this time from the Hadar formation in Ethiopia (home of Lucy).[17] Dated to about 3.2 million years ago, this specimen (AL 162-28) was older than the South African endocasts. With a cranial capacity of 350–400 cm^3, it was also some 10–20 percent smaller. Most important, the AL 162-28 endocast revealed a beautiful, whole lunate sulcus in addition to numerous other sulci. Like the South African specimens, the entire sulcal pattern of this Hadar endocast was clearly apelike. What was especially frustrating was that when a clear lunate sulcus at last appeared on an australopithecine endocast, Holloway failed to recognize it. Instead, he claimed that for AL 162-28 "there are no landmarks . . . which can be interpreted as a pongid-like lunate sulcus."[18]

(Holloway attributed the groove in question to an artifact caused by lipping at the edge of a bone.) In exasperation I wrote the following poem:

Ode to the Lunate Sulcus

Oh crescent shaped groove near the back of the brain,
Anterior limit of the visual cortex.
So misunderstood, misidentified and misbegotten
In the study of human brain evolution.
In 1925 Dart wrongly identified the lambdoid suture
On the Taung endocast as you!
And others believed it was far back,
So "human, human," they cried,
Although you rarely leave your mark on endocasts,
This does not stop them from guessing your location.
"Human, human," they wail.
And when you finally do reveal yourself,
Splendidly, completely, unequivocally (on AL 162-28),
But, alas, in an apelike, position,
"Artifact, artifact," they cry.
Neither calipers, nor stereoplotting, nor projection
Indices have saved you from your fate.
Poor thing.

Although neither calipers, nor stereoplotting, nor projection indices saved the lunate sulcus from its agony, powerful new imaging tools were being developed by Michael Vannier, who was then the director of the Radiology Research Division at Mallinckrodt Institute of Radiology in St. Louis. Although these tools would begin to change Taung's fate, the final words on this little specimen have yet to be written!

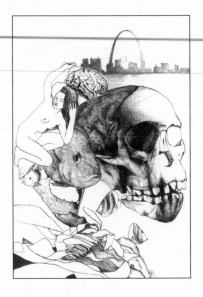

chapter 2

TAUNG GOES TO ST. LOUIS –
AND BEYOND

When I was introduced to Michael Vannier nearly twenty years ago, I already knew him by reputation as one of the world's foremost experts in three-dimensional medical imaging of complex biological structures. I had just given a talk about endocasts of rhesus monkeys at Washington University in St. Louis. In my talk, I noted that physical anthropologists were still using relatively primitive tools (for example, dental floss and hand-held calipers) to measure features of the brain that are reflected on endocasts. Afterwards, Vannier told me that he had developed new ways to image and measure complex surfaces, and he thought they would work on endocasts. He invited me to visit his laboratory, which was then at Mallinckrodt Institute of Radiology in Washington University's Medical Center. (Mike has since moved to the University of Iowa College of Medicine.)

Although I'm sure it doesn't come close to matching the setup he has today, I was overwhelmed by Mike's laboratory. With the possible exception of televised NASA launches, I had never seen so much high technology in one place. A back room contained numerous computers to run Mike's lab and to communicate with computers in the outside world. The computer room had a distinct personality—it was large, cold, and hummed (probably because it was shivering). Out front in warmer territory, I met some of the people who worked in the lab, including Charles Hildebolt, who is still one of my closest colleagues. Other people inhabiting Vannier's lab were physicians, researchers, and graduate students who used various instruments to reconstruct and collect data from medical images, be they magnetic resonance images (MRIs) of the heart, computerized axial tomography (CAT) scans of the brain, or X-rays of the wrist. There were vivid anatomical images displayed on numerous machines around the lab. Before each, investigators sat absorbed in their work.

One machine that Mike showed me was of particular interest. The McDonnell Douglas 3Space Digitizer, or 3Space, was developed from technology originally designed for a helmet-mounted sight apparatus for military fighter aircraft. In the medical domain, an operator could use the 3Space's electromagnetic pointer to identify an anatomically significant point. When a pedal was pressed, the 3Space recorded all three dimensions (length, breadth, and height) of the point. Mike said that with appropriate software to string the points together, the 3Space would be perfect for reading sulci on brains or endocasts. With the 3Space, it was possible to describe (digitize) sulci in three dimensions and determine their precise lengths. (We were also able to analyze some shape features.) Good-bye, dental floss; good-bye, calipers! Hello, precision instruments!

I told Mike about a research project I wanted to do on hundreds of endocasts from rhesus monkeys of known age and sex, who, most importantly, were descended from known mothers. If we could precisely read and quantify details of the cerebral cortex from these endocasts, which I would prepare from rhesus monkey skulls, we would be able to investigate a number of important questions about the neuroanatomy

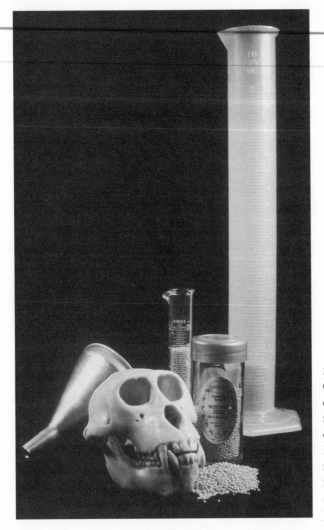

FIGURE 2.1.
Good-bye to
calipers and
mustard seed
of the old days!
Hello, advanced
medical imag-
ing technology.
(Photograph by
John Guyer.)

of the most widely used higher primate model in medicine. The extent of cortical asymmetry (or right/left differences) could be explored, and age-related changes in external brain morphology could be quantified. We could also investigate whether or not there were sex differences in the superficial appearance of the brain. Finally, we would be able to do something never before attempted with primates: because maternal genealogies would be known, we could quantify the contribution of genetic factors (called heritabilities) to variations in the lengths and patterns of brain features.

Mike agreed to participate in the project. Together, we organized a team to carry it out. Over time, the team put together a successful research proposal for funds to support our work.[1] This was our plan: I would make more than four hundred endocasts and collect certain information from them by eye. Mike would write the software and direct the collection of data from the endocasts in his laboratory. Charles (Scooter) Hildebolt, drawing on the skills he had developed as a dentist in another life (before obtaining a Ph.D. in anthropology), would use his steady hand for the delicate but tedious job of digitizing thousands and thousands of sulci on hundreds and hundreds of endocasts. Finally, Jim Cheverud (a big, brilliant teddy bear) would join our efforts and carry out all of the quantitative and genetic analyses. (Jim, a professor in the Department of Anatomy and Neurobiology at Washington University, had already done genetic studies on the same skeletons that provided the endocasts.) All four of us would participate in the interpretation, writing, and publication of results.

As the project evolved, I periodically flew to St. Louis to meet with the team. Once we got the bugs worked out by doing pilot work, the investigation went remarkably well and, eventually, we obtained exciting results. (Jim made us do lots of pilot work before he was satisfied that we would get meaningful data. However, it was worth it, and we have forgiven him for cracking the whip.) Clearly, we clicked as a team. Looking back on it, I think this happened because all four of us tended toward workaholism, and we, as kindred spirits, responded to each other's exuberance about the work at hand. I grew to love my visits to St. Louis.

Scooter Had an Idea

Scooter usually picked me up at the airport; then we put in a long day at the lab. Frequently, we used the 3Space to digitize all of the sulci on actual brains. (Scooter digitized, while I kept a running map of what he was doing.) At other times, we would prepare illustrations or experiment with a new toy that had appeared in the lab since my last visit. Whatever our research agenda, we always found time for idle chitchat.

(It amuses me to remember the countless hours we spent discussing whether or not Mike was really an Einstein-caliber genius.)

One day, while we were working with the 3Space, Scooter said to me, "Hey, Dean, guess what's in the *American Journal of Physical Anthropology* that just arrived?"

"I give up."

"An article by Ralph Holloway," he said.

"Oh, no," I uttered in dismay. "What's it about?"

"It's another one of those 'apples and oranges' articles," Scooter answered. (He was referring to the title of one of my papers in the exchange with Holloway.)

"Oh, n-o-o-o," I wailed in my "Mr. Bill" voice.

"Dean, don't worry. Nobody actually *reads* those things anymore."

As we continued digitizing, we started talking about the frustrations I had encountered during my long debate with Holloway about australopithecine endocasts. A key problem had to do with the different brain sizes of chimpanzees and humans. Adult human brains are three to four times the size of adult chimpanzee brains. Because of the physical laws that govern the relationship between surface areas of brains and their volumes, human brains have more sulci than chimpanzee brains—just because they are bigger. (This is known as allometric scaling.) Before true evolutionary differences can be identified, one must substract out changes that are due simply to size scaling, or allometry.

In 1980, I had shown that the endocast of Taung had a simpler pattern of convolutions (that is, fewer sulci) than one would see on a human brain. In fact, the Taung endocast was within the ape range for size and, consistent with this, its sulcal pattern appeared to be apelike rather than humanlike.

"But how can I rule out allometric scaling as the only cause for the differences between the Taung endocast and human brains? How can it be shown that Taung's endocast is apelike even after size effects have been subtracted out?" I asked Scooter.

"Digitize the Taung endocast and digitize a human brain that is the same size," Scooter suggested.

"But Scooter, human brains are over three times as big as Taung."

"Not all human brains, Dean."

"What are you talking about, Charles?"

He answered my question with a question, "How old did Taung live to be?"

"Scooter, you know it was a so-called 'baby,' maybe three and a half years old."

"Well, there you go, Dean. Get a brain of a human baby."

The Baby Brain

Of course. A baby brain. Charles's idea was inspired. But finding a normal brain of a human baby was easier said than done. We made requests to various institutions to borrow a baby brain. Very few parents have the altruism and desire to donate their children's bodies to science. When these rare specimens do become available, every effort is made to share them and maximize the medical, educational, and scientific benefits of these precious gifts. Several months after we made our requests, a specimen was loaned to us for our noninvasive research.

It was a beautiful specimen. The brain had been obtained from a two-week-old baby who had died of nonneurological causes. Serendipitously, its volume turned out to be 432 cm³, so close to the 404 cm³ estimated for the Taung endocast that it was difficult to tell by eyeball which of the two was bigger. Since human brains have their sulci in place by birth, this would indeed be a good specimen to compare with Taung.

We also intended to compare the baby brain and Taung endocast with the brain of a juvenile chimpanzee that had been part of my scientific collection for many years. It is standard practice for anthropologists to obtain such specimens by requesting that zoos save the carcasses of animals that die from natural causes. As with human specimens, these specimens are highly valued and are frequently shared by a number of investigators.

Departure day for St. Louis. On an earlier trip to South Africa, Phillip Tobias had given me a copy of the Taung endocast. (Before bringing it home, I compared it feature by feature with the original fossil and found it to be an exquisite copy.) That treasure went into my purse. (I would never check such luggage through in a suitcase.) The chimpanzee brain was in a canister of fluid, which I wrapped in a dark plastic bag and carried by hand. My first plane landed a bit late. And I had to make a very quick connection. Briefcase and purse over my left shoulder, plastic-wrapped container cradled in my right arm, and boarding pass between my teeth—running through the airport. Slosh-slosh-slosh. I was the last person to arrive at the gate.

"Almost didn't make it, huh," the airline attendant said in a cheerful manner as she took the boarding pass from my mouth. "What you got there?" she said, eyeing my dark green bundle.

"Uuuhhh," I fumbled as the world went into slow motion and I desperately thought "What'll I tell her? Should I lie? No, shouldn't do that—better to tell the truth."

"A chimpanzee brain," I answered feebly.

She paused. "Oohh, a chimpanzee brain," she said in a high, incredulous voice. I held my breath. Then she swept her arm in a wide arc and said "Step right on." We did.

I always find airplane takeoffs exhilarating. This one was particularly so. With Taung in my purse and the chimpanzee brain locked securely between my feet, we were hurtled down the runway. As we ascended, I imagined a little hominin brain being propelled through the millennia and into the Space Age. Taung was on its way to St. Louis.

Taung Meets the 3Space

Scooter digitized; I mapped. Sulcus by sulcus and lobe by lobe. Because the Taung endocast consisted mostly of the right hemisphere, we digitized all of the sulci on the outside surfaces of the right hemisphere of the chimpanzee and baby brains. To check for accuracy, we digitized everything twice. Scooter's years of probing around in people's mouths paid off. His steady hand and the 3Space's ability to measure exact locations proved to be an amazingly accurate partnership. When we were done, we had obtained and stored a voluminous amount of information about the surfaces (or cerebral cortices) of juvenile-chimpanzee and human-baby brains. This would provide the database for assessing the hominin endocast and would also be saved for future research.

Digitizing the Taung endocast was another matter. Unlike actual brains, endocasts of early hominins pick up only parts of the sulcal pattern. In the case of Taung, fairly good sulcal patterns appear on the right frontal and temporal lobes. (Unfortunately, details are poor on Taung's

FIGURE 2.2.
Right hemispheres of a chimpanzee brain (top), the Taung endocast (left), and a human baby brain (right). In all major respects, the Taung endocast appears apelike, not humanlike.

parietal and occipital lobes.) We digitized all of Taung's visible sulci and, for comparative purposes, also digitized the same set of sulci on the chimpanzee and baby brains. (This was in addition to digitizing the entire surfaces of the two brains, as described above.) Again, everything was done twice and, again, Scooter's steady hand came through. The two sets of measurements of the various sulcal lengths were virtually identical.

Harry Jerison, who is a leading expert on the brain and intelligence and knows as much about allometry as anyone,[2] kindly helped design our quantitative analyses.[3] We used formulas determined from both mammalian data and solid geometry to generate predictions about the expected ratios of sulci on the chimpanzee brain and the Taung endocast relative to the baby brain. We then compared our predictions with 3Space acquired reality. The results were startling. When brain size was accounted for, the chimpanzee had longer (summed) sulci than the endocast of Taung in all areas that could be compared, relative to the human brain. Our results on lengths of sulci confirmed our other observations based on sulcal pattern (in temporal and frontal lobes) and position of the cerebellum. In all respects, the Taung endocast was ape-like, not humanlike.

Interestingly, the frontal lobe of Taung turned out to be particularly impoverished in terms of summed sulcal length. The pattern of sulci in the frontal lobe was also extremely simple and included an orbitofrontal sulcus that is found in ape brains but not in human brains. (This is also true of all scorable australopithecine endocasts.) Este Armstrong, a distinguished scientist who uses her computer skills today in private enterprise, and her colleagues had shown that, of all the lobes of the brain, the frontal lobes of humans are the most convoluted compared with those of apes.[4] From Armstrong's work and our own, it appeared that frontal lobes became more convoluted relatively recently: that is, after the divergence of *Homo* from the australopithecines. Thus, reorganization of the frontal lobes is of key importance for understanding human brain evolution.

It has been a long haul, this research on australopithecine endocasts. Traditionally, paleoanthropologists have emphasized the humanlike attributes of australopithecines and downplayed their apelike features. (After all, these were our relatives.) When I entered the Red Cave, australopithecines were thought to be humanlike in their teeth, limbs, and pelves, as well as in their cortical sulcal patterns. Many researchers also believed that australopithecines were as refined in their bipedalism as contemporary humans.

But, the emperor has no clothes. In the past twenty years, much new evidence has come to light that shows australopithecines were considerably more apelike than previously believed. The accepted view of Taung and the other australopithecines has now taken a 180-degree turn because of the research on dentition and locomotion by numerous investigators whose work has already been discussed: Bill Jungers, Holly Smith, Tim Bromage, Mike Vannier, and Glenn Conroy. The "australopithecines-are-humanlike" school no longer holds the majority opinion. At least on this issue, voices of reason have finally risen above the cacophony of contention.

And, the endocasts of australopithecines are, of course, just as apelike as they can be. Furthermore, as I had hoped would happen, other workers finally published their views on hominin brain evolution. Research by Armstrong and her colleagues (using advanced techniques on different primates) and by Jerison (based on comparative morphometric considerations) supports the contention that the lunate sulcus of early hominins, were it visible, would have been in an apelike location.[5] At least that's my interpretation. As far as I know, Ralph Holloway still thinks otherwise.

But a good thing has happened on the Holloway front. He and I both attended a workshop on brain evolution that took place in Barcelona, Spain, during the fall of 2001.[6] Not only were we in a wonderful city, we were in great company, which included Kathleen Gibson, Harry and Irene Jerison, Phillip Tobias, and European colleagues Javier De Felipe, Emmanuel Gilissen, and Dominique Grimaud-Herve. At one point, several of us took a break and went walking around the city to see the spectacular architecture designed by Antoni Gaudi. I don't know exactly when it happened, perhaps it was on that walk, but at some point during the conference Ralph and I patched up our differences. Of course, neither one of us has budged from our strong opinions about the cerebral cortex of australopithecines. We, however, have agreed that reasonable people can hold different views, and that from now on we will do so on friendly terms.

Taung Goes to Germany

In 1996, I found myself on a train gliding through the achingly beautiful Austrian Alps with a small group of experts whom Horst Seidler (head of the Institute of Anthropology at the University of Vienna) had gathered together to discuss the applications of medical imaging technology to the study of fossil hominins. We were on our way to an audience with the famous Tyrolean ice mummy known as "Otzi." As we sipped our beers, a British colleague asserted that, if we could just obtain three dimensional computerized tomographic (3-D CT) data for the world's most important fossil hominins, we wouldn't ever again need to refer to the original specimens. Some of my travel companions even suggested that such data would be better than the fossils themselves because they could be manipulated and measured in virtual space. "But I get some of my best ideas actually holding endocasts in my hands, eyeballing them, and comparing them with each other—it's also important to keep hard copies of specimens," I protested. My colleagues, however, seemed underwhelmed by this observation. Despite their skepticism about retaining physical copies (casts) of specimens, I thank my lucky stars every time I see something new on one of my endocasts, and on those rare occasions when some previously unimaginable technology (such as the innovations in Mike Vannier's laboratory) comes along to tease new insights from them.

And lucky the stars have remained. Just as I was privileged to work in Vannier's laboratory some years ago, the most important hominin endocasts in my collection are currently being analyzed in another laboratory, and in a way I'd never dreamt possible. And once again, we are able to ask questions that have never before been posed about the endocast of the little pioneer, Taung. This time, however, the work is being done in Germany with Karl Zilles and his colleagues.

I have a soft spot for "type A" workaholics and know quite a few of them. My nominee for the "Person Who Works Harder and Longer Hours than Anyone Else on Earth" is tied between two candidates: Karl Zilles and Horst Seidler. Although they do not know each other personally, it amuses me that both men were born within two months of each other, and that both make occasional pilgrimages to unwind at the same isolated monastery on Holy Mount Athos in Northern Greece. (Alas, I will never be able to see this monastery, which is reputably surrounded by breathtaking landscape in an independent monk republic that has no streets or electricity, because women are not permitted to visit.) In Karl's case (actually Horst's too), it's a wonder that he doesn't need to go there more often because he is involved in directing two different research groups that regularly produce important discoveries in the neurosciences (the Institute of Medicine's Research Center in Juelich, Germany, and the C. & O. Vogt-Institute of Brain Research at the University of Düsseldorf).

Karl and his colleagues, including physicist Hartmut Mohlberg, have developed an innovative method for mining previously unattainable information from endocasts. First, the endocasts are scanned while they are submerged in water using magnetic resonance imaging (MRI), which permits them to be reconstructed as precise "virtual endocasts" that can be manipulated using computer technology. Next, the virtual endocasts are corrected to a standard size to avoid scaling problems. Finally, each endocast may be warped to fit precisely the surface of a

FIGURE 2.3.
Karl Zilles directs two research groups in Germany that are on the cutting edge of the neurosciences. (Photograph courtesy of Karl Zilles.)

reference endocast (such as an average human endocast) and the relative amounts of local compression and expansion required to do the warping visualized in color-codes that are projected onto an image of the reference endocast.

Early in 2002, I hand-carried my precious hominin endocasts to Düsseldorf in order to analyze them with Karl and his colleagues. Although our results are still being interpreted,[7] one of the first things we confirmed was that the temporal lobes of gracile and robust australopithecines differed significantly in their shapes.[8] One part of the temporal lobe that looks very different in the two groups is the very front end, known as the temporal pole. In robust australopithecines, it is short and stubby; in gracile australopithecines it is much more prominent and pointed.

But where does little Taung fit in? As noted in chapter 1, there is some ambiguity about which hominin Taung would have grown up to look like—a gracile australopithecine (for which it is the type specimen), or a robust australopithecine. Unfortunately, the right hemisphere of the natural endocast from Taung lacks a temporal pole. Or does it? Thanks to the fact that I collected a good old "hard copy" of the fossilized face that fits snugly with the front end of the Taung endocast, Brian Worthington, a talented graduate student in my laboratory at Florida State University, has been able to cast a previously unrecognized impression of the right temporal pole that was molded into the back of the face. Brian has used this endocast of the temporal pole to reconstruct a more complete whole endocast, and this newly reconstructed endocast of Taung will soon be MR imaged and warped in Düsseldorf to see which kind of australopithecine it most resembles. We may or may not get a definitive answer to this question, but one thing is for sure: without hard copies of fossils and Karl Zilles's fantastic methodology, we would never have thought to ask it in the first place.

Looking for Mr. Goodbrain

The australopithecine natural endocasts from South Africa created a dilemma: if the hominins that lived between roughly two and three million years ago appeared to be apelike in their brains, when did a humanlike brain first appear in the fossil record? Moreover, which part of the brain should we look to for an answer to this question? The one area of the cortex that best distinguishes an ape brain from a human brain is the frontal lobes. A triangular fold of gray matter known as Broca's area appears in left frontal lobes of humans and is associated with speech. This area does not appear in ape brains. Not only is the lower frontal lobe the best area for distinguishing an ape brain from a human brain, it is also the area most likely to leave a good impression on the inside of the skull and therefore appear on an endocast—a happy accident.

By 1980, I knew that humanlike brains were not showing up in the fossil record of hominins that lived more than two million years ago. It was time to move forward in the fossil record, but that meant gaining access to fossils in other parts of Africa. Because of the dispute with Holloway, my work was already controversial. How would curators react

FIGURE 2.4.
This imposing statue of the late Louis Leakey greets visitors to the national museums of Kenya. (Photograph by Dean Falk.)

to my request to study their collections? Although I was denied access to some fossils, I believe it was out of a sheer sense of fair play that one museum director let me into the shop. In 1982, I went to the National Museums of Kenya in Nairobi to study the fossil hominins under Richard Leakey's care.

Just up the hill from the hotel where I stayed is a statue of Louis Leakey. He is perched on a pile of rocks, with a stone tool in his hand. Behind that statue is the National Museums of Kenya. It too has a hominin vault. Although less colorful than the Red Cave was, this vault was larger and its fossils more varied, reflecting the fact that the East African australopithecines were not alone. They had company.

What spectacular hominins there were between one and two million years ago in East Africa! As hard as it is to imagine, the robust australopithecines from East Africa looked even more rugged than those from South Africa (hence they are sometimes described as hyper-robust). As with variations among human groups today, these differences seem to have been associated with living in different regions, and under different environmental conditions. The other (non-robust) australopithecines in East Africa had somewhat bigger brains than the gracile species from South Africa, but this is hardly surprising since they lived more recently.

East Africa was a busy place two million years ago. By then, another group of hominins appears to have been undergoing dramatic evolution. I refer of course to our own genus, *Homo,* which at some undetermined point in time branched off from gracile australopithecine stock. When the 1992 edition of this book appeared, most paleoanthropologists agreed that the first African *Homo* to appear was *Homo habilis,* and that this species gave rise to *Homo erectus* who in turn gave rise to *Homo sapiens.* Furthermore, at that time workers believed the transition between *Homo habilis* and *Homo erectus* had occurred rapidly (some thought between 1.8 and 1.6 million years ago) and exclusively in Africa.

A little more than a decade later, the picture is murkier because the species names of many of the African early *Homo* specimens have been changed! Thus, fossils previously attributed to *Homo habilis* were split by some workers[9] into *Homo habilis sensu stricto* (which bear a striking resemblance to the gracile australopithecines from South Africa), on the one hand, and *Homo rudolfensis* on the other. More recently, these two species have been accepted by some (including myself) as members of *Australopithecus* rather than *Homo.* Similarly, certain African specimens that were once attributed to *Homo erectus* are now called *Homo ergaster* by some, but not all, workers. This confusion about species identifications raises the issue of just which species of early *Homo* (or *Australopithecus*) gave rise to which other species of not-quite-so-early *Homo* that eventually gave rise (through who knows how many speciation events) to *Homo sapiens.* In other words, the proposed family tree of *Homo* has gotten bushier and therefore more difficult to interpret. (This has also happened for more recent parts of *Homo*'s record.) In this edition of *Braindance,* the latest species names will be referred to when appropriate, but this should not trouble the reader. Just keep in mind that, although some of the names have changed, the fossils are still the same—and so is our task of interpreting them!

Brain size continued to increase markedly as the genus *Homo* evolved. But what concerns us here is the surface structure of the cerebral cortex. During the summer of 1982, I studied the braincase of the oldest skull representing *Australopithecus rudolfensis* (*nee Homo habilis*). And guess what. Unlike any of the other australopithecine endocasts, this one (from an approximately 1.9-million-year-old specimen, KNM-ER 1470) was considerably larger than those from other australopithecines and appeared to be humanlike in the revealing convolutions of its left frontal lobe. As Phillip Tobias first suggested, the endocast appears to reproduce something like a Broca's speech area and, as such, may indicate that at least one species of early hominin was capable of some form of rudimentary vocal language.

Our lineage has evolved dramatically since that first hint about the possible glimmerings of language was imprinted in a braincase from *Australopithecus rudolfensis.* In the last two million years, brain size has nearly doubled in *Homo,* and its plethora of connections has become increasingly complex. The cultural products of the cerebral cortex evolved too. Over time, transportation developed from unshod feet to space shuttles. The spoken word gave rise to writing and numbers—to information technology that in turn has led to the computer revolution and, now, spectacular achievements in biotechnology. Our ancestors' ability to conceive of making a few clunky stone tools occurred at the beginning of a neurological trajectory that would one day result in Mozart's horn concertos, Einstein's theory of relativity, and Neil Armstrong's stroll on the moon. As we have seen, all of this was heralded in an endocast from what was probably a large-brained australopithecine. Two million years ago, the braindance had begun.

But I am getting ahead of myself. How can we assess the importance of the different appearances of hominin endocasts without understanding something about the differences between ape and human brains and what these differences mean for cognition?

chapter 3

CHIMP BRAIN, HUMAN BRAIN

Chimpanzees are smart. Very Smart. For one thing, they have an acute ability to remember the exact location of hidden objects. This particular sense may even be better developed in chimpanzees than in people. And chimpanzees can also solve fairly complex puzzles, such as ones that involve locks and keys, or mazes. Moreover, in a series of intriguing experiments with mirrors, Gordon Gallup, professor of psychology at the University at Albany in New York, demonstrated that, unlike monkeys, chimpanzees have a sense of "me" or self. To show this, Gallup painted red dye over the eyebrows and on the ears of a variety of anaesthetized animals that were then placed near mirrors. Upon waking and looking into the mirror, most of the animals did not appear to recognize the altered reflections as their own, although some of them did investigate the red patches on that other animal in the mirror. Not so for Gallup's chimpanzees. As I like to tell my students: the chimpanzees woke up, looked in the mirror with horror, touched their own ears and eyebrows (not their mirror image's), and then sobbed, "Oh my God, who did this to me?"

We now have some other inklings about how chimpanzees think, thanks to the pioneering work of Allen and the late Beatrix Gardner. Beginning in the 1960s, the Gardners taught American Sign Language for the Deaf to several chimpanzees, including the famous Washoe. The Gardners' research opened up a whole new field of investigation. Consequently, results are now available regarding the acquisition of several types of nonverbal languages in apes. If they are exposed to language for a sufficient period of time, chimpanzees can learn an impressive number of signs and spontaneously put them together into very simple proper sentences. In fact, the stages of language acquisition are similar in young chimpanzees and human children. Up to a point, that is.

Since the Gardners' groundbreaking efforts, other scientists have taken up the mantel. Psychologist Sue Savage-Rumbaugh of Georgia State University has spent most of her working life in the company of chimpanzees. Along with her husband, Duane Rumbaugh, she helped design and teach a computer-based language called "Yerkese" to a number of chimpanzees. Savage-Rumbaugh has interacted so closely with the chimpanzees, and for such a long time, that they have come to accept her as one of their own. Consequently, she understands how chimpanzees think and has a good grasp of their cognitive similarities and differences with humans.

The Albert Einstein of living apes is a pygmy chimpanzee, or bonobo, named Kanzi. And Savage-Rumbaugh is one of Kanzi's best friends. Kanzi learned much of his Yerkese when Savage-Rumbaugh's back was turned. At the time, workers in the laboratory were making strenuous efforts to teach Kanzi's adoptive mother, Matata, the meanings of numerous keyboard symbols and to recognize their corresponding spoken English words. Yerkese utterances are produced by pressing the keys for these symbols. (Because of the anatomy of their throats, chimpanzees are essentially unable to clearly articulate spoken words.) During these sessions, Kanzi would be playing in the room, seemingly paying scant attention to his mother's activities. Matata proved to be a disappoint-

FIGURE 3.1.
Gordon Gallup contemplating himself in a mirror. Gallup's mirror experiments showed that chimpanzees have a humanlike sense of self. (Photograph by Elizabeth Davis.)

ment; old and set in her ways, she was not a quick study. The lab workers were beginning to think that pygmy chimpanzees were not going to be good subjects for language experiments.

One day, young Kanzi threw the researchers for a loop by revealing that he had learned a good deal of what they had unsuccessfully been trying to teach his mother—and had apparently done so by osmosis. Similarly, when my daughter, Adrienne, was eleven, she learned Spanish in Puerto Rico in much the same way that Kanzi sopped up Yerkese (in Adrienne's words: "on the street, Mom"). Like Matata with her language, Adrienne's mother struggled with Spanish lessons at night school, never learned it very well, and spoke it with an American accent to boot. Herein lies a human/chimpanzee similarity in language acquisition: the young of both species learn a foreign language easily (humans with the proper accent), whereas mature individuals have to struggle (and older people retain a foreign accent). Put bluntly, Matata's and Mom's brains had pickled as far as language was concerned. Kanzi's and Adrienne's had not.

By the time he was six years old, Kanzi could identify 150 symbols upon hearing their spoken words.[1] As of this writing, Kanzi is twenty-three years old and Sue Savage-Rumbaugh estimates that he now understands around 2,000 words. He also responds appropriately to sentences that contain similar words arranged in different orders that change their meaning. Unlike some of the apes used in earlier studies, Kanzi produces spontaneous utterances that reflect what is on his mind, rather than merely labeling objects in response to the experimenter's question, "What's that, Kanzi?"

As with young humans, Kanzi's language comprehension was ahead of his language production, and his linguistic skills continued to increase as he matured, although not as much as those of a human child. Most of his utterances are still only one or two words. Kanzi is not alone. Savage-Rumbaugh now works with two groups of bonobos, each containing four animals. One group is lexically competent, the other is not. The findings for Kanzi have been confirmed: young apes, like young children, can assimilate certain language skills by observing and listening to their caretakers.

As noted, because of their throats, chimpanzees' linguistic utterances are usually restricted to gestural signs or pressing keyboard symbols. Nevertheless, even when Kanzi was much younger, it appeared to his caretakers that he sometimes made an effort to actually speak a few English words such as "carrot," "onion," "raisin," "snake," "right now," and "open." Skeptics, however, were reluctant to accept these vocalizations as words, and suggested, instead, that they were simply indicative of a heightened emotional state. Happily, Kanzi's linguistic efforts have recently been vindicated by spectrographic and statistical analyses that affirm (and quantify) that he has distinct vocalizations for "banana," "grape," "juice," and "yes."[2]

But there are certain language-related skills that apes, even young apes, do *not* develop. Savage-Rumbaugh points out that whereas humans can do simultaneous tasks, chimpanzees cannot. (In other words, chimps have a hard time with the proverbial problem of walking and chewing gum at the same time.) Savage-Rumbaugh also notes that

FIGURE 3.2.
The Albert Einstein of living apes is a pygmy chimpanzee, or bonobo, named Kanzi. (Photograph courtesy of Sue Savage-Rumbaugh.)

chimpanzees can invent gestures fairly easily, but these inventions do not get encoded and transmitted to others. This may be due to the fact that chimpanzees often have difficulty cooperating with each other, as Christophe Boesch of the Max Planck Institute in Leipzig notes. (Dr. Boesch makes this observation despite the fact that he and his wife, Hedwige Boesch, saw two rare instances of forest-dwelling chimpanzee mothers demonstrating nut-cracking techniques to their offspring.) According to Savage-Rumbaugh, apes seem to anticipate the actions of other apes or people, but they do not plan ahead as humans do, and they seem not to have an awareness of death.

Kathleen Gibson of the University of Texas Health Science Center[3] has also worked with chimpanzees and has a pet New World capuchin monkey who, like his conspecifics, is clever at using tools. She speculates that her pet could easily break a rock into flakes, but thinks that the monkey would never be able to put them back together again. Gibson believes that the act of putting things together sets people apart from nonhuman primates. Although it may not sound like much at first, a general ability to construct may, indeed, have far-reaching implications when it comes to putting together sentences or even generating ideas. Indeed, Gibson seems to have hit upon something very important here.

Chimpologists have a privileged perspective from which to compare the cognitive abilities of humans and apes. They are able to tell us certain ways in which humans are unique. Humans can attend to multiple tasks, cooperate, plan ahead, construct, and easily encode and transmit inventions to others. However, this list seems almost too narrow because as Savage-Rumbaugh observes, there is an enormous difference between chimpanzees and humans. Humans are just plain smarter. Both chimpanzees and young children use gestures combined with two-word utterances (pressing keys on the one hand, vocalizations on the other) to ask for cookies, tickles, games, favorite people, and so on. However, the chimpanzee never grows out of this stage. A human child always does. By five years of age, the child is capable of asking profound questions, but the chimpanzee is not. And, of course, spontaneous questions like "Mommy, where did I come from?" spring directly from the child's brain. That is the major difference between a chimpanzee and a human.

There is another general area of human accomplishment that chimpologists rarely mention, probably because it is so obvious. No chimpanzee ever wrote a book, composed a symphony, painted a realistic portrait, performed a *Singing in the Rain*–quality tap dance, calculated the day of the week upon which a certain date will fall next year, developed a math proof, took apart and reassembled a watch, programmed a computer, designed a bridge, or theorized about the origin of the universe. These arts and sciences also spring from special features of the human brain.

But these special features had to come from somewhere, and chimpanzees are a good place to look for whispers of creativity that may hearken back to the initial substrates that eventually gave rise to the arts and sciences. Take music, for example. Recently, Sue Savage-Rumbaugh showed me a videotape of Panbanisha and Kanzi playing the piano with British rock star Peter Gabriel. The video gave me goose bumps. Accompanied by Gabriel and his colleagues who were playing instruments in an adjacent room, Panbanisha sat at a keyboard and improvised a slow, melodic "grooming song." Exit Panbanisha, and enter Kanzi to a loud, rhythmic background provided by Gabriel's group. Kanzi positively sauntered into the room and over to the piano bench, where he sat down and got right into the spirit of the music. He and Gabriel improvised off of each other, and it sounded to my ears like passable jazz.[4] When I first saw the tape, in fact, I thought that if I'd been sitting in a smoky club engaged in conversation, I wouldn't have noticed that the background music was being played on the keyboard by a chimpanzee. Although neither Panbanisha nor Kanzi is ever likely to play a Mozart piece, it is clear that they have an appreciation for music and take pleasure in making it.

So what is it that the human brain has that the chimpanzee brain does not? Dissection of brains from each species has not provided an answer to this question. On a superficial level, brains of humans and brains of chimpanzees appear to have all the same parts. True, human brains are larger and more convoluted than chimpanzee brains. However, the other differences that exist between the brains of humans and chimpanzees are more subtle than mere gross neuroanatomy.

This does not mean that differences between human and chimpanzee brains cannot be detected. Fortunately, they can be. Comparative neuroanatomists have repeatedly touched upon three separate themes in explaining the unique features of the human brain: evolution of the frontal lobes, the relative amount of association cortex across the entire brain, and the extent of differences between the right and left hemispheres, or brain lateralization. To oversimplify, the first theme is implicated with planning ahead and personality factors, the second with the ability to put things together in a meaningful way (construct and synthesize), and the third with participation in the arts and sciences. As is well known, all three areas of activity contribute to being human.

The Cerebral Cortex

Neurosurgeons working in the earlier part of the last century demonstrated that the cerebral cortex is organized according to the same basic floor plan in nonhuman primates and people. The following two illustrations show the primary sensory and motor areas of the left hemisphere of a human brain (representing the right side of the body), as determined by the neurosurgical pioneers Wilder Penfield and his colleagues.[5] The primary somatosensory area (S in the top illustration) re-

fers to the first locations at which sensations of touch, pain, temperature, pressure, position, movement, and vibration are received by the
cortex. Primary motor cortex (M) is the area of cortex where motor responses are caused by relatively low thresholds of electrical stimulation.
In higher primates, including humans, the central sulcus separates primary motor from primary somatosensory cortex, as well as frontal from
parietal lobes.

In the second illustration, an upside-down man (or homunculus)
shows the order in which body parts are represented on the primary
somatosensory and motor cortices.[6] The map for an ape would be arranged the same. Certain features of the homunculus are noteworthy.
For example, the sensory and motor maps of the left hemisphere represent the right side of the body, and vice versa (notice that both hands and
both feet of the homunculus are from the right side of the body). Further, the sensory and motor maps for the opposite side of the body are
mirrored around the central sulcus. Thus, sensory information for the
right hand is received in the hand area behind the central sulcus of the
left cerebral hemisphere, and the motor impulses to wiggle the fingers
of the *right* hand come from the hand area in front of the central sulcus
of the *left* hemisphere. Although there are exceptions, such crossed (or
contralateral) representation is the general rule for the cerebral cortex.

The homunculus appears somewhat comical because of the distorted
size of certain body parts, not to mention that it is upside down. However, for mammals in general, the size of the cortical area for a particular
body part is a reflection of its functional importance in the day-to-day life
of that animal. (Harry Jerison calls this the *principle of proper mass.*) The
homunculus reflects the importance of hands and face for humans.
Notice also that sensory and motor representations for the right foot
curve over the top of the brain and extend down the (buried) inside surface of the hemisphere. Certain other interesting features are not shown
in my homunculus. For example, sensory representation for genitals is
located deep on the inside surface of the brain, near the sensory area for
the foot. Similarly, sensory and motor representations for vocal structures such as the larynx and jaw are located right below the face representation (and just above the Sylvian fissure).

As shown in the first illustration, the Sylvian fissure separates the
frontal and parietal lobes from the temporal lobe of the brain. Most of

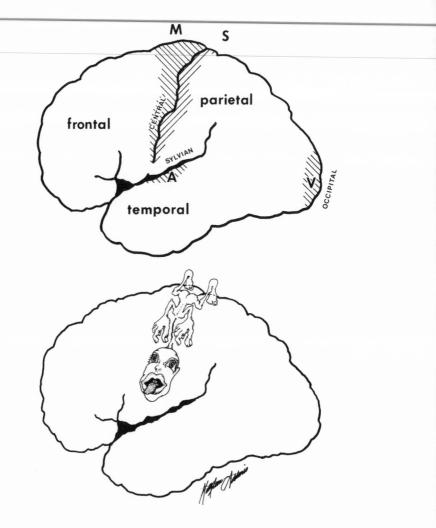

FIGURE 3.3.

(top) The primary cortical areas of the human brain (left side) include M, motor; S, somatosensory; A, auditory; and V, visual, with the lobes of the brain and Sylvian and central sulci indicated. (bottom) This homunculus illustrates the order and scale in which body parts are represented on the primary somatosensory and motor areas of the brain (left hemisphere).

the primary auditory cortex (A) is located on the superior part of the temporal lobe and is buried within the floor of the Sylvian fissure. The primary auditory cortex is organized according to pitch of sounds and (contrary to the contralateral rule) receives substantial input from the ear of the same side, as well as a somewhat greater contribution from the opposite ear.

The primary visual area (V) is not always limited by the lunate sulcus in humans, as it is in other higher primates. The primary visual cortex is represented by just a small portion of the outside surface of the occipital lobe in humans, whereas larger areas are buried on the inside surfaces of the back of the brain. The right half of the visual field is represented in the primary visual cortex of the left hemisphere, and vice versa.

Each of the primary sensory areas has a special relationship with a nearby association area. For example, the primary somatosensory cortex (S) sends fibers to an area of the parietal lobe directly behind it. Data from the general senses are integrated, related to past experiences, and interpreted in this association area. By way of illustration, it is this region that allows a person to interpret an unseen object held in the opposite hand as, say, a key. If the association cortex were damaged (but with the primary somatosensory cortex left intact), the individual would know that his hand held an object that was small, cold, and heavy. However, he would not be able to put the information together and arrive at the conclusion that the object was a key.

Similarly, the primary visual cortex (V) sends fibers to the association cortex right in front of it. In a manner like that just described for somatosensory association cortex, visual association cortex relates present to past visual experiences and permits recognition of what is seen and appreciation of its significance. Damage to this area results in an inability to recognize objects in the opposite visual field. The auditory association cortex (which is located right next to A) also permits the listener to recognize and interpret language and nonlanguage sounds.

The primary motor cortex has its helper too, called the premotor cortex and located directly in front of the primary motor cortex (and the homunculus). Stimulation of the premotor cortex causes muscle movements on the opposite side of the body, although stronger stimulation is required than from the primary motor cortex. The premotor cortex seems to be involved with accessing the memory of complex movements that have been learned (such as brushing the teeth), since these movements may be impaired by a lesion in that area, while other voluntary motor functions are spared.

There you have it: the basic cortical floor plan of higher primates including rhesus monkeys, chimpanzees, and humans. And it was probably the blueprint for the cortex of their common ancestor as well. But from whence the paintings, the symphonies, and the great books? Those came with nature's elaborations of three overlapping cortical features whose seeds were sown long before the world saw its first hominin: the frontal lobes, association cortex, and brain lateralization.

Inner Models of Reality: Domain of the Frontal Lobes

The area in front of the premotor cortex (that is, the foremost end of the frontal lobe) is known as the prefrontal association cortex. Unlike primary motor and premotor cortices, bodily movements are not usually elicited when the prefrontal cortex is stimulated. Thus, the prefrontal cortex is said to be silent. Silent it may be, but a lot is going on there nevertheless. For it is the prefrontal cortex that is responsible for self-regulated, goal-directed behaviors that are formative of personality. In some sense, then, it is the prefrontal cortex that makes us human.

Not too many years ago, it was considered appropriate to treat severe depression (often in housewives) by removing part of the prefrontal cortex or by severing the tracts that connect it with other, deeper parts of the brain. Although such prefrontal lobotomies did cure patients of depression, they also resulted in a host of less-desirable changes. To greater or lesser degrees (depending on the amount of brain damage sustained), frontal lobe patients were subject to thought disorders, inappropriate or generally flattened moods, lack of initiative, poverty of speech, and inability to grasp the significance of events going on around them. Prefrontal lobotomies were also used to treat intractable pain, such as that associated with inoperable cancer. In these cases, although patients could still experience pain after their surgeries, they no longer minded it! Prefrontal lobotomies thus resulted in nothing less than complete personality changes.

Frontal lobes changed greatly during primate evolution. In particular, compared with more posterior regions of the brain, the prefrontal cortex is more convoluted in humans than in apes.[7] Even in monkeys, the prefrontal cortex is highly differentiated and has multiple subdivisions and connections. Because the prefrontal cortex of macaques is relatively well understood, the neuroanatomy of this species provides insights that may shed light on the basic floor plan and evolutionary significance of the human frontal lobe.

The late Patricia Goldman-Rakic incorporated a good deal of experimental evidence of macaques into an elegant model that explains much about the basic organization of the primate prefrontal cortex.[8] According to Goldman-Rakic, the elemental capacity of the prefrontal cortex is to access information and keep it on-line (or, in mind) until the task at hand is completed. It can also stimulate or inhibit motor responses based on the on-line representation. Thus, the prefrontal cortex affects attention, accesses memories, and helps to govern behavior via motor control.

Further, because of their connections to other lobes as well as deeper brain structures, specific areas of the prefrontal cortex seem to specialize in the types of information they process. One part of the prefrontal cortex of macaques holds on-line the positions of objects in space, while another attends to nonspatial visual attributes of objects, such as color. Although not as well understood, still another area of the monkey prefrontal cortex appears to be associated with social/emotional and motivational states. In sum, Goldman-Rakic hypothesizes that "the subdivisions of the primate prefrontal cortex function as central executive centers for guiding voluntary behavior by representational memory."[9] Put another way, the prefrontal cortex integrates events that are separated in time and space and uses stored representational knowledge to guide appropriate responses. Without it, neither monkey nor man could keep enough information in mind to plan even a little bit ahead. Of course, humans are the supreme planners. A chimpanzee can hold on-line the location of previously stored food and go for it when permitted to do so. However, Savage-Rumbaugh tells us that unlike humans, chimpanzees have difficulty attending to more than one task at a time, do not plan much ahead, and seem to have no concept of death (perhaps the ultimate in planning ahead).

Because of the way in which it became reorganized during hominin evolution, the frontal lobe is the one part of the brain in which chimpanzee and human sulcal patterns are easily distinguishable. But it is not just the absolute size of the frontal lobes that counts, as revealed by exciting new MRI work by Katerina Semendeferi of the University of California at San Diego and her colleagues.[10] Although human frontal cortices are absolutely larger than their counterparts in great apes, the relative size of the frontal cortex (that is, its percentage of the entire cerebral cortex) is the same in the two groups. Contrary to received wisdom at the time this book was first published, Semendeferi concludes that humans and great apes share a relatively large frontal cortex, and that the special cognitive abilities of the former may be due to differences in the sizes of subregions of the frontal lobe, as well as to richer connectivity within the frontal lobe and between it and other parts of the brain. One thing is for sure: whatever their nature, the organizational changes that took place in the human frontal lobe were accompanied by an elaboration of the capacities that Goldman-Rakic has enumerated for the prefrontal cortex of nonhuman primates.

The human frontal lobe not only brings information on-line, presumably it can bring lots of information on-line simultaneously. Thus, the prefrontal cortex of humans may access relatively more memory to guide voluntary motor responses than is the case for nonhuman primates. An increased capacity to bring memory on-line would account, in part, for the fact that learned motor behaviors of humans can entail longer sequences of activity that are more finely controlled than those of apes. (Recall that the performance of learned motor skills is associated with the premotor cortex, which presumably is influenced by the prefrontal cortex.) As a result, people learn intricate, sequential motor activities that are uniquely and gloriously human, such as (my favorite) tap dancing.

Tap dancing depends, first and foremost, on a kind of motor memory and, second, on the ability to smoothly execute a sequence of learned movements (taps) that are remembered. Rhythm, or timing, is everything—botch the spacing between taps, and you ruin the dance. In order to perform, a tap dancer must be able to actualize the memory of how to correctly time taps. This requires anticipation of what is ahead. The tap dancer's holding of representations of long motor sequences on-line long enough to execute them correctly bridges time. The tap dance has a past, present, and future. And so, alas, does the tap dancer.

FIGURE 3.4.
Meticulous research by Katerina Semendeferi has clarified details about the evolution of the human frontal lobes. (Photograph courtesy of K. Semendeferi.)

Whereas chimpanzees can plan only a bit ahead (get that food bait), thanks to its evolved frontal lobes, the species that tap dances has a conscious concept of time.

Another unique human characteristic that may be attributed to elaborate frontal lobes is an active imagination. Because of their ability to time bind, people can hold real or fictitious ideas on-line and spin all kinds of scenarios. We've all relived unpleasant past events and imagined "if only I'd done such and such." In the face of frustrating past (or present) events, one may entertain other outcomes and obtain satisfaction after all, if only in the mind's eye. Perhaps more important, an active fantasy life allows humans to anticipate variations of future events and imagine (practice) alternate responses. The human imagination is so powerful that it cannot sit still. If it's not being used for something practical or being occupied (for example, by television), it will entertain itself with gratuitous fantasies. Apparently, the frontal lobe provides its own entertainment center. And, as dreams show, its doors are unlocked twenty-four hours a day.

Perhaps the most mysterious function of the frontal lobe has to do with personality factors, such as individual styles of social awareness and behaviors toward others. Chimpanzees do not show the same degree of frontal-lobe mediated self-regulation of responses to social/emotional events as mature humans do. Human frontal lobes have complex connections with other deeper parts of the brain (known as limbic structures) that are concerned with emotional processes. Thus, codes of conduct that have been deeply ingrained in childhood may be accessed and represented in the prefrontal cortex and, ultimately, brought to bear on adult social interactions. Mature people attempt to govern their social interactions and to take other individuals into account (that is, to guard against childish behavior).

Higher Thought Processes: The Association Areas

A synthesis of neurological events, or gluing together of information that occurs in the frontal lobes, is a form of thinking. And the prefrontal association cortex is not the only part of the brain that transforms multiple inputs into higher-order thoughts. This kind of synthetic thinking also occurs in other association areas of the temporal, parietal, and occipital lobes. One way to get a handle on the general functions of these posterior association areas is to examine the intriguing syndromes that occur in people when these areas are damaged.[11] For example, we've already noted that damage to the association regions contiguous with the primary receptive areas interferes with the integration and interpretation of sensory information. Thus, if a lesion occurs in the area that is directly in front of the primary visual cortex, a person may be able to walk around an obstacle such as a ladder (indicating that he sees it), yet be unable to name it, say what it is used for, or point out that he has just avoided bad luck. In short, the visual input is there, but the ability to interpret it is not.

Sensations of touch, hearing, and vision are integrated in the parietal association cortex. Because of connections between the parietal association cortex and other areas such as the frontal lobes, these complex associations are interpreted in light of past experience and present judgment. Damage to parietal association areas can therefore lead to bizarre dysfunctions; the best known entails a failure to recognize body scheme.

A person (or nonhuman primate) with this syndrome does not recognize a part of his body as belonging to himself. For example, if the damaged area of the parietal lobe is the association cortex for the hand (of the opposite side of the body), the individual fails to recognize the hand as his own. He will not talk about the hand, wash it, or put a glove on it. He does, however, know that the hand is a hand and may in fact be quite frightened of it because, to him, it is someone else's hand. This same neglect syndrome occurs for other parts of the body such as the face, depending on which parts of the superior parietal lobe are damaged.

The sense of our own whole bodies is so intrinsic to our day-to-day living that we do not ordinarily think of this experience as being dependent upon synthetic neurological processes. Yet it is. And just as we all have an awareness of our body scheme, we also have an awareness of visuospatial relationships in the external world. Along with expanded association areas, visuospatial skills, or the related ability to map one's environment, are especially well developed in humans. The extent of these skills varies with sex (males outperform females on some tests) and from individual to individual. Certain visuospatial abilities are also better developed on the right side of the brain.

Olfactory, auditory, and visual associations dominate the front part of the temporal lobe. These associations are influenced by other parts of the brain, including the frontal lobe, a nearby limbic area on the underside of the temporal lobe that is important for memory (the hippocampus), and other limbic structures that are concerned with emotions. Consequently, the association cortex of the front part of the temporal lobe is susceptible to its own interesting syndrome. Damage to this area results in vivid auditory, visual, or olfactory hallucinations. For example, a temporal lobe patient may experience a strong sense of déjà vu, while hearing distorted music that is not there or seeing hallucinations of funny little (or large) people. Depending on the size of the area involved, the person may also smell nonexistent disagreeable odors and experience intense, irrational fear. A dreamy sense of unreality often accompanies these hallucinations, and the patient frequently realizes that the sensations are not real.

Remove the temporal lobes in human and nonhuman primates, and a suite of similar symptoms occur in what is known as the Kluver-Bucy syndrome. These symptoms include psychic blindness, a tendency to examine everything with the mouth, voracious appetite, increased sexual activity, marked absence of emotional responses, and general docility. Although it is unlikely that a temporal-lobe-damaged monkey ever hallucinated music, the Kluver-Bucy syndrome suggests that, once again, temporal lobe association areas of humans are elaborations woven from a basic primate floor plan.

Language Areas: Manifestation of a Lateralized Brain

More than a century ago, Paul Broca discovered an amazing fact from postmortem autopsies of patients with speech disorders. Their brains almost invariably had damage in a specific area of the left hemisphere. Today, we know that language has both sensory and motor components. It is therefore represented by networks that depend partly on two focal areas in the brain, one posterior and one anterior. An important sensory area for *comprehension* of spoken words (known as Wernicke's area) is next to the primary auditory area in the temporal lobe. A crucial motor area for *speech* (Broca's area) is located in the frontal lobe near the primary motor areas that stimulate the organs of speech (such as larynx, tongue, mouth). As anticipated by Broca's initial discovery, both language areas are located in the left hemisphere. Although they are on the same side of the brain, damage to these areas results in different types of aphasias.

Patients with Broca's aphasia are fine in the comprehension department. However, they have great difficulty speaking or writing what they wish to say. Their speech is terribly slow and, when it finally comes, characterized by poor articulation. Although patients may be able to produce single meaningful words, small words and endings are usually omitted. As a result, their sentences (such as they are) are grammatically incorrect. Left-hemisphere damage may extend to the primary motor cortex, which accounts for the fact that Broca's aphasiacs also frequently experience paralysis of the right side of the body.

Wernicke's aphasia is quite a different story. Although a patient's basic hearing abilities may be unimpaired, comprehension of speech is severely disrupted by damage to Wernicke's area. (If the damage is extended posteriorly, reading ability will also be lost.) Because Broca's area

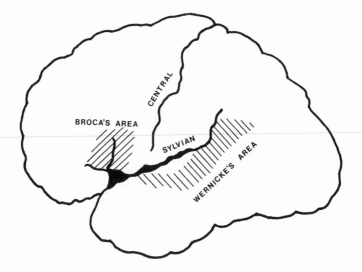

FIGURE 3.5.
The left hemisphere of a human brain showing approximate locations of classical Broca's area (front) and Wernicke's area (rear).

is undamaged, the rhythm and grammatical scaffolding of speech appear normal. Verbal output seems effortless in Wernicke's patients, yet its content is full of numerous errors, including lots of little words and circumlocutions. In short, speech has little meaning in the Wernicke's aphasiac. It is "word salad."

The above summaries of Broca's and Wernicke's aphasias are, of course, oversimplifications; both areas are now known to participate in certain nonlinguistic as well as linguistic processes. Beneath the surface of the cortex, the two areas of the brain connect with each other and with other cortical areas. There are not only two types of aphasia but also many different manifestations (each with unique combinations of symptoms). Perhaps more important, the left-hemisphere areas for comprehension and production of language extend beyond those that have been classically defined. In some sense, both Broca's area and Wernicke's area should be larger than shown in my illustration. Although Wernicke didn't know it, his area should extend back up and around the end of the Sylvian fissure, because it is here that reading and a full understanding of the symbolism of language are facilitated.[12] Likewise, Broca's area should be extended forward to include part of the area that is directly in front of it.[13]

Because language so dramatically separates humans from nonhuman primates, the evolutionary importance of Broca's and Wernicke's areas has been greatly emphasized. Do nonhuman primates have these areas? The answer is yes and no. Yes, there are frontal lobe and temporal/parietal regions in the brains of monkeys and apes that appear to be in (somewhat) similar positions and to have similar arrangements of cells as Broca's and Wernicke's areas do in human brains. There is also some evidence that the left hemisphere differentially processes socially meaningful vocalizations in certain nonhuman higher primates. It therefore appears that, once again, human language areas are an elaboration on the basic primate pattern. However, the sulcal pattern associated with Broca's area in humans does not appear in the hominin fossil record until around two million years ago. And of course, monkeys and apes don't talk or read books.

Body Language

Because of its predilection for language, the left hemisphere is known as the major hemisphere. During development, the left hemisphere matures more slowly than the right hemisphere. And some workers believe that the left hemisphere was a kind of late bloomer during primate evolution as well (that is, that it changed more than the right hemisphere during hominin evolution). All of this credit has gone to the left hemisphere because of one package of skills—those related to language.

I believe that the above interpretation is too narrow. We have toured the different lobes of the brain and have seen numerous ways in which humans differ cognitively from their chimpanzee (and monkey) cousins. Yes, the left hemisphere of the human brain is particularly good at analytical, time-sequencing processes that are important for language. As we have seen, it can count (keep time) and smoothly execute strings of ordered motor events. And the left hemisphere can bring past experiences on-line and use them to influence not only what is said, but also what is done. Contrary to popular wisdom, however, human beings apply the analytical, sequencing skills of the left hemisphere to the task of communicating with their *whole bodies,* rather than with just their vocal anatomies. Language is important, but it is not everything.

Take, for instance, the gesticulation that accompanies speech. When people talk, so do their bodies: heads bob, arms flail, eyebrows are raised, and hands go everywhere. Further, these bodily movements are rhythmically coordinated with speech. As Adam Kendon, a leading expert on gesture, puts it: "Speech and movement appear together, as manifestations of the same process of utterance. That is, in the translation of 'ideas' into observable behavior . . . the output that results is manifested in both speech and movement."[14] Kendon observes that the starting point that leads to generation of a multifaceted utterance is its semantic organization. It is the underlying meaning that drives communication.

As we speak, most of us are barely aware of our gesticulations. It is therefore surprising to learn that the gesticulations that accompany speech are not only planned, but are planned prior to the spoken phrase with which they concur. Apparently, the analytical frontal lobe sequencing machinery plans ahead, coordinates, and executes all kinds of motor activities in its mission to express meaning. By way of example, Kendon offers the following beautiful description from his observations of a videotape of a woman telling a fairy tale:

> The speaker is recounting how the hunter rescued Little Red Riding Hood's grandmother from the Big Bad Wolf, who had just eaten her. The speaker says: "And he took his hatchet and with a mighty sweep, sliced the wolf's stomach open". . . . As the speaker says "sliced" she brings both her hands down from an upraised position, sweeping them to her left as she does so, in what is clearly an enactment of the hunter's action. However, to do this, the speaker had to have her hands positioned in advance of the word "sliced." She organizes her hands into an upraised position as she says "and he took his hatchet and with," actually beginning this process before she begins to speak at all, and she holds her hands upraised while she says "a mighty sweep."
> . . . In the example given, for instance, it will be clear that the enactment of the hunter's action and the account given in speech must have been organized simultaneously. An image of the hunter's action must have been available before the speaker embarked on her speech. Note,

further, that the speaker, having raised her arms in preparation for the slicing movement, does not perform it at once, but waits until she has reached the word "sliced." The placement of the stroke of the gesture phrase (in this case the "slicing" enactment) in relation to the verbal representation of the action described is thus an organized placement and must itself be seen as part of the utterance plan.

In the example just discussed, the speaker adjusted the performance of her gesture to fit with the structure of the concurrent speech phrase. In other instances we may observe the reverse of this: the speaker adjusts the production of speech to the performance of gesture.[15]

This example illustrates that gesticulation and speech work together to communicate meaning in a subtle but complex manner. However, as Kendon points out, the mode of encoding content is different in the two forms of expression. In speech, highly conventionalized forms from an established vocabulary are organized sequentially and according to grammatical rules. On the other hand, although conventionalized forms may be used in gesticulation, the utterer has considerable leeway to create new gestures and to form constructions that are relatively free of grammatical constraints. Susan Goldin-Meadow of the University of Chicago has shown that, interestingly, children who are born deaf organize gestures into a fully linguistic system.[16] Thus, gesticulation retains its free spirit only if the utterer has access to both speech and gestural modes of expression.

What area of the brain facilitates gesticulation? We know that people who are right-handed (and left-hemisphere dominant for language) gesticulate more with that hand than with the left. It is also known that stimulation of the primary cortical (motor) hand representation causes the hand on the opposite side of the body to move, just as stimulation of primary facial and vocal areas causes movement of these structures. During speech, Broca's area somehow facilitates proper functioning of the primary motor cortex that controls the vocal anatomy. But what cortical areas influence primary hand representations? Does the frontal-lobe association cortex that is next to the primary hand region (above Broca's area) act as a kind of Broca's area, but for the hand? Perhaps it does.

Whatever the details of their neurological underpinnings, speech and gesticulation flow effortlessly together in order to achieve the mutual goal of expressing ideas that are brought on-line (represented) in the frontal lobes. Indeed, the two modes of communication can be difficult to separate, as illustrated by a well known interesting fact about simultaneous translators. Apparently, simultaneous translation of one language into another is a thoroughly exhausting enterprise. It is said that translators frequently occupy their hands with some rote activity such as knitting. Presumably, this minimizes the distraction that would ensue from attempting to gesticulate in concurrence with two slightly differently paced languages!

Chimpanzees Can't Tap Dance

As far as I am concerned, cortical areas for feet also have access to a kind of Broca's area (if not *the* Broca's area). I say this for the simple reason that, as an adult, I took tap lessons for five years and found this activity to be not only governed by the same constraints that apply to linguistics, but also one in which no chimpanzee could ever skillfully engage. Tap dancing, like speech, entails production of finely coordinated motor sequences that are based on an accepted vocabulary of smaller units. It is hierarchically organized and is generated according to grammatical rules. The left hemisphere prevails, since most tappers are better on their right sides. As with any foreign language, little kids learn tap easily, while adults have to struggle.

My tap class was taught by Cynthia (Riffle) Bowers, a professional dancer who taught ballet, tap, and jazz dance for a number of years in San Juan, Puerto Rico. She began taking tap lessons at age seven and by ten was also studying ballet, jazz, voice, and piano. For five years, Cynthia taught tap classes to six middle-aged adults who met once a week in her studio. (As an ecologist in the group put it, "You have to do something to keep in touch with your culture.") We were lucky to have a teacher who was incredibly fluent in tap. It was like taking lessons from Ginger Rogers. The following transcription of a conversation that I had with Cynthia gets at some of the thinking that underlies tap dancing. It also shows that the ability to tap dance is one of the better things about our species.

Q: *One of the things I've noticed is that the way you teach a complicated tap step, say like the timestep, is that you break it apart. Or break it down as you say, so that we learn it by first learning the individual parts and then glue them together.*

CYNTHIA: Right, so that they flow eventually.

Q: *And you glue them together in short segments and then glue those short segments together into longer segments. And so it flows and it gets to the point where all I have to do is think "timestep" and I can do a whole timestep. Is that the normal process?*

CYNTHIA: That's how I was taught. So that for the memory, once you learn brush-hop for instance, you do that over again. Brush-hop, brush-hop. That enters the brain, it enters the body, it has to enter down to the feet, the knees.

Q: *As one unit?*

CYNTHIA: As one unit. Then you have to just go on. An extra shuffle-step. OK. It's a memory; it would be like memorizing a complete sentence. So then I go back and I say, "OK. Now it's brush-hop, second part shuffle-step."

Q: *When you're dancing what are you thinking?*

CYNTHIA: Early on, when performing, I would be thinking more of the counts or of the steps. Now, after performing for years, I'm able to just listen to the music. The memory is now developed, as with most dancers after a period of time, so that I don't have to think about what comes next. Sometimes in a piece I'll have to be aware if there's a space problem, where I have to cross somebody. That breaks my listening to the music and all of a sudden I have to say, "Oh, where is she? Am I going to miss her?" But otherwise I just listen to the music.

Q: *Is that a larger extension of what we were just talking about? Is that "brush-hop, shuffle-step" but throughout the whole thing? Where you've got it down as one flowing—*

CYNTHIA: Right, it's almost as if your brain is a computer and it's there. A lot of people say to musicians, "How could somebody who's

FIGURE 3.6.
Cynthia (Riffle) Bowers taught tap and other dance classes in San Juan, Puerto Rico. (Photograph courtesy of C. Bowers.)

playing a concert, say a Bach concert, do it without reading music?" You should never go to a concert, and see somebody reading the music. The musician should know the music. Sometimes the music's there in front of him just to refer to in case there's a lapse of memory, but a concert pianist should be able to sit down and play a whole sonata. It's the same process; it's just part of him.

Q: *So you actually just listen to the music as you're performing, and that's it. . . . What about choreography?*

CYNTHIA: In choreographing, which is still new to me, the music usually comes first. If I close my eyes, I will see the steps or I will see the pattern or the next place it should go.

CYNTHIA: Oh, it's very visual. It's all lines, although many dancers don't even understand that. It's as if each move is a word and you're telling something, whether it's a literal story or not. A lot of dancers don't even realize that it's the lines they're making, and the connecting of the lines.

Q: *How do you prepare for a performance?*

CYNTHIA: Before a concert, I will not physically go through every move. The better thing for me to do, and I think a lot of artists will tell you this, is almost like meditating. I close my eyes, and I go through every move in a piece. I'm hearing the music, and I can feel and see my body go through every move. I know where my hands are, where my fingers are, where my head is, where my neck is.

Q: *And do you experience it; do you actually feel as if you're doing it?*

CYNTHIA: Yes, although in a sense I'm removed from it. It's almost as if I'm watching somebody on television doing it, in the sense of seeing it, but the feeling of it—

Q: *When you watch a performance, are you at some level participating?*

CYNTHIA: A really good dancer, yes. Somebody like Makarova, for instance, whose technique is so incredible that she's beyond her technique. The technique is there and you don't even think she's not going to make something or miss something. And she's so musical that she's able to take it beyond that and make one feel her moves. But only very few dancers do that. Astaire did that.

Q: *Do you dream about dance or moving?*

CYNTHIA: Not so much anymore. But I used to have a dream when I was a child. I would see myself fly in a grand jeté. A grand jeté is a big jump and everybody knows it when they see it. It's in every ballet. That was a wonderful dream. I would be in the grand jeté position and I would go around the room and was definitely above looking down. That was the flight thing, you know. Now later on, as years have gone by, I've lost that. I was never to regain that space.

Q: *What about the mental aspects of training?*

CYNTHIA: That's very important. When I teach my professionals who have studied at very good schools, and we're going to do pirouettes, there's no reason why three pirouettes should mean anything to them. It should have evolved by now, and they're still getting caught up in two pirouettes. Now that is a block. Somewhere there was too much technique taught and they've lost the feeling of what it's like to turn. So the thing I point out to them, even in balances, is that you can't let your mind get in the way. You just simply do it. In other words, if you're going to take your hand off the bar and try to balance and you're thinking of all these things and your mind is overworking, you're not just going for it. And a lot of it is just simply, "This is where I have to be and this is where I'm going to be." So a lot of times, the mind stops a natural movement.

Q: *Are dancers getting better all the time? Is there an evolution of dance?*

CYNTHIA: Well, when you look at old clips of people like Anna Pavlova, she was inspiring but certainly technically not anywhere up to where a dancer in a class would be today. The bodies have evolved and the feet and the backs and everything. People can do a lot more physically now than they did then. It doesn't mean that spiritually they've evolved to make the art form greater. I'm sure that if you saw Anna Pavlova dance and you saw somebody today dance, you might say that Pavlova was actually more inspirational than this other dancer who had her leg up to her nose and feet like this and had a back that went on for days and could turn maybe six times compared to Anna Pavlova's two turns. So it's a very individual thing. But certainly the physicalness has evolved. The kids on the street, look what they do: turning on their heads and elbows!

Cynthia's tap dancing is primarily an activity of her left hemisphere. Her dancing may be thought of as a kind of speech of the feet. Her right hemisphere is also involved, of course, since it controls the left side of her body. But it is the left hemisphere that is keeping time and running the show. It does so by sending instructions to Cynthia's right hemisphere. These precisely timed instructions are transmitted over nerve fibers that cross to the right hemisphere through a large C-shaped structure known as the corpus callosum. The corpus callosum is simply a big bundle of fibers that connects the two halves of the brain.

Despite the above observations about tap dancing, traffic along the corpus callosum is not one-way. Furthermore, the much beleaguered right hemisphere is often in the driver's seat. In fact, this has probably been the case since the days of the first primates. Contrary to popular wisdom, I believe that it was the right, rather than the left, hemisphere that sparked the evolution of brain lateralization in the earliest hominins. (This will be discussed later.)

Although they are very smart, even the most educated chimpanzees are not able to tap dance. Signing chimpanzees instead use their hard-won language skills almost exclusively to seek food or other immediate gratification. We pride ourselves that, by comparison, human intellectual and artistic achievements are so great that they must be the result of qualitative improvements in the human nervous system. According to this line of thought, it is not just that humans have larger brains than chimpanzees but also that humans have better brains. As we have seen, comparative neuroanatomists speculate that the neurological basis for the difference in consciousness between the chimpanzee and the human child is based on evolutionary improvements in three features: the frontal lobes, association cortices, and brain lateralization. But at what point during hominin evolution did these changes begin?

We know that, during much of their prehistory, australopithecine endocasts were about the size of chimpanzee brains and that, superficially, the pattern of their convolutions appeared apelike. However, because of allometric scaling, the latter is exactly what one would expect in light of the former. But australopithecines were not apes. Rather, they were ape-men who occupied their own unique niches. It is therefore safe to surmise from the fossil record and from comparative neuroanatomical studies that australopithecines would have had at least the cognitive ability of chimpanzees—and perhaps more.

Of course, the most striking feature about australopithecines was that they walked upright. Today, I believe more than ever that selection for bipedalism in early gracile australopithecines kicked off the train of events that would eventually lead to even more advanced brains. In fact, bipedalism may be the key to understanding human brain evolution.

chapter 4

OF FAMILY TREES, DARWIN'S THEORY, AND THE ORIGINS OF BIPEDALISM

Fossils have traditionally been used to sketch the sizes and shapes of family trees that evolved through time. This is done by placing reliably dated specimens on time charts and then connecting them with probable descendants that include other fossils and living species. The resulting evolutionary trees can be narrow or full. In keeping with a long evolutionary history that spans some 65 million years, the family tree for primates is bushy. Unfortunately, the fossil record provides many disconnected fossil twigs (species whose descendants are unknown). The precise branching pattern for all of primate evolution is therefore impossible to establish. Happily, it is somewhat easier to arrive at reasonable family trees for relatively recently evolved groups of primates like the apes and ourselves.

Thanks to a new breed of anthropologist, paleoanthropology has recently undergone a revolution in the way it constructs the family tree of apes and humans. As their name implies, molecular anthropologists investigate differences in various microscopic structures or processes. These include specific sequences of DNA, certain blood proteins, immunological reactions, and results of DNA hybridization experiments. Each difference between molecules is the result of one mutation. Assuming that mutations occurred randomly and at a uniform rate over time, investigators are able to determine mutation rates for specific molecules in species whose times of divergence are known from the fossil record. The mutation rate can then be used to estimate the time at which other species diverged, on the basis of their molecular dissimilarity.

Family trees based on molecules don't always agree with trees constructed exclusively from fossils, a fact that creationists frequently bring up during their attempts to discredit evolutionary theory. However, previous discrepancies between molecular and fossil approaches have turned out to be the result of errors in basic assumptions, such as a miscalculated mutation rate here or a misidentified fossil there. Furthermore, both schools are sure to continue arguing about the branching patterns for certain groups of primates until a working set of basic assumptions is accepted by one and all. It is important to note, however, that these differences of opinion are about details, not about whether evolutionary theory is valid.

Contrary to what creationists would like you to believe, traditional and molecular anthropologists both use scientific methods that are grounded in Darwinian theory. No matter how they draw their trees, all evolutionary biologists accept the premise that when the environment changes, populations of living organisms tend to alter over time in response to the new environment.[1] That way, life goes on. The theory of natural selection, formulated by Charles Darwin and Alfred Russel Wallace, explains how this important phenomenon works. In developing their theory, Darwin and Wallace were profoundly influenced by the 1798 edition of *An Essay on the Principle of Population* by the English clergyman and political economist, Thomas Robert Malthus.

In his essay, Malthus pointed out that if human populations are unrestrained by natural causes, they will double in size every twenty-five years. He also claimed that food production increases linearly and that it therefore could not keep up with the geometric increase in population size. Malthus concluded that the struggle for existence keeps animal populations in check, but that artificial restraints would have to be applied to humans. It was specifically the notion of natural checks on population size that excited the imaginations of Darwin and Wallace.[2]

Darwin and Wallace independently had the same "aha" experience after reading Malthus's essay. They realized that those individuals with characteristics that were the most favorable for survival (individuals who were the best adapted) would prevail over others in the struggle for existence. It was that simple. In 1859, Darwin went on to elaborate the theory of evolution in his book *On the Origin of Species by Means of Natural Selection, or The Preservation of Favoured Races in the Struggle for Life*.

Darwin's theory can be reiterated in a sequence of logical steps. First, because of Malthus, Darwin assumed that all species produced more offspring than could be fed; therefore only some individuals of each species would survive. Second, the survivors would naturally turn out to be those who were better adapted to their particular environments—the stronger, the quicker, and the like. A very important third assumption was that favorable traits of those who survived could be inherited by the next generation. (Darwin knew this was true, although he was not familiar with Gregor Mendel's work on genes.) Darwin concluded that entirely new species resulted from the above processes acting over long periods of geological time. Today, traditional and molecular evolutionists may quibble about the pace, rates, and methods for studying evolution, but Darwin's grand theory still stands.

Our Arboreal Heritage

In an exciting and relatively recent development, the brunt of the molecular evidence now suggests that humans share a more recent common ancestor (CA) with chimpanzees than with any other primate, including gorillas. (In fact, the genetic similarity between chimpanzees and humans is so close that some workers have suggested that a cross between a human and a chimpanzee might theoretically be possible!)

Furthermore, molecular anthropologists have determined that the CA lived about five to seven million years ago, an estimate that traditional anthropologists find they can accept.[3] Although all known fossil hominins were bipedal, we know that at some point they, like our cousins the chimpanzees, had ancestors who were arboreal. Thus, the CA bequeathed certain general arboreal primate traits to early chimpanzees and our early hominin relatives. Simply put, although hominins lived on the ground and walked on two legs, many of the features that they inherited were developed over the course of millions of years of primate evolution *in trees*. This is a basic theme in primatology and is called the "Aboreal Theory."[4] It also applies to humans.

Look in the mirror and you will see a primate who retains many adaptations for life in the trees. Those eyes. They face forward, instead of sideways like the eyes of some dogs. All the better to see with in three dimensions (a result of the two eyes' visual fields overlapping). And seeing in three dimensions is very helpful when it comes to leaping around in a complicated environment that is up high. What shoulders! They're sturdy and allow a good deal of mobility in the upper arms: a necessity for suspending one's weight by the arms or swinging through trees.

Look at your hands. They have really good grasping ability and fingernails instead of claws. Hands like these are great for hanging onto branches without clawing oneself in the palms. The hands and eyes together make for good hand-eye coordination in primates. This is useful for picking, inspecting, and eating plant food. Or for catching insects. No snout. Many of its grasping functions (including picking food) were taken over by hands in an arboreal environment. Further, the keen sense of smell that is associated with a snout is not as important as good vision for a tree-living primate.

Besides these physical features, we also inherited certain related behaviors from our distant tree-living ancestors. For example, we sleep in beds that derive from tree nests. During the night, people sometimes awaken briefly with a quick jerk. Fear of falling from the nest? How do you regard snakes and spiders? These creatures evoke terror in many humans, and I suspect we owe this oddity to our arboreal legacy, as well. Chimpanzees apparently select their lodge trees and construct their night nests with an eye toward avoiding just such dangers. (I avoid these and other frights by pulling the covers up over my body before going to sleep.)

Some of our daytime activities are also rooted in the trees. Children at playgrounds love to do arboreal acrobatics (playing on the monkey bars). Adults also have the ability to swing through the trees. However, except for joining sports programs or the circus, there is little opportunity to develop this proclivity in our culture. In one respect, hand-eye coordination is important to us in much the same way that it is to an arboreal primate: we visually inspect our food before bringing it into our mouth. If it looks questionable, we either do not put it into our mouths or do so knowing that we may regret it later. Primates, including ourselves, would be truly miserable eating while blindfolded.

So these traits are part of the general primate baggage that was handed down to the CA of chimpanzees and humans some five to seven million years ago. We should also include good mothering, a tendency for child's play, and, of course, a lively curiosity. The latter is very important and goes with another special feature that developed during primate evolution—an unusually large brain.

Getting the Feet on the Ground

But what set the CA apart from other primates? Unfortunately, there are few fossil remains from five to seven million years ago that have been proposed as hominin, and these are very fragmentary and controversial. It is best, therefore, to make educated guesses about the CA on the basis of later fossil hominins and living apes. Adrienne Zihlman, professor of anthropology at the University of California, Santa Cruz, has done comparative studies of ape anatomy and fossil hominin bones that have led her to one of the best assessments going for the CA. Unfortunately, and predictably, she has not always been given due credit for her contribution. Zihlman candidly discusses the frustrations of doing paleoanthropological research, noting that any successful new hypothesis passes through three predictable stages on the road to respectability:

First, it is criticized for being untrue.

Secondly, after supporting evidence accumulates, it is stated that it may be true, but is not particularly relevant.

Thirdly, after it has clearly influenced the field, it is admitted to be true and relevant, but the same critics assert that the idea was not original.[5]

As Zihlman details, this progression is exactly what happened to her pygmy-chimpanzee hypothesis.

According to the Zihlman model, the CA resembled pygmy chimpanzees (bonobos) more than any other living primates, including the common chimpanzees one usually sees in zoos. Zihlman points out that bonobos are relatively small, with long arms and especially long legs. Of all the apes, pygmy chimpanzees come closest to resembling the earliest fossil hominins (such as Lucy) in terms of general body build. They also seem to be the most like humans in their social and sexual behavior.

Bonobos have a peculiar way of getting about on the ground, a form of locomotion that they share with the common chimpanzee and gorilla. They frequently walk on all fours. But the hands are doubled over (palms down) so that the forward weight is placed on the knuckles rather than the palms when they walk. This form of locomotion, known as knuckle-walking, is just plain weird among primates and is thought to have resulted when the tree-living ancestors of chimpanzees and gorillas (with long hands for hanging onto branches) took to the ground. Thus, the formerly clinging hand became a weight-bearing structure and tucked its fingers out of the way in the process. Bonobos don't always knuckle-walk. They sometimes stand up and walk bipedally, although with more of a bent knee and bent hip than humans have when they walk. Bonobos are even known to walk bipedally along tree branches, especially if they are carrying food.

Until recently, few paleoanthroplogists believed that the CA was a knuckle-walker because fossil hominins and living humans appeared to lack vestiges of knuckle-walking in their hand and arm bones. If knuckle-walking did not occur in the CA, however, then chimpanzees must have acquired this special habit *after* their separation from hominins some five to seven million years ago. And since gorillas split off from CA stock several million years earlier, they would have come by this unusual mode of locomotion independently, which seems a stretch.

FIGURE 4.1.
Adrienne Zihlman. Her comparative studies of ape anatomy and fossil hominin bones provide important evidence for understanding certain aspects of the
earliest hominins. (Photograph copyright r. r. jones, 1996, courtesy of University of California at Santa Cruz Public Affairs.)

A recent study, however, by Brian Richmond of the University of Illinois
and David Strait of New York College of Osteopathic Medicine, supports
those few workers who thought all along that this was too much of a
coincidence and that the CA must have been a knuckle-walker.

Specifically, Richmond and Strait discovered that two species of australopithecines (*Australopithecus afarensis* [including the famous Lucy]
and *Australopithecus anamensis*) that lived roughly three to four million
years ago had certain features in their wrist and arm bones that are associated with knuckle-walking in living chimpanzees and gorillas.[6] Humans and more recent australopithecines lack these features, which help

to brace the wrists as weight is loaded across the knuckles of walking African apes.[7] Because the australopithecines that show the knuckle-walking wrist morphology were bipedal, Richmond and Strait think that they did not actually knuckle-walk but instead retained vestigial morphology from a CA who did. If so, bipedalism must have evolved from a CA who was inclined not only to climb trees but also to knuckle-walk.

Although Richmond and Strait's hypothesis is still being debated, one thing is for sure. Since all known fossil hominins were (by definition) bipeds, walking on two legs probably played an important role in the origin of the hominin tribe some five to seven million years ago. Furthermore, I believe that the question of why bipedalism became the preferred form of locomotion in early hominins remains one of the biggest unsolved mysteries in hominin paleontology.

Footprints in Time

The hominin fossil record is precious. Hominins become fossilized only under special circumstances: when minerals such as calcite or silica are deposited within the bones or teeth of dead individuals. Through time, cavities that were previously empty or filled with soft tissue absorb more minerals from the burial environment. The fossil bone or tooth becomes harder and heavier. Usually, the fossil just sits there quietly like a rock, never to be discovered. Occasionally, however, fossilized teeth or fragments of bone are collected or unearthed by archaeologists or paleontologists. But this is a rare event. That is why fossil hominins are priceless and are kept locked away in bank vaults.

Although a few possibly hominin fossils that are older than five million years have recently been discovered, the fossil record of our early hominin ancestors perks up about 3.6 million years ago, with a remarkable find from Laetoli, Tanzania, announced by Mary Leakey in 1978.[8] Thousands of fossilized footprints of animals had been discovered. Pigs, elephants, giraffes, hyenas, antelopes, horses, and rhinoceroses were among the many species that left tracks at Laetoli. So were hominins who, by this time, had experienced at least a million and a half years of evolution since splitting from the ancestors of chimpanzees.

Three hominins had walked slowly north across the grassy savanna. The ground was covered with a layer of ash from a nearby active volcano,

FIGURE 4.2.

A trail of hominin footprints that were fossilized in volcanic ash was discovered at Laetoli, Tanzania. The trail shows that 3.6 million years ago some hominins were already bipedal. (Photograph by John Reader, copyright 1992/Science Photo Library.)

and it was damp at the time of their walk (perhaps from rain). Think of it as walking on the beach, next to the water, as the tide goes out. Footprints are left in the wet sand, and these become crusted or set as the sand dries. The same thing happened at Laetoli. But with one difference: the tide never returned to erase the Laetoli footprints. Instead, the tracks were covered and preserved by more ashes from the volcano. Over time, they became fossilized.

Approximately 3.6 million years later, these hominin footprints were studied by Russell Tuttle of the University of Chicago.[9] He estimated that the shortest hominin in the group was about four feet tall. Another who was about four feet, ten inches walked to the right of the first hominin. A third individual overprinted and partially obscured the tracks of the second; he was apparently taller still. Were the hominins walking together or separately? Could the second and third individuals have been following the first "with lust, murder, or other mayhem in mind," as Tuttle so vividly wondered? According to Tuttle, the answers to these questions, as well as certain other specifics about the Laetoli hominins, remain unknown. Nevertheless, the Laetoli footprints have much to tell.

Tuttle has convincingly argued that the Laetoli footprints are virtually indistinguishable from those made by small *Homo sapiens* who are not used to wearing shoes. The big toes of the Laetoli hominins were aligned alongside the other toes, instead of sticking out from the foot like the big toes of apes. And Laetoli toes appear, like ours, to have been less curved than those of apes.[10] Laetoli feet had good arches—a must for efficiently supporting and shifting the weight of the body while walking on two legs. Most telling of all, the depths of certain parts of the footprints (for example, the big toes and heels) show that the Laetoli hominins shifted their weight across their feet in exactly the same pattern that characterizes humans when they are walking. Although the Laetoli footprints are just whispered impressions left in the sands of time, the information they convey is extremely important. By 3.6 million years ago, at least some hominins appear to have been completely bipedal.

Bipedalism, more than anything else, separates early hominins from apes. Yet the primary cause for bipedalism remains the biggest unsolved mystery in hominin paleontology. However, it's not for lack of discussion in the literature. Speculation abounds. So, too, does controversy.

FIGURE 4.3.

Right soles of a never-shod fourteen-year-old Machiguenga Indian male (left) and of habitually shod Russell Tuttle (right). Tuttle has convincingly argued that the Laetoli footprints are virtually indistinguishable from those made by small *Homo sapiens* who do not wear shoes. (Photograph courtesy of Russell Tuttle.)

Some workers argue that bipedalism occurred more or less in one fell swoop (a sort of "quick and dirty" school of thought). Others believe that full bipedalism was achieved more slowly during the course of hominin evolution. There is even a battle-of-the-sexes contingent among students of bipedalism. Was bipedalism selected for mainly in males or females? Each sex has its advocates.

The Laetoli fooprints invalidated an important theory of bipedalism. I call this now defunct theory the "2001" model, in honor of the wonderful opening sequence from the classic movie of the same name. The "2001" theory was a cyclical one, in which the evolution of bipedalism and of the brain occurred more or less simultaneously: Bipedalism freed the forelimbs, the freed hands made tools, tool production selected for intelligence, and greater intelligence was associated with bigger brains that produced still better tools.[11] This model captured the imaginations

FIGURE 4.4.
This 1970 drawing of australopithecines (species undetermined), demon-strates that the "2001" theory had captured the imagination of anthropologists. (Image #335092; photograph by Logan; American Museum of Natural History Library.)

of anthropologists for many years, but was eventually doomed by the discovery that the earliest known hominins, although bipedal, had small, ape-size cranial capacities (and therefore small brains). As the fossil record now reveals, the increase in brain size did not really take off until a million and a half years after the first whispers of bipedalism at Laetoli.[12] The same is true for the production of stone tools. Thanks in large part to the footprints from Laetoli, bipedalism has been thoroughly disengaged from both brain size and tool production.

Then why did early hominins become bipedal? Most of the causes that have been proposed for bipedalism fall into two simple categories: food and sex. Of the two, the acquisition of food has received more atten-tion. But what kind of food? Animal food or plant food? As has occurred among contemporary American consumers, paleoanthropology has had its own food fads. At the moment, meat is out and vegetables are in (on both fronts). Not many years ago, the notion of man the hunter had an important role in theories about bipedalism. Early hominin men were thought to have been out hunting while females and children remained at the home base. For physiological reasons having to do with breathing, bipedalism would have been adaptive for long-distance running after game (so-called persistence hunting), as well as for freeing the hands to make hunting weapons and to carry meat home. This theory tied in well with the "2001" model.[13] And the bottom line was that males made the tools and brought home the bacon. At least they did until (mostly) female anthropologists pointed out the obvious.

Woman the Gatherer

In modern hunting and gathering societies that live in a variety of habitats, the men may go hunting, but on a day-to-day basis, it is the women who end up providing most of the nourishment for the entire group. While *he* is out trying his luck at hunting, *she* (often accompanied by children) collects the more widely available plant food, insects, and small animals. She ensures that neither her children nor her hunter will go hungry tonight!

According to this woman-the-gatherer hypothesis, not only did early hominin women provide most of the food, but their freed forelimbs may have fashioned the first tools.[14] What did they use these tools for? To acquire food—by digging it up, knocking it down, or cracking something open. (With regard to the last, it is interesting that female chimpanzees appear to be more adept than male chimpanzees at cracking open nuts with rocks.[15]) Natural selection for bipedalism would have been especially strong for gathering mothers. Accordingly, early hominin women may have invented slings or other devices with which to carry small children and containers for food or water.

"Man" the hunter has suffered other affronts. Carnivores such as lions or hyenas are known to leave tooth marks on the bones of animals they eat. Similarly, early hominins sometimes left their own stamp, in the form of cut marks, on the bones of animals they butchered with stone tools. Studies by paleontologist and science writer Pat Shipman have examined the layering of hominin cut marks and carnivore tooth marks on animal bones associated with early hominin sites.[16] And guess what? More often than not, our intrepid hunter got there after the kill. It may well have been man the scavenger instead of man the hunter. (And one of his earliest inventions may have been the fish story, as he explained how he caught the big one that got away!)

In 1981, Owen Lovejoy of Kent State University offered a kinder, gentler picture of the early male hominin. He did so by suggesting a unique man-the-gatherer hypothesis to explain the origin of bipedalism.[17] According to Lovejoy, early hominins were near the brink of extinction. He therefore sought to identify some aspect of bipedalism that would have increased the number of living offspring of early hominins. Because food, water, and sleeping trees were widely scattered in the Plio-Pleistocene environment, Lovejoy assumed that early hominins traveled between food sources, much as savanna baboons do. He also assumed that hominin females would have had fewer accidents and been less exposed to predators if they had refrained from moving too often. Lovejoy therefore speculated that males foraged farther afield for food and left the supposedly safer central area to the females and young.

Where does all-important bipedalism fit in? Nature favored males who were bipedal because they could gather food and carry it back to their females and young. Thus, man the gatherer increased his number of living offspring. The problem with Lovejoy's hypothesis is that there is little or no comparative primate or ethnographic evidence to support its basic assumptions. If you see similarities with the man-the-hunter model, you are right. Either way, it is "man the provider." (As Zihlman points out, Lovejoy co-opted the male-gathering hypothesis from the earlier female-gathering hypothesis and even suggested that carrying devices might have been the first tools.[18])

Sex

What were the females doing when the males were away? Well, they were being faithful. As Lovejoy sees it, early hominins seemed to follow the Western cultural tradition of monogamy. That way, a male could go away during the day and still be sure that it was he who had fathered his children. But wait, there's more to this male fantasy. Lovejoy believes that early hominin females were like modern women in several respects. Unlike many nonhuman primates, hominin women did not have specific periods in which they were in heat and mated (they did not go into estrus). Nor could males determine by visual inspection if a hominin woman was ovulating and therefore fertile. Therefore, copulatory vigilance was required to assure perpetuation of the species and reinforce the pair-bonds of couples. Early women obliged because, like contemporary human females, they were "continually sexually receptive." (Now *there's* a fantasy.)

Needless to say, Lovejoy's theory did not receive positive critical acclaim from certain anthropologists, as shown by Zihlman's comment about footnote 79 of Lovejoy's article:

> Lest there be any question about the chauvinistic undertones of Lovejoy's prehistoric family portrait, there is the coy reference, with regard to his assertion that females are perpetually sexually receptive, to a "personal communication" from his buddy, Donald C. Johanson, famous for his discovery of three million-year-old "Lucy" and also well known for his Don Juan image. Lovejoy repeatedly invokes the "epigamic traits" (jargon for tits and ass) by which females succeed in attracting and holding their mates.[19]

For fun, the last word on bipedalism and the battle of the sexes will be given to the late Nancy Tanner. Tanner's theory invokes the concept of sexual selection, an idea that goes back at least as far as Darwin. Features are sexually selected when they are preferred in one sex by the other and are passed down to future generations. A classic example is the beautiful tail feathers of male peacocks. Apparently, males have beautiful tails because females prefer to mate with (and, therefore, bear the offspring of) males who are so endowed. Tanner goes for woman the gatherer all the way:

> Among gathering mothers natural selection was strong for bipedalism: for walking from one forested area across grasslands to another, for freeing the hands for tool-use in obtaining food, for carrying babies and food.[20]

However, not to be sexist, Tanner allows males a role in the origins of bipedalism. Specifically, bipedal males were sexually selected by females:

> Whereas natural selection was more pertinent for bipedalism among gathering mothers, sexual selection was more significant for male bi-

pedalism since their penises (especially when "upright") could be noted more readily when they walked bipedally.[20]

Tanner adds:

> As Freud long ago noted, an erect, unclothed male with an erect and quite visible penis might have proven noticeable and attractive.[20]

In this context, Jane Goodall's observation of a male chimpanzee named Shadow is interesting. Shadow was attacked by the females he courted until he invented an extraordinary courtship display that combined a bipedal stance, erect penis, and direct gaze. According to Goodall, Shadow's display worked wonders.[21]

Tanner's theory regarding sexual selection of bipedalism in male early hominins may seem frivolous, or even humorous. Nevertheless, it is noteworthy that relative to other primates, human males have enlarged penises.[22] Such "flasher" theories have also been applied to the large breasts of human women, as opposed to their relatively unendowed nonhuman primate cousins.

Wheeler's Explanation: Hominins Had It Made in the Shade

While all this hullabaloo was going on, a British biologist named Pete Wheeler of the Liverpool John Moores University sat back and quietly thought about the physiological factors involved with the shift to full bipedalism. At the time hominins were perfecting their bipedalism, the climate was getting drier. As a result, grassy savannas and woodlands replaced closed forests. Because food was no longer uniformly distributed within forested habitats, it was hard to find. Thus, early hominins had to travel through open country to find patches of food scattered within the mosaic environment. They may also have followed the seasonal migrations of savanna game (meat on the hoof), as suggested by Mary Leakey and her colleagues.[23] Thus, there is no reason to rule out either plant or animal foods in the diets of early hominins. What's important is that hominins of both sexes began to traverse open spaces to feed. In so doing, they encountered intense solar radiation. *That* is the key to Wheeler's theory.[24]

Sunshine. As any dermatologist will attest, too much can be harmful to the skin. Further, if core body temperature increases even a moderate

FIGURE 4.5.
Early hominins had to travel through open country to find patches of food scattered within the mosaic environment. They may also have followed the seasonal migrations of savanna game. (Photograph by Dean Falk.)

amount, heatstroke can result and cause brain damage. Quadrupedal savanna mammals, like antelopes, have fur that protects their skin from solar radiation. They also have a special net of veins within the skull that prevents their brains from overheating. However, even with these adaptations, savanna animals take to the shade during the heat of day. (This was brought home to me on a train ride through Safari Park in San Diego. It was in the middle of a very hot day and, as our guide predicted, the animals we wished to see were all resting in the shade of trees.)

But humans have neither the marvelous net of veins nor the protection of overall body fur. How, then, did early hominins keep cool as they traveled out in the open, or scavenged and foraged for food without competition from other animals in the noonday sun? Wheeler has an eloquent and simple answer that is so obvious that others have overlooked it: Like pygmy chimpanzees, the CA was probably capable of a certain amount of bipedal locomotion or was preadapted for bipedalism. When the CA's increasingly bipedal descendants eventually migrated from wooded to more open habitats, they were able to minimize the amount of body surface that was directly exposed to solar radiation by walking bipedally. That way, only the shoulders and top of the head took a direct beating of rays when the sun was high in the sky. Put another way, early hominins created their own shade and were able to go about their business while they were at it.

Other adaptations also helped early hominins cope with thermal stress. With the shift to full bipedalism, a coat of fur was no longer needed to protect the skin from direct solar radiation—except, that is, on top of the head and shoulders. In keeping with this, hair was retained on the head, but lost on large areas of the body. Hominin skin thus became (largely) naked. Especially efficient sweat glands also evolved as a means of cooling the recently denuded skin. (We humans are sweaty beasts, indeed, with the greatest sweating capacity for a given surface area of any known animal.)

A naked skin and associated cutaneous sweat glands allowed increased evaporation and, therefore, whole-body cooling in early hominins. According to Wheeler, such whole-body cooling helped prevent heatstroke and thereby released a physiological constraint on brain size in *Homo*.[25] (The idea that brain size can be held in check by thermoregulatory requirements is extremely important and will be returned to later.)

Our Earliest Bipedal Ancestors: A Thumbnail Sketch

Mobility. That is the key to understanding the bipedal ancestors that gave rise directly to *Homo*. As noted, changes in the climate and the requirements for thermoregulation contributed to the hominin proclivity for traveling bipedally in search of plants and animals to eat. Their feet were humanlike, but the rest of the body had a way to go. And although they could remain upright for hours, their gaits were by no means graceful. The ancestors of *Homo* were little (perhaps four to five feet tall), sweaty, and probably had dark skin with a reduced amount of body hair. They also had long arms and legs, and big front teeth.

Something can even be surmised about the social behavior of these ancestors. Richard Wrangham of Harvard University does this by identifying behaviors that are shared by chimpanzees, gorillas, and modern

FIGURE 4.6.
In one of the few attempts to approach the question of the origin of bipedalism scientifically, biologist Pete Wheeler used this model (appropriately named "Boris") to quantify the relationship between posture and the amount of radiant heat load absorbed by the body. (Photograph courtesy of Pete Wheeler.)

hunting and gathering humans. Because of the wide presence of such behaviors, Wrangham sees them as probable hand-me-downs from the CA.[26] Since Wrangham's study, however, molecular evidence has accumulated that suggests chimpanzees share a more recent CA with humans than either does with gorillas. In light of this, it is reasonable to modify Wrangham's approach by attributing behaviors to the CA that are shared by both kinds of chimpanzees and modern humans who live in small-scale societies. Using this method,[27] I conclude that our ancestors probably lived in relatively open "fission-fusion" communities that were closed to outsiders except, perhaps, for receptive females who had a tendency to migrate away to find mates and to settle down. Males and occasionally females may have sometimes foraged alone. Mating relationships were likely to have been short term and promiscuous in both sexes of the CA. (It is entirely possible that the bewildering variety of mating patterns that occur among living people derived from such an ancestral state.) CA females probably got along fairly well together, but without forming really strong interpersonal bonds. Males, on the other hand, are likely to have remained in their birth groups, where they may or may not have formed especially strong bonds with each other. They also would have been quite hostile to males in other groups. Finally, and darkly, relationships between groups were probably tense, and stalk-and-attack interactions may have been carried out regularly by males (but more on that later).

Here we are at the base of our own family tree. And our ancestors are, above all else, bipedal. But does this mean that we now leave behind all vestiges of our arboreal past? According to Graham Richards of the University of East London, it does not. In a refreshing departure, Richards has questioned the cliché that bipedalism led to freeing of the hands. He points out that chimpanzees use their feet like hands and that the tree-living common ancestor of humans and chimpanzees was probably also "four-handed." That means the transition to ground living was more likely to have enslaved the feet than to have freed the hands. If we accept the thesis that the foot became enslaved as a result of bipedalism, what of the hand? Did it not become liberated as a result of bipedalism (and able to fulfill itself by becoming skillful)? Maybe not. According to Richards:

On becoming terrestrial the hand was never then "freed" from branch-holding, it brought the branch with it, as innumerable artist's impressions testify, along with the appropriate co-ordination schema. . . . It could be argued that even now many of us find a freed hand uncomfortable, feeling far more at ease holding something, be it a cigarette, a glass, a pen, a walking stick, the lapel of a jacket, something in our pocket, worry-beads, a necklace, or a stray lock of hair. Indeed we seem to be happiest with one hand, at least, engaged in gripping behavior, even after more than four million years.[28]

Whence the Fossils?

The above portrait of our earliest bipedal ancestor is gleaned from studies of comparative primate anatomy, molecular genetics, behavioral primatology, and the Laetoli footprints. But something is missing. Where are the fossilized skulls and teeth and long bones of the earliest hominins? Since this book was first published, a number of new finds have been attributed to hominins that lived between 6 (or even 7) and 3.2 million years ago. That's the good news. The bad news is that the interpretation of these specimens is exceedingly difficult because of their often fragmentary nature, and because each new discovery is inevitably heralded as a direct ancestor of humans (on that you can bank!).

The oldest hominin candidate so far is a dramatic find. Announced by French paleoanthropologist Michel Brunet and a large team[29] in the summer of 2002, the date of this 6–7-million-year-old skull is older than many estimates for the split between chimpanzees and hominins. Thus, if the specimen is truly hominin, the date for the CA must have been earlier than the five to six million years ago that some workers accept on the basis of molecular evidence. It's not just the time of this skull that is surprising, it is also its place. The skull was uncovered in the Sahel region of Chad, central Africa, which is approximately fifteen hundred miles west of the east African locations that have yielded the vast majority of other very early hominins, and its attribution to a new genus and species, *Sahelanthropus tchadensis,* is in honor of this unusual location. (The skull is also nicknamed Toumai, which means "hope of life.") Furthermore, rather than having lived in savanna grasslands as expected, this early hominin inhabited a lush forest.

What is really surprising, however, is the physical appearance of *Sahelanthropus*. The back of the skull resembles that of a chimpanzee, as does its brain size. The front of the skull, however, has a relatively flat face, small front teeth, and a large bony eyebrow ridge that are reminiscent of advanced australopithecines or early *Homo* that lived four to five million years more recently! It's not just the front of the skull that makes Brunet think Toumai was a hominin. He also interprets the relative position and shape of the foramen magnum on the skull's base as indicative of bipedalism—just as Raymond Dart did for Taung more than seventy-five years ago. Needless to say, such a combination of features at such an ancient date has thrown the field for a loop. As is always the case for new finds, not everyone agrees with Brunet's assessments of *Sahelanthropus*. Some workers go so far as to suggest that, rather than being hominin, this specimen might represent a fossil female gorilla.[30] Even that would be exciting, however, since the fossil record for gorillas (and chimpanzees) has, so far, been a blank. Whatever consensus eventually

FIGURE 4.7.
Michel Brunet digging in Toumai site TM266, Chad. (Photograph copyright M. P. F. T., courtesy of Michel Brunet.)

FIGURE 4.8.
The Toumai cranium has a surprising mixture of features. (Photograph copyright M.P.F.T., courtesy of Michel Brunet.)

develops for *Sahelanthropus*, it is already agreed that the specimen is very important.

In what some might consider an embarrassment of riches, another new genus and species has appeared that is also a contender for the position of the oldest-known hominin in the human lineage. Nicknamed Millennium Man because its remains were discovered at the end of 2000, these fossils are from the Tugen Hills, northwest of Nairobi in Kenya, and date to approximately six million years ago. French paleontologist Brigitte Senut and geologist Martin Pickford named the fossils *Orrorin tugenensis*,[31] which translates as "Original Man from Tugen." Thirteen fossils of *Orrorin* have been uncovered that include teeth, a finger bone, an arm bone, and several leg bones. The latter are especially important because they show numerous features that indicate *Orrorin* was, indeed, bipedal. For example, the size and shape of the top of the femur (which fits into the leg socket of the pelvis) is more humanlike than is the case for the femurs of apes or other early hominins, and this morphology is associated with walking in humans. Furthermore, computed tomography (CT) scans of the femur confirm a microstructure in the top of the bone that correlates with the weight-bearing stresses associated with bipedalism in living people. The curved finger bone, on the other hand, suggests to Senut and Pickford that, although *Orrorin* spent time happily padding along the ground, it was equally at home in the trees. Equally important, Millennium Man's small, square, thickly enameled molars also resemble those of humans. This combination of advanced leg morphology and dental features is not seen in any other early hominin, leading Senut and Pickford to the dramatic conclusion that other known early hominins such as the famous Lucy were not direct ancestors of humans. We will return to this important point in chapter 6 ("Lucy's Child: Mix-up at the Hospital"), where we will also meet other newly named hominin species that are promoted by their discoverers as *the* true ancestors of humans.

More than ever, the tone of advocacy that was established when Raymond Dart first discovered australopithecines lives on and thrives. The exciting announcements of *Sahelanthropus* and *Orrorin* have met with a good deal of controversy, and not a little fossil envy. Nor does a fragmentary and controversial record for the very earliest hominins prevent controversy and passion from governing discussions about how the CA looked and moved, or whether bipedalism was preferred more by males or females. The battle of the sexes over the evolution of bipedalism is entertaining, if a little silly. When it comes to the question of sex differences in the brain, however, we find ourselves on firmer ground.

chapter 5

BOY BRAIN, GIRL BRAIN

Just as hominin paleontologists have been biased toward overstating the humanness of their fossils or pushing their preferred family trees, neuroscientists have also been biased when it comes to studying the brains of their own species. The anthropocentric notion that only humans are evolved enough to have lateralized brains held sway for a long, long time. Although that notion has fortunately gone by the wayside, another idea, namely that the brains of men and women are exactly the same, has only recently (and reluctantly) been given up by social scientists. I sometimes wonder if this bias has anything to do with why many primate neuroanatomists were not traditionally trained to analyze data according to sex (a scientifically sound practice, even if it only occasionally yields significant results). Despite this history, it is now clear that there are differences between the brains of male and female primates (including humans), just as there are for other animals. However, before exploring these differences, it is important to discuss brain lateralization itself.

Because of a specific area of research established by the late Roger Sperry and his students during the 1960s, it is now known that the human brain is lateralized for much more than just language, handedness, and tap dancing. Sperry's studies were based on psychological tests of human patients who, as a last-resort measure to control otherwise fatal epilepsy, underwent surgery that literally cut their brains in two! The operation of disconnecting the cerebral hemispheres, known as commissurotomy, entails severing the large corpus callosum, as well as other smaller forebrain structures that connect the right and left sides of the brain. Sperry's tests of postoperative split-brain patients provided some of the first clues that the two hemispheres of the brain differ profoundly in their general capabilities. His findings also shed light on the nature of consciousness itself. Appropriately, in 1981, Sperry won the Nobel Prize in Physiology and Medicine for his research on hemispheric specialization in the split brain.[1]

Right Brain, Left Brain

A general rule for the nervous system is that nerve pathways from the brain cross to the opposite side of the body. Thus, the right hemisphere has predominant control over the left hand, and so on. However, in normal brains, this contralateral organization is far from complete because an additional 200 million nerve fibers cross directly between the two hemispheres, so that each is informed of what the other is doing. Besides facilitating communication between the two halves of the brain, these fibers allow the cerebral cortex to coordinate motor activities of both sides of the body. Thus, in brains of healthy individuals, both hemispheres get a total picture of what is going on. Not so for commissurotomy patients. Because surgery had permanently divided their brains, the cross talk that normally occurs between the two hemispheres is prevented. As a consequence, the left hemisphere sees things in the right but not in the left half of the visual field, and perceives and manipulates objects that are held with the right but not the left hand. The converse is true for the right hemisphere. Furthermore, the functions of the right hemisphere are cut off (literally) from the main language areas that in most people are located in the left hemisphere.

Remarkably, commissurotomy patients seem unaware of their deficits, and appear to the casual observer to be normal. Apparently, during day-to-day activities, these patients unconsciously compensate for their disconnected hemispheres by cuing both hemispheres through speaking (which sends information into both ears), turning their heads (shifting visual fields), and touching or manipulating objects with both hands. As Sperry put it,

> Normal behavior under ordinary conditions is favored also by many other unifying factors. Some of these are very obvious, like the fact that these two separate mental spheres have only one body and therefore they always get dragged to the same places, meet the same people, see and do the same things all the time and hence are bound to have a great overlap of common, almost identical experience.[2]

Nevertheless, Sperry was able to do controlled lateralized testing of commissurotomy patients by using procedures such as keeping the subject's hands isolated from each other and hidden from the subject's view, and projecting images exclusively into one visual field (with an instrument known as a tachistoscope). And oh, what wonders his tests unraveled!

Under strict testing conditions, split-brain patients show themselves to be, literally, of two minds. Each hemisphere appears to experience its own separate consciousness and seems unaware of the mental events that occupy its other half. For example, if an object is placed in a patient's concealed left hand, she will not be able to say what it is, because speaking is a left hemisphere function and that hemisphere receives input from the right hand but not the left. Although the patient will report that she hasn't the foggiest idea of what she has just held in her left hand, her right hemisphere will then be able to select the correct object (with her left hand) from a number of choices. Similarly, objects placed in the right hand will be identified verbally or selected later from a group of objects by the right but not the left hand. Furthermore, both hemispheres can go about their respective endeavors simultaneously and cheerfully oblivious to each other. Thus, commissurotomy patients are very good at doing two things at once, as long as those two things are done by opposite hemispheres.

Prior to the research on split-brain patients, the right hemisphere was viewed as "an automaton lacking conscious awareness."[3] This poor image held sway largely because of the left hemisphere's superiority for language. One of Sperry's most important findings was that the right hemisphere was not of such minor significance after all. It mentally outperformed the left hemisphere in a series of nonverbal, often spatial, tests, including (among others) the copying of designs, discrimination of shapes by both touch and sight, intuitively understanding geometrical properties, and reading faces. Careful testing also revealed that the right hemispheres of commissurotomy patients expressed emotions and possessed a sense of self that was as conscious and strong as that shown by their left hemispheres.

Decades later, Sperry's findings have been confirmed and widened by investigators using a variety of sophisticated techniques on enormous numbers of normal, as well as clinical, populations of humans. Methods for detecting brain asymmetries have included clinical research on brain-damaged individuals and patients in whom one hemisphere has been momentarily paralyzed by injection of a chemical (sodium amytal) into its blood supply. Lateralization studies have been carried out for sensory (for example, discriminating how many points are touching an area of skin) and motor (handedness) activities. Normal individuals have been the subjects for numerous tachistoscopic visual and two-eared (dichotic) listening tests. In addition, basic anatomical asymmetries have been observed for certain brain structures. Finally, physiological correlates of brain lateralization have recently been obtained using a variety of techniques, among them electroencephalograms (EEG), the method of evoked potentials (EP), neuromagnetometry, functional magnetic resonance imaging (fMRI), and positron emission tomography (PET).[4]

The contemporary literature on brain lateralization is multifaceted and frequently difficult to interpret. Functional differences between the hemispheres are often subtle but statistically significant. Upon close inspection, however, contradictory results obtained by separate studies may often be attributed to slightly different methodologies or to differences in the populations investigated. For example, left-handers and the musically sophisticated do not test like the general population on some measures of brain asymmetry. Fortunately, certain generalizations about the left and right hemispheres float to the top, despite various complexities that plague this burgeoning field.

With these caveats in mind (and remembering that there are many exceptions), the following generalizations characterize the cerebral hemispheres of humans:[5] The left hemisphere is associated with language functions, skilled movements (like those in which more than 90 percent of right hands engage), and analytical, time-sequencing processes. This hemisphere is also involved in processing positive emotions. The right hemisphere, on the other hand, engages in global, holistic pursuits. Its visuospatial and mental imaging skills are superb, and it is also associated with musical abilities.[5] Although the right hemisphere counterbalances the cheerful left hemisphere by processing negative emotions, it has a noticeably greater role than the left hemisphere in generally expressing emotions, as well as in reading them in others. The right hemisphere also seems to have an edge over the left in recognizing faces, in certain aspects of humor, and in the ability to understand metaphor. Although it is the left hemisphere that speaks, it is the right hemisphere that provides tone of voice, an important and sometimes decisive aspect of verbal communication.

Tone of voice, or prosody, may even represent a kind of signature that is left over from evolutionary events that preceded the emergence of the first language (protolanguage) in early hominins. Although the body language that chimpanzee and human mothers use with their infants is virtually identical, only human mothers deliver a constant stream of baby-talk. Such "motherese," or musical speech, is universal among people, and its special tone of voice helps babies around the world grasp the fundamentals of their respective languages. Chimp mothers do not vocalize in distinctive ways to their infants, who, for their part, remain in close physical contact with their mothers by clinging, unaided, to their hairy abdomens. Because of developmental effects related to the evolution of bipedalism, human babies have lost this ability. Early hominin mothers would therefore have expended a good deal of energy carrying their helpless infants, at least until baby slings were invented. I believe that these mothers developed soothing, melodic vocalizations to calm and reassure nearby infants that were, of necessity, periodically put

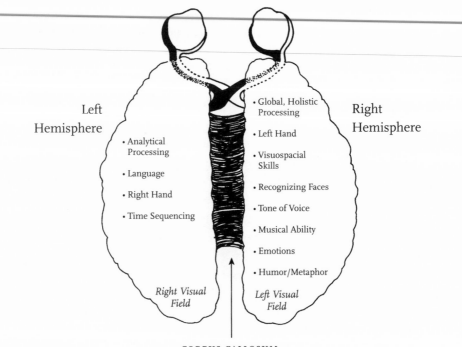

Left Hemisphere

- Analytical Processing
- Language
- Right Hand
- Time Sequencing

Right Visual Field

Right Hemisphere

- Global, Holistic Processing
- Left Hand
- Visuospacial Skills
- Recognizing Faces
- Tone of Voice
- Musical Ability
- Emotions
- Humor/Metaphor

Left Visual Field

CORPUS CALLOSUM

FIGURE 5.1.
General specializations of left and right hemispheres. Top view of the brain (shown connected by the corpus callosum).

down so that mothers could go about their business. As I envision it, tone of voice evolved as a kind of disembodied extension of mothers' cradling arms and eventually contributed to the emergence of the earliest speech.[6] An implication of this "putting the baby down" hypothesis is that evolution of the right hemisphere would have contributed at least as much as the left hemisphere to the initial emergence of speech.

There are hints that certain biological substrates underlie functional lateralization of the two hemispheres. These substrates include asymmetries in the distribution of neurotransmitters that facilitate neurological activity, such as greater representation of norepinephrine in the right hemisphere and of dopamine (involved with complex motor functions) in the left. Neurochemical asymmetries, in turn, may be the result of developmental (including intrauterine) events. Along these lines, limited evidence suggests that, prenatally, the right hemisphere matures more quickly than the left. If so, the two hemispheres will be exposed to slightly different intrauterine chemical environments at equivalent levels of maturity. Therein lies a key.[7]

The Mind-Body Problem Revisited

What is the relationship between conscious awareness and the brain? Although philosophers have been kicking the mind-body problem around for centuries, the new insights provided by commissurotomy studies became available only during the last half century. As noted above, a few contemporary workers infer from split-brain studies that each hemisphere has a separate mind of its own. Part of the reasoning underlying this conclusion is based on conflicting answers provided by the right and left hemispheres of individual patients in response to the same questions. An interesting example of this doubling of conscious-

FIGURE 5.2.
Chimpanzee infants are able to cling unaided to their mothers, an ability that was lost during selection for habitual bipedalism in early hominins. (Photograph copyright Curt Busse, 2002.)

ness was reported by commissurotomy patient W. J., who had been shopping with his wife:

> He was sitting next to her in the car as she was driving home. Between them was a large bag of groceries. He recounted, "My left hand reached in the bag and pulled out the licorice she had purchased for herself." I asked him, "Well, what's the matter with that?" He said, "I don't like licorice." I said, "Well, that is strange—what happened?" He said, "I ate it—but I didn't like it."[8]

Another example of interhemispheric competition occurred in the day-to-day routine of a female patient who experienced dramatic conflicts for several years following her surgery:

> I open the closet door. I know what I want to wear. As I reach for something with my right hand, my left comes up and takes something different. I can't put it down if it's in my left hand. I have to call my daughter.[9]

Although my corpus callosum is intact and I frequently experience terrible dilemmas over what to wear, I am skeptical regarding the extreme view, held by some, that otherwise normal individuals have two separate minds in their heads. So, too, was Sperry (although he has been misquoted on the subject), who pointed out that even the question of whether there exists a right-left division of conscious experience in bisected brains is subject to debate.[10] According to Sperry, certain aspects of consciousness are *not* divided in split-brain patients. For example, sensations from both sides of the face and sounds experienced by both ears are represented in the two hemispheres. The same is true for sensations of crude pain, temperature, position sense, pressure, and visceral sensations like hunger. Thus, each disconnected hemisphere shares a sense of the positions and movements of body parts, as well as an awareness of the surrounding environment. Add to this the cross cuing that occurs in nontest situations and you get one unified consciousness, even in commissurotomy patients.

In sum, more than four decades of research on brain lateralization has expanded our understanding about asymmetrical representations of certain complementary cognitive abilities in the right and left hemispheres of human brains. No more and no less. Philosophers (and sometimes neuroscientists) too often lose sight of the fact that the two hemispheres are widely interconnected and that they function as a unit in normal brains. These investigators also continue to give undeserved priority to the left hemisphere and its language functions in discussions about what makes us truly human or conscious. (Musically naive as I am, I can have a dandy conscious experience that relies neither on language nor, in all probability, on much other left-hemisphere processing by simply listening to classical music.[11]) As to the mind-body problem, Sperry defined consciousness as "a holistic or emergent, functional property of high-order brain activity."[12] And that's about as elegant a definition as one can hope for.[13]

Different Sexes, Different Brains

As populations, males and females test differently for certain abilities that are neurologically lateralized. Some workers have questioned the utility of studying such differences because there is usually massive overlap in the distributions of these traits for the two sexes. In these cases, numerous individuals of the weaker sex (for some tasks it is males; for others, females) outperform many of the stronger sex. Despite the fact that sex differences are frequently small, they are often real (statistically significant). Furthermore, the sex differences that have been detected form a fascinating pattern that provides clues about the evolution of brain lateralization.

Females tend to outperform males slightly but significantly on tests of verbal abilities, including reading comprehension, essay writing, anagrams, and (especially) measures of spoken language. Interestingly, females appear to be more left-hemisphere biased for general motor expression than males, as shown by their greater rightward skill for fine motor tasks such as finger-tapping and cursive writing. Compared with males, females are also subtly biased for certain emotional skills such as understanding nonverbal body language (this may, in fact, be one basis for good old women's intuition).

Males, on the other hand, test better on average than females for perception and manipulation of spatial relationships, such as mental rotations of figures, maze tracing, map reading, rod-and-frame alignment tests, and remembering positions of numbers. They are also better at left-right discriminations, disembedding figures, and localizing points. As is well known, males outperform females in certain areas of mathematics, particularly on calculus and geometry problems.[14] Finally, there is some indication that males also excel at musical abilities such as composition.[15] This raises the interesting possibility that the manipulation of auditory space involved in musical composition is based on cognitive processes that are similar to those that underlie another right-hemisphere activity at which males excel, namely perception and rotation of visual shapes. This seems plausible because music, like visual images, has contours and corners.

The above generalizations are gleaned from many hundreds of studies across a diverse spectrum of human activities based on musical, visuospatial, auditory, motor, emotional, and linguistic skills. Despite the complexity, confusion, and related sociopolitical issues that abound in the literature, this body of information converges on a clear bottom line: Finely shaded but significant sex differences characterize human behaviors. And of all those differences, the largest (no fine shading here) is the one in which males are favored for certain visuospatial skills such as the mental folding task illustrated below.[16] The fact that males are particularly good at getting around—reading maps, tracing mazes, and mentally manipulating spatial arrangements in visual and auditory modes— should not be viewed as in any way detracting from females. I believe that these skills contributed to the remarkable evolution of our species—in both sexes.

Men have somewhat larger brains than women, and many anthropologists once believed that this simply reflected their generally larger body sizes. For example, one study showed that the average brain size in 13 samples of men from around the world was about 1,350 grams, while that for matched samples of females was approximately 1,225 grams.[17] Other studies, however, reveal that for individuals of the same weight or stature, women's brains are only about 90 percent the size of men's, a sex difference that also appears in children.[18] I was initially surprised to learn that women do, indeed, have smaller brains than men, and that most of this difference is not due to different body sizes.

Beyond this, a number of specific anatomical differences have been reported for the brains of men and women in several regions including the massa intermedia, planum temporale, anterior hypothalamus, and

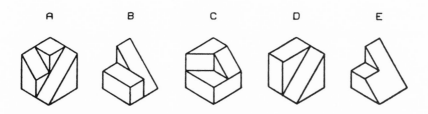

FIGURE 5.3.
Certain spatial aptitudes seem to be (on average) better developed in males than in females. Select the appropriate figure that represents what the upper figure would look like when it is folded into a three-dimensional object (the shaded portion is the bottom). See reference 16, chapter 5 for answer. (Figure courtesy of Roland Guay.)

corpus callosum.[19] Significantly, a study by R. C. Gur and colleagues shows that the larger sizes of men's brains compared to those of women of similar body weight are correlated with different distributions of gray and white matter.[20] Gray matter, which is made up of neuronal cell bodies and their processes, occupies a higher proportion of women's brains and is thought to be important for computation. Men, on the other hand, have a relative abundance of white matter, which helps transmit information across the brain. Gur's study reveals that the internal brain wiring for the two sexes differs in other more subtle ways, including their patterns of brain lateralization for volumes of gray matter.

There is other evidence that the *pattern* of brain lateralizaton differs for the two sexes. According to one survey of the literature, females seem to process certain kinds of information with both hemispheres, whereas males tend to rely more on one hemisphere or the other.[21] For example, the incidence of aphasia (an inability to use or understand words) after left-hemisphere lesions is at least three times higher in men than in women. This suggests that females may process language more with both hemispheres.

However, the generalization that males are more lateralized than females needs to be tempered with findings from studies by Doreen Kimura of Simon Fraser University, in Canada. She found that speech disorders and manual difficulties occurred significantly more often in women because of damage to the left frontal lobe, whereas these conditions were caused more often in men by damage to their left posterior parietal and temporal lobes. Kimura concluded that for women (who have stronger tendencies toward right-handedness than men) manual skills are at least as dependent as speech on the left frontal lobe. Thus, women may be more asymmetrical for frontal lobe motor activities, and men for functions that are subserved by more posterior regions of the brain. If so, the sexes appear to differ in the front-to-back organization within hemispheres, as well as the right-left pattern for the whole brain.[22]

There is less clinical information available about the degree to which visuospatial skills are lateralized in the sexes. However, a number of studies do show that males are more dependent on their right hemispheres for certain visuospatial tasks. Investigations of the patterns of hemispheric blood flow during tasks like mental rotation indicate significant differences between males and females. These findings are consistent with the hypothesis that males are specialized for some visuospatial skills.

Certain neuroanatomical findings regarding brain shape strengthen the impression that the sexes differ in the overall organization of their brains. Marjorie LeMay, a radiologist from Harvard Medical School, has pioneered the study of asymmetrical projections of the brain that are called petalias. She discovered that right-handed people tend to have right frontal lobes that project farther than the left frontal lobes (that is, a right frontal petalia) and left occipital lobes that extend back more than their right counterparts (left occipital petalias). This configuration gives both the brain and the overlying skull a characteristic lopsided appearance that can be seen in medical images including X-rays. LeMay showed that left-handers are characterized by higher frequencies of the reverse conditions (namely, left frontal and right occipital petalias).

LeMay's research is very important because it demonstrates a statistical link between brain shape and handedness. Results of another study confirm LeMay's earlier findings. The latter study also shows that greater degrees of frontal and occipital asymmetries are present in men than in women. Furthermore, reversals of the typical petalia patterns are more common in women, even though their incidence of left-handedness is slightly less than that for men.[23]

Sex Hormone Research

Quickly recite the tongue twister "a box of mixed biscuits in a biscuit mixer" five times! Not exactly a piece of cake, huh? Elizabeth Hampson, of the University of Western Ontario, and Doreen Kimura have shown that women are significantly better at this task when their monthly cycles are at peak estrogen and progesterone levels—just before ovulation and again during the last week before menstruation.[24] On the other hand, when estrogen and progesterone levels are low, during and right after menstruation, the same women do not do as well on this test or on other measures of speeded motor coordination like finger tapping or peg-assembly tasks. Since women generally outperform men on tests of skilled motor coordination, it appears that high estrogen and progesterone levels enhance female skills.

But what effect do female sex hormones have on the visuospatial tasks at which males usually excel? In another part of the same study, each woman was given a rod-and-frame test, at two carefully selected times during her cycle. (The goal of the test is to align a rod to the true vertical against a deceptively tilted background, and males are generally better at it than females.) The results were striking. The subjects were significantly less accurate at aligning the rod at the midluteal phase of their cycles, when estrogen and progesterone levels were high, than during menstruation, when they were low.

As the foregoing discussion shows, visuospatial skills (at which men usually excel) are enhanced in menstruating women, just when their generally superior motor skills are inhibited. Hampson and Kimura therefore conclude that women's performances on cognitive tasks are influenced by their fluctuating hormonal states. They also suggest that sex differences on these and other cognitive tests may have a substantial hormonal basis. For example, the neurotransmitter dopamine plays a role in motor coordination, and it is possible that sex hormones influence its release in the brain.

A key to sex differences in performance on cognitive tests may lie in the prenatal environment. Sheri Berenbaum, of Pennsylvania State University, and Melissa Hines, from City University London, studied play behavior in children with congenital adrenal hyperplasia (CAH), a genetic disorder that causes an individual to release excessive amounts of androgen (a male hormone) before and after birth.[25] They found that compared with their normal sisters, CAH girls played significantly more often with boys' toys than with girls' toys. (Normal children have sexually specific toy preferences. Boys like to play with vehicles and building toys, while girls prefer kitchens and dolls.) It therefore appears that sex differences in cognition (in this case, play behavior) are at least partially hormonally primed, and this priming takes place at early stages of development.

Hines summarizes other evidence for hormonal influences on sex differences in human cognition and notes further that exposure to low levels of hormones during development is always associated with reduction in male-typical cognitive traits, whereas exposure to high levels of hormones increases these traits:

> First, adolescent girls and young women exposed to excess testosterone and other androgens prenatally, because they have a genetic defect called congenital adrenal hyperplasia (CAH), have been reported to show enhanced performance on measures of visuospatial abilities. Second, men exposed to lower than normal levels of androgen from early life, because they have idiopathic hypogonadotrophic hypogonadism, have been found to show reduced visuospatial abilities. Third, women exposed to higher than normal levels of estrogen prenatally, because their mothers were prescribed the synthetic estrogen, diethylstilbestrol (DES), during pregnancy, have been found to show increased language lateralization. Finally, girls and women exposed to lower than normal levels of hormones, because of prenatal ovarian regression associated with the genetic disorder of Turner syndrome, have reduced visuospatial abilities and reduced language lateralization.[26]

Albert Galaburda, of Harvard Medical School, and the late Norman Geschwind developed a rather speculative, but interesting, theory about brain lateralization that is based on prenatal priming of the nervous system with sex hormones. Their reasoning goes something like this: There is some evidence that the cerebral convolutions of fetuses develop earlier on the surfaces of their right, rather than their left, hemispheres. Therefore, some influence probably slows growth of parts of the left hemisphere. In those individuals for whom left-hemisphere growth is particularly slowed, corresponding parts of the right hemisphere compensate by growing faster and possibly larger. This results in especially well-developed right-hemisphere visuospatial functions and a relatively high incidence of left-handedness. On the other hand, left-hemisphere functions suffer from being left behind, as is indicated by higher incidences of language disorder such as dyslexia or stuttering.

As it turns out, the configuration of both positive and negative traits that are said to be associated with slowed growth of the left hemisphere is manifested much more in males than in females. Galaburda and Geschwind therefore conclude that the influence that theoretically slows growth of the left hemisphere is probably male related, and they offer the male hormone testosterone as a likely candidate because developing males are exposed to much greater quantities of it than are developing females. Thus, brain lateralization and the priming related to sex differences in cognitive abilities may both be mediated by the action of testosterone on the cerebral cortex, especially during the third month of intrauterine life.[27]

Theories such as this are built largely, but not exclusively, on animal models. This is because, for ethical reasons, scientists are very limited in the experiments that can be performed on people. In order to study questions about brain evolution and lateralization, my colleagues from Washington University in St. Louis and I analyzed endocasts that were prepared from hundreds of skulls of rhesus monkeys, one of the most widely used animal models in medical research. These endocasts were from known individuals of certain age and sex, and they revealed many details about skull sutures, cortical sulci, and brain shape. Two of our findings are of interest with respect to Galaburda and Geschwind's hypothesis.[28]

First, during postnatal development in monkeys, some cranial sutures closed significantly sooner on the right than on the left side, but never the reverse. Recall that the convolutions of human fetal brains tend to develop on the right side first. If an asymmetry in skull growth like that seen in monkeys also occurs in humans (a reasonable hypothesis), then there may be a general *developmental gradient,* whereby the right side of the cranium and its contents are slightly outpacing the growth of the left side.

Our second finding was a dramatic sex difference in the age at which adult brain size (estimated from cranial capacity) was reached in rhesus monkeys. Females attained their adult sizes by about four years of age, whereas males did not achieve their adult brain sizes until they were six years old. If a similar pattern also characterizes human brain growth, it could help explain why males appear more lateralized than females (in some respects), without necessarily having to argue that testosterone inhibits left-hemisphere growth. To wit: If right hemispheres are programmed to develop at slightly faster rates than left hemispheres in both sexes, and if brain growth continues longer in males, then the two hemispheres of males will grow farther apart (that is, become more asymmetrical) than those of females. This hypothesis, brought to you courtesy of the standard rhesus monkey animal model, seems well worth exploring.

Despite an ongoing revolution in the neurosciences, the human brain remains, in many respects, a little black box that can best be pondered from the outside. However, the few glimpses we get of the brain's inner workings do gel into three useful insights: First, sex hormones play an important role during the brain's development, and they subsequently influence cognition. Second, the interaction of the prenatal chemical environment with the timing of specific neurological developments is of definitive importance for the brain's structure and, therefore, its eventual functions. Finally, the brains of males and females are to some extent organized differently.

So which influences brain development, nature or nurture? The answer, of course, is both. Are the small but significant differences between males and females due to genes or environmental factors? Again, both variables are important. Although brain lateralization is undoubtedly rooted in a genetic substrate, it is important to keep in mind that traits selected for in one sex are usually automatically increased in the other sex. (This is due to the way genes mix and match as they are passed from parents to offspring of both sexes.)

At least one pioneer in the study of sex hormones and behavior is well aware of the importance of cultural factors (including sexism) for determining behavior. Noting that women outperform men on verbal and dexterity skills, Estelle Ramey, professor emeritus from Georgetown University, says: "So what do [men] say about women? That they talk too much. Even when you have the advantage, you can't win." Such biases are engendered by women as well, she adds. "Females also have the advantage in digital dexterity. So do they become neurosurgeons? No, they do needlepoint! In other words, the biology is just the barest beginning."[29]

Brain Lateralization in Other Animals

Philosophers tend to exaggerate the extent to which *Homo sapiens* is special and set apart from other animals. Until fairly recently, such anthropocentrism characterized the thinking about brain lateralization. Consequently, it took many years for workers to accept the idea that other animals have lateralized brains—especially since this fact seems to be contradicted by a lack of language and right-handedness in nonhuman species. But lateralized brains they have. Today, asymmetrical nervous systems have been found in a wide variety of animals that range from rodents to birds to primates.

The unfolding of this information is one of those rare scientific success stories that I love. It began with research in the early 1970s, when Stanley Glick made two serendipitous observations about rats. Glick, who is professor and director at Albany Medical College, Center for Neuropharmacology and Neuroscience (CNN), first found that drugging trained rats with amphetamine increases their side preferences in pressing levers. He then discovered that amphetamine induces more circling behavior in untrained rats. (Though they do so less intensely, normal undrugged rats rotate at night in the same direction induced by amphetamine.) At the time of Glick's observations, it was known that vigorous circling could also be induced in rats by lesions to deep parts of one side of the brain that damaged neurons containing dopamine. Glick therefore postulated that amphetamine caused his rats to prefer one side in lever pressing or rotation because of its action on an asymmetrical dopaminergic system.

FIGURE 5.4.
Betty Zimmerberg's work
in neuroscience is important
for understanding brain
evolution. (Photograph courtesy of Betty Zimmerberg.)

In a 1974 report in *Science,* Betty Zimmerberg (professor and chair of
the Neuroscience Program at Williams College) and her colleagues actually demonstrated the existence of an asymmetrical dopaminergic system in normal rats, and the concentration of dopamine turned out to be
significantly higher on the nonpreferred side. Together, Zimmerberg
and Glick concluded that these and other results indicated that circling
is a stereotyped spatial behavior that derives from a deep neuroanatomical asymmetry. This means that rats have lateralized nervous systems
that are responsible for their lateralized circling. Curiously, male and
female rats have a slight tendency to circle in opposite directions.

How did scientists respond to these dramatic findings? "At first,
people didn't believe us," said Glick. "Then, when they finally did believe
the results, they said 'So what? They're only rats, not people.'" There was
only one thing to do. In 1982, Glick and his colleagues investigated the
distribution of a variety of neurotransmitters, including dopamine, in
human brains. Not only did they find an asymmetry in the distribution
of dopamine in these brains, it turned out to be twice as high as that for
rats. Just as dopamine levels were higher on the side opposite circling

preference in rats, dopamine levels of humans were higher on the side opposite the most frequently preferred hand.

But circling behavior is one thing, and handedness is another. Or is it? What about rotation in humans? Do people turn in preferred directions like rats? If so, do males and females also prefer opposite directions? Eager to answer these questions, Glick and a colleague designed an electronic rotometer that humans could wear on a belt. This device measured exactly the same kinds of rotational movements that had been observed in rats. Although they had no idea of the kind of counts obtained by the device, seventy-four male and sixty-one female students, physicians, and hospital employees agreed to wear the rotometer for seven to eight consecutive hours. People proved to be just like rats! Without realizing it, most of the men and women preferentially rotated to the left or to the right during a routine day. (You probably do too.) As in rats, female humans rotated more than males, and the sexes also differed with respect to their overall directional preferences. Left-hemisphere-dominant men rotated more to the right, whereas left-hemisphere-dominant women rotated more to the left.

Because of Glick's research, investigators can no longer say "so what" to rats. Or to birds or primates, for that matter. Furthermore, a review of experimental studies for various mammals based on locomotor, neurochemical, lesion, and neuroanatomical measures shows that gender is a major determinant for patterns of behavioral and brain asymmetries. In fact, sex differences in locomotor asymmetries, such as circling in rodents, are the rule rather than the exception.[30]

An Evolutionary Model

Why did brain lateralization get started in the first place?[31] The work of Glick and his colleagues suggests that in the beginning there may have been circling. But what good is that? Simply put, if one wanders off, one wanders back to the safety of the nest, if one is a rodent, or full circle back to the starting point, if one is a lost human explorer. At least for the rodent, finding the way home would presumably be an adaptive trait favored by natural selection. That is, homing rodents would have longer lives and leave more offspring that those unfortunates who get lost. I asked Glick what function he thought might be served by a preferred direction of rotation, and he suggested that rats who don't waste time deciding which way to turn might be better able to get away from attackers. This too would no doubt be adaptive.

But why the sex difference? A clue to this puzzle is provided by other rodents called voles. Voles look like small burrowing mice, and they come in two kinds. Prairie voles from the Midwest are monogamous, with both sexes sticking close to home. Meadow voles from Pennsylvania are polygynous, and males wander far afield during breeding season in order to mate with as many females as possible. The two species of voles are, therefore, perfect subjects for testing whether or not sex differences in visuospatial skills are associated with males getting about in the world and, if so, whether or not visuospatial skills contribute to breeding success. And that's just what Steven Gaulin of the University of Pittsburgh and Randall FitzGerald did in an intriguing set of experiments.[32]

During the first part of their study, Gaulin and FitzGerald trapped voles of both species and fitted them with small radio transmitters. After the voles were released, daily ranges and total ranges were determined from each subject's broadcasts. The results confirmed that male meadow voles expanded their ranges during the breeding season, whereas female meadow voles did not. In contrast, the monogamous prairie voles showed no sex differences, at any time, in their ranging patterns.

During the second part of the investigation, the voles of both species were retrapped and tested for visuospatial ability in laboratory mazes. In keeping with Gaulin and FitzGerald's earlier findings, only polygynous meadow voles showed consistent male superiority on the spatial tasks. It is therefore a good guess that visuospatial skills evolved in male meadow voles because their far-ranging search for mates contributed to their reproductive success (which, after all, is what evolution is all about).

But vision is not the only sense that is important for breeding success. Because of their habitats, arboreal species such as birds rely more on auditory senses. For example, canaries use songs to announce their presence to neighbors and to claim breeding territories. More important for our discussion, it is male songbirds who sing to attract mates. Further, birdsong is neurologically lateralized to left forebrain structures, which are three to four times larger in adult male canaries who sing complex songs than in adult females who sing simpler songs.[33] Apparently, birdsong contributes to reproductive success, and it is reasonable to conclude that sex differences in the behavior, as well as the neurological asymmetries underlying birdsong, were selected for in this context.

Unlike the bird and rodent examples, nonhuman primates rely heavily on both visual and vocal communication systems. And in humans, at least, relevant aspects of these visual and vocal systems are generally lateralized to right and left hemispheres, respectively. Taking a cue from the evolution of other mammals, could sex differences in visuospatial and vocal communication skills have been selected for in the primate ancestors of early hominins?

Although this question is difficult to address, there is evidence that permits one to engage in reasoned speculation. Like humans, macaque (rhesus) monkeys are left-hemisphere dominant for processing particular socially meaningful vocalizations and right-hemisphere dominant for certain visual discriminations. Macaques also manifest petalia patterns and other cortical asymmetries that are similar to those of humans. In 1999, my colleagues and I showed that rhesus monkeys and humans manifest nearly identical amounts of sex differences in average brain size, with averages for females approximating 92 percent and 90 percent of the average sizes for males respectively.[34] Furthermore, 88 percent and 84 percent of the larger brains of rhesus and human males were due to sex rather than to body weight. Our results led us to hypothesize that, similar to computers that require more memory to process graphics, the larger brains of males may be related to processing of visuospatial stimuli. If so (and as suggested for polygynous voles), perhaps sex differences in visuospatial skills originated long ago in a polygynous common ancestor of macaques and humans in conjunction with the extensive navigating required of amorous males during mating seasons. These findings, along with a number of other studies, suggest that the substrate for human brain lateralization was already present during early anthropoid evolution.[34]

A surprising survey of handedness across the primate order also suggests that early anthropoids were neurologically lateralized. Peter Mac-Neilage, of the University of Texas at Austin, and his colleagues showed that nonhuman primates tend to be left-handed when reaching for food and right-handed for manipulative tasks. According to MacNeilage's evolutionary scenario, the initial primate adaptation (indicated by studies on prosimians) involved right-hemisphere specialization for visually guided reaching with the left hand. Subsequently, the left hemisphere of higher (anthropoid) primates became specialized for right-hand manipulation and bimanual coordination. This model, therefore, gives primacy to specialization of the right hemisphere for visuospatial functions during early primate evolution.

From the above, we may conclude that anthropoid primates indeed have lateralized brains and that this trait probably enjoyed a long evolutionary history. Of all the anthropoids, of course, *Homo sapiens* is the most lateralized. Since gender is a determinant for patterns of behavioral and brain asymmetries in mammals including humans, we may speculate that gender was probably an important factor in the development of brain lateralization in ancestral primates. The fossil and archaeological record suggests that by two million years ago, the immediate australopithecine ancestor of early *Homo* had brains that were lateralized along the lines of our own. Meanwhile, we are left wondering about sex differences in patterns of brain lateralization in early hominins.

Unfortunately, attention to gender is often missing from studies of hominin brain evolution. The knapping (shaping) of stone tools requires special visuospatial skills, and it would be interesting to know the sex distribution of early knappers. Were they predominantly male? As spatial competence increased during the evolution of tool production (beautifully described by Thomas Wynn[35]), were sex differences in patterns of behavioral and brain asymmetries also evolving?

I have an image of one of our distant mammalian ancestors who lived more than 65 million years ago. The ancestor is male, and it is mating season. He's good at spatial navigation and temporarily extends his daily range in search of mates. Because of a good cognitive map, he is able to return home later and to repeat the process during the next mating season. During his life, he fathers many offspring.

Thanks to Wynn, I also have an image of one of the mammal's distant, future descendants. It is a knapper making a bifacial stone tool, some 300,000 years ago. As the tool takes shape, the knapper uses notions of perspective, the control of spatial quantity, and an understanding of composition. Overall shape is very important to the knapper.

Why won't you ever stop and ask for directions?

FIGURE 5.5.
As is hypothesized for humans, the larger brains of male compared to female rhesus monkeys may be related to the evolution of differential navigational skills. (Drawing by John Guyer.)

When it is finished, the tool has a regular cross section. It is gorgeous. And all because the knapper's distant ancestor was good at getting around and delivered the genes for skilled visuospatial abilities to his offspring. The knapper is satisfied with the way the tool has turned out. She packs up and goes home.[36]

Despite my cheerful image of woman the knapper, the previous discussion of bipedalism and the battle of the sexes shows that the role women played during human evolution is a subject of much recent debate. Nevertheless, this discourse represents an improvement over the old unquestioned assumption that males were the primary focus of selection for various good and noble human features. And of all the ancestral females who have lived during the past five million years, one in particular has created havoc in the hominin fossil record. Her name is Lucy.

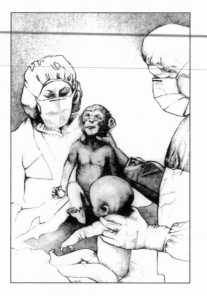

chapter 6

LUCY'S CHILD

Mix-up at the Hospital

When I wrote this chapter for the 1992 edition of Braindance, *few workers agreed with my view that the famous fossil known as Lucy could not have been a direct forerunner of* Homo sapiens. *Since then, numerous fossils have been unearthed in the earliest part of the hominin record, and predictably, their discoverers have usually assigned them to new species and proclaimed them to be the direct ancestor that led eventually to humans. Well, they can't all be. Although her discoverers still include Lucy on the human family tree, an increasing number of workers now believe that she was not. Nevertheless, the bone wars rage on with repercussions that are at times amusing, puzzling, and counterproductive for science.*

It happens rarely. Years later, no one knows who did it. Or if the switch was accidental or deliberate. All that is known is that two newborn babies went home and grew up with the wrong families. In these notorious incidents, mothers and fathers are shocked to learn from routine blood tests that they cannot be the biological parents of their child. In some cases, more informative genetic tests are then done on the child and on another boy or girl who was born in the same hospital, at approximately the same time. Unfortunately, these extremely accurate DNA fingerprinting tests sometimes prove that the two children were, indeed, switched before leaving the hospital. Through no fault of their own, the victims of these awful switches have grown up misunderstanding their own family trees.

Alas, there has been a terrible mix-up at the hospital within our own family, the Hominidae. It involves the fossil named Lucy, and as is usually the case in these switches, initial evidence based on blood suggests that she has been woefully misplaced on our family tree. Other evidence confirms the initial, shocking suspicion: Lucy and her kind could *not* have been the parents of *Homo,* contrary to what many people believe.

However, it is difficult to convince Lucy's proponents that a mistake has been made. Mix-ups at the hospital are traumatic events for all parties concerned. Sometimes, parents of other children born at the same hospital refuse to allow their children to be tested for blood and genetic information that will confirm or deny their presumed heritage. It is understandable that these parents are upset by the suggestion that their child may not really be their biological offspring (who wouldn't be?). In fact, they may even lash out and attack those who dare to question their family trees.

Lucy's "birth" some thirty years ago was an exciting event. Nearly 40 percent of her skeleton was recovered from eroding sand deposits in the Hadar area of the Afar region of Ethiopia in November of 1974. When they put her together, Donald Johanson (currently director of the Institute of Human Origins at Arizona State University) and other members of the International Afar Research Expedition found that they had discovered the most complete early hominin skeleton ever found. (As discussed below, an even more complete fossil skeleton, KNM-WT 15000, was found ten years after Lucy's discovery, and a nearly complete australopithecine skeleton known as Little Foot is currently being excavated by its discoverer, Ron Clarke, at Sterkfontein in South Africa.) As is traditional with such finds, Johanson's specimen was given a name (after the Beatles song "Lucy in the Sky with Diamonds").

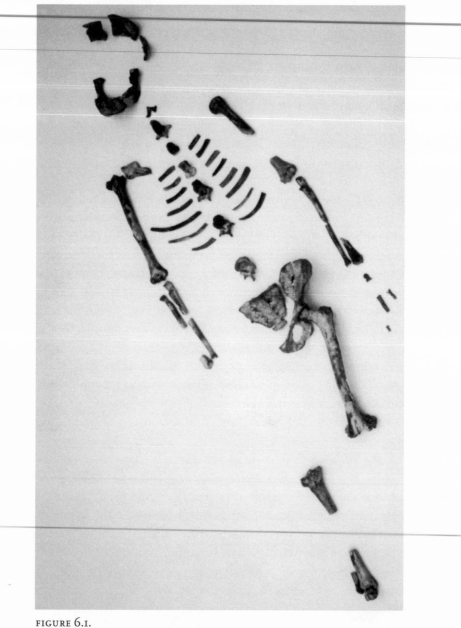

FIGURE 6.1.
Lucy. Nearly 40 percent of her skeleton was discovered eroding from sand deposits in the Hadar region of the Afar Depression in Ethiopia. (Photograph by John Reader, copyright 1992/Science Photo Library.)

Lucy lived more than three million years ago. Her wisdom teeth were in, and she was a young adult when she died. She was a tiny thing, standing only three and a half to four feet tall. And her arms were relatively long compared with those of a modern human (all the better to climb trees with). Her pelvis (which showed she was female) and her leg bones left no mistake that she had walked bipedally when she was on the ground. Her lower jaw (mandible) was V-shaped and had apparently once held small front teeth. Unfortunately, not enough of Lucy's skull was recovered to obtain a cranial capacity or to provide other definitive clues about the identity of her species.

Although Lucy is the most famous fossil hominin from the Hadar site in Ethiopia, she is not the only one. She had lots of company, including the so-called First Family of thirteen individuals from one particular location. According to Johanson, this group of individuals lived together, and died together as a result of some natural catastrophe such as a flash flood.[1] He believed that they may have even been relatives. However, these individuals were extremely varied in their physical appearance and geological evidence suggests that they were fossilized and buried separately. In other words, these early hominins may not have constituted one group.

Although Lucy eventually became Johanson's claim to fame, he did not really know what to make of her at first. Which relative did she most resemble? Which species did she represent? Johanson's first assessment of Lucy was published (with Maurice Taieb) in 1976.[2] At that time, he thought she might be a primitive version of a gracile australopithecine. It is significant that Johanson also thought that three species of early hominins may have been represented at Hadar: gracile australopithecines, robust australopithecines, and early *Homo*.

The Naming of *Australopithecus afarensis*

At the time I was contemplating the contents of the Red Cave, a former classmate of mine was studying the early hominin fossils from the Hadar region and from Laetoli, Tanzania. His name is Tim White, and he was instrumental in convincing Johanson to lump all of the fossils from these two sites together into one new species, *Australopithecus afarensis*. This was quite a departure from Johanson's earlier assessment.

When White (now a professor at the University of California, Berkeley) and I began our graduate studies at the University of Michigan, its physical anthropology program was known for supporting a "single-species hypothesis." According to this school of thought, there was only one species of early hominin living at any given time; therefore, two species of australopithecines had never coexisted. Thus, the variation seen in australopithecines was attributed to sex, rather than species, differences. Robust australopithecines were believed to be males and gracile australopithecines were supposedly females. We graduate students at Michigan were brought up on this hypothesis. And we believed it.

At least we did until 1976. That's when the single-species hypothesis died rather suddenly because of a fatal blow struck by a paper in *Nature* by Richard Leakey and Alan Walker. It was titled "*Australopithecus, Homo erectus,* and the single species hypothesis" and revealed that two beautiful skulls coexisted in Kenya some 1.5 million years ago. One was a robust australopithecine (KNM-ER 406), the other an early *Homo erectus* (KNM-ER 3733).[3] Clearly the single-species hypothesis was no longer tenable.

However, with some justification, investigators continued to emphasize sex as an important source of variation in early hominins. For example, Johanson and his colleagues viewed the large fossils from Laetoli and Hadar as males and the smaller ones as females. They then proceeded to lump the fossils from both sites into one new species (*Australopithecus afarensis*). With the advantage of hindsight, this melding of fossils from two sites now seems questionable for several reasons: it is currently believed that, besides being in different countries, Laetoli and Hadar had different climates (Laetoli's was more arid), had different habitats (evergreen bushland at Hadar, open savanna vegetation at Laetoli),[4] and may have been separated by half a million years of time. Also, the fossils from Laetoli are relatively few and consist mostly of jaws, teeth, and footprints, while cranial fragments that are critical for assessing taxonomic status are mostly lacking.

There are very strict rules that govern the naming of new zoological species. These rules are formally spelled out in the *International Code of Zoological Nomenclature.*[5] According to the Code, new scientific names must be made readily accessible to the scientific community in a publication. If an investigator has something really important to communicate, he or she generally tries to publish in the best possible journal. And the best journals are peer reviewed. Articles submitted to these journals are either rejected or accepted for publication on the basis of anonymous reviews that often contain suggestions for improving the manuscript. Sometimes editors will provisionally accept an article for publication (that is, accept it on the condition that the author make certain revisions suggested by the reviewers).

The process of peer review is not a perfect one. But it does assure a certain amount of scientific give-and-take within disciplines, as well as the improvement of many manuscripts prior to their publication. Inferior articles get weeded out by the review process at peer-reviewed journals. Examples of peer-reviewed journals are *Behavioral and Brain Sciences, Journal of Human Evolution, Science, Nature,* and the *American Journal of Physical Anthropology.* Although the Code does not specify that new names must be published in peer-reviewed journals, any of the above would have been an appropriate forum in which to name a new species of early hominin. However, Johanson, White, and Coppens named *Australopithecus afarensis* in 1978 in *Kirtlandia,* which is described on its inside cover as "an occasional publication of the Cleveland Museum of Natural History." (In fairness, it is to their credit and the field's benefit that Johanson and his colleagues went on to publish full and detailed descriptions of the Hadar material in a 1982 issue of the *American Journal of Physical Anthropology.*)

More telling is the response of Johanson, White, and Coppens to Article 13a(i) of the Code, which requires that the published name be "accompanied by a statement that purports to give characters differentiating the taxon." Given White's education at Michigan, it is not surprising that the investigators attributed the variation in their species to strong sexual dimorphism. However, the *Kirtlandia* account of variation in *Australopithecus afarensis* went further:

> The authors recognize that individual traits and even single specimens in the new collection can be matched in other samples representing different taxa (e.g., *Australopithecus africanus* Dart 1925, *Homo habilis* Leakey, Tobias and Napier 1964).[6]

In other words, *Australopithecus afarensis* was so variable that some of its specimens looked like gracile australopithecines while others looked like what was then recognized as *Homo habilis*. (This is especially interesting today, because, as discussed below, it has recently been proposed that *habilis* belongs in *Australopithecus* rather than *Homo*.)

Since the above was written, the Hadar dates have been reassessed, and it turns out that they are likely to have been contemporaneous with the gracile australopithecine site of Makapansgat, South Africa.[7] This raises a dilemma for the next discoverer of a fossil australopithecine from a previously undiscovered 3.2-million-year-old site. What species should it be assigned to if it is one of those specimens that matches both *Australopithecus africanus* Dart and *Australopithecus afarensis*? Can two fossils that are identical (not to mention contemporaneous) reasonably be assigned to two different species? I do not believe so.

According to Johanson and White's preferred taxonomic scheme (published in *Science* in 1979), their new species was the *only* australopithecine on the line leading directly to *Homo sapiens*.[8] Everybody else's australopithecines were placed on a sidebranch that became extinct without issue. By now, the reader will not be surprised to learn that everybody else did not approve of Johanson and White's genealogy. In fact, neighbors (some of them named Leakey and Tobias and Walker[9]) began whispering suspicions that there might have been a mix-up at the hospital. But having named the new species and passed out the cigars, would the proud parents agree to a blood test?

The Evidence from Cranial Blood Flow

My reaction to all of this at the time? Mostly, I was amazed at the rapidity with which much of the field accepted the new species. Other than that, I was too busy defending my position on the position of the lunate sulcus to develop much of an opinion about the details of early hominin phylogeny. Then in 1982, quite by accident, I found myself immersed in blood.

Cranial remains of australopithecines and early *Homo* were my subject matter and, once again, I was spending my summer doing research in African museums. For the first time, I also saw numerous casts of the cranial remains from the Hadar early hominins. Although convolutions and sulci were my primary interest, that summer I became fascinated

FIGURE 6.2.
Blood flow routes that appear in the back of human skulls (left) and the Hadar hominins and robust australopithecines (right). Sa, superior sagittal sinus; T, transverse sinus; O, occipital sinus; and M, marginal sinus. In humans, cranial blood flows through the transverse sinuses and out of the skull. In the hominins on the right, blood flows straight down the O/M sinus before exiting the cranium.

with a particular feature that showed up on some of the fossils. It had to do with cranial blood flow.

The feature that caught my attention was a dramatic groove located inside the back of the braincase. This large groove is called the occipital/ marginal (or O/M) sinus and it is rarely present in a form large enough to leave a groove in apes or living people. In life, the enlarged O/M sinus of early hominins provided a major pathway for draining blood from the skull. But only for *some* early hominins. What intrigued me was that all of the scorable robust australopithecines (there were seven at the time, there are now ten)[10] and all of the scorable Hadar early hominins (there were five and are now seven scored specimens) had this feature, while only one of six gracile australopithecines showed it. (That specimen was Taung, which may have been incorrectly placed with gracile instead of robust australopithecines because of its young age, as the reader will recall.) Contrary to Johanson and White's taxonomic scheme in which robust australopithecines and the Hadar early hominins were completely separated, presence of the unusual O/M sinus in all scorable members of both of these two groups suggested to me that they might, in fact, be directly related.

But why did some early hominins have an O/M sinus? What was its function? For that, I turned to my colleague and fellow paleoanthropologist Glenn Conroy, now in the Department of Anatomy and Neurobiology at Washington University School of Medicine. Glenn agreed that it seemed to be too much of a coincidence to find the highly unusual enlarged O/M sinus in all members of two different groups of unrelated early hominins. We decided to put our heads together about heads.

Glenn and I knew that Lucy and company were among the earliest known bipeds. That led us to wonder if the O/M sinus had something to do with the origins of bipedalism. As a starting point, we decided to find out whether or not there was a general relationship between posture and cranial blood flow in living people. Within weeks, we located and studied a number of relevant clinical and physiological reports that made it clear that cranial blood flow depends very much on posture. And not just for humans.

Monkeys, snakes, people, and giraffes are all subject to the constraints of gravity. In all of these animals, blood flow changes with a shift in body posture from a horizontal (lying down) to a vertical (standing up) position. (For snakes, blood flow differs between horizontal positions on the ground and vertical hanging postures in trees.) A major reason why blood flow changes with altered postures is because gravity places different stresses (called hydrostatic pressures) on horizontal and vertical columns of fluid (such as blood in veins).

To understand this, imagine a long tube half-filled with water. If the tube is vertical, all of the water is in its bottom half. When the tube is completely tilted over on its side, however, the water is redistributed along its entire length. Now imagine that the tube contains little holes that are sparsely but evenly distributed over its entire surface. When the tube is vertical, the water drains out of the holes in its bottom. When it is horizontal, on the other hand, the water exits through holes all along the tube's side. To wit: Different postures, different exits for fluid. And all because of gravity.

Conroy and I learned that the same thing happens with blood that is draining from peoples' skulls. If an individual is lying down, cranial blood flows out through the internal jugular veins. When the person stands up, however, most of the exiting cranial blood shifts away from the jugulars and into a network of veins that surrounds the spinal cord. That network of veins is called the vertebral plexus. Our bipedal existence depends on it! We were on to something.

Our next task was to determine if there was a relationship between an enlarged O/M sinus and the vertebral plexus of veins. Again, we studied the literature and, again, the answer was affirmative. Most humans have small O/M sinuses (not big enough to leave grooves in skulls) and these usually have numerous connections with the vertebral plexus of veins. More to the point, in a study of one hundred human cadavers, nine had relatively large O/M sinuses.[11] Seven of the nine O/M sinuses were connected to the vertebral plexus of veins. Clearly, it was a good bet that the even larger O/M sinuses of early hominins were also connected with the vertebral plexus of veins. After all, if cranial blood flows to the vertebral plexus of veins when a person stands up, it makes sense that a route leading to the vertebral plexus would be enlarged in some of the earliest bipeds.

Conroy and I took our findings to *Nature*. In a 1983 paper, we suggested that the O/M system of the Hadar early hominins represented a unique solution to increased circulatory demands (on the vertebral plexus) that were associated with the origin of bipedalism. We also speculated, contrary to Johanson and White's taxonomic scheme, that rather than giving rise to gracile australopithecines (most of whom lacked enlarged O/M sinuses), *Australopithecus afarensis* may have been directly ancestral to robust australopithecines (all of whom had the O/M system). According to our preliminary blood test, there had been a mix-up at the hospital.

The "Surprising" Black Skull

In *Lucy's Child,* Johanson writes:

> Tim and I had hoped that the Leakeys and their colleagues would oblige our theory with some professional response—perhaps a counterthesis that we could bounce ideas off, even integrate into a more refined synthesis.[12]

The evidence regarding cranial blood flow certainly provided a coun-
terthesis for Johanson and his colleagues to bounce their ideas off of.
However, instead of considering that evidence, these investigators ignored it, while claiming to have addressed it![13]

By way of example, according to William Kimbel, enlarged O/M sinuses represented an "adaptively neutral trait" that could not be used to
reconstruct phylogenies. Yet, he provided no discussion of the vertebral
plexus, or of the connections of the O/M sinus with the vertebral plexus,
or of the shifts in hydrostatic pressures associated with changed postures. Having pronounced the O/M sinus as uninformative with respect
to early hominin relationships, Kimbel reaffirmed his colleagues' family
tree:

> the distribution of venous sinus variants in Plio-Pleistocene hominids
> gives little or no basis for revising the phylogenetic scheme of Johan-
> son and White (1979) . . .[14]

In other words, Kimbel maintained that robust australopithecines were
descended from gracile australopithecines and not (as Conroy and I had
suggested) from the Hadar early hominins.

Johanson and his colleagues' failure to give consideration to the physiological, anatomical, and functional evidence regarding cranial blood
flow was disappointing, to say the least. In *Lucy's Child,* Johanson states:

> Meanwhile, Dean Falk . . . scrutinized the Hadar skull fragments and
> announced that the patterns of blood-drainage channels, faintly per-
> ceptible on the inside of the fragments, fell neatly into two groups—
> one looking like *Homo,* the other resembling those of the robust aus-
> tralopithecines.[15]

However, I have never maintained that the Hadar cranial remains fell
neatly into two groups. On the contrary, I have emphasized that all of the
scorable Hadar crania (seven, if you include Kimbel's scoring of Lucy)
have enlarged O/M sinuses like those of ten out of ten robust australopithecines. Rather than being "faintly perceptible," an enlarged O/M sinus is a striking feature and its occurrence in all of the scorable Hadar
specimens and all of the scorable robust australopithecines deserves
careful thought.

A good theory should be testable. If our blood tests were right, robust australopithecines occurred much earlier in time than the fossil record had yet indicated. In that case, a really old robust australopithecine could still be discovered. And if a robust australopithecine were discovered that turned out to be as old or older than gracile australopithecines, then the Johanson and White taxonomic scheme would be invalidated. In 1986, that's just what happened.[16]

The discovery was a beautiful skull called KNM-WT 17000. It is also known as the Black Skull (because minerals had darkened it during fossilization), and it is just as robust as can be. Found on the west side of Lake Turkana in Kenya, WT 17K (as it became known) is 2.5 million years old, much too old to be located on the robust australopithecine portion of Johanson and White's family tree.[17] WT 17K has a small cranial capacity (410 cm^3) and, best of all, a suite of features that suggest it is descended from at least some of the Hadar early hominins. Bingo!

But there's more to this story. "A robust australopithecine descended directly from the Hadar early hominids, who'd ever have guessed? . . . The paleontological world's on its ear, everything's upside down, why oh why didn't anybody anticipate this find?" complained numerous scientific journalists. The interesting thing is that a handful of workers had questioned the Johanson and White tree and some had anticipated just such a skull as WT 17K.[18] For different reasons, Adrienne Zihlman, Brigitte Senut, Christine Tardieu, Todd Olson, and Russell Tuttle had all questioned the integrity of *Australopithecus afarensis*. (Senut and Tardieu are from the Musée Nationale d'Histoire Naturelle, Paris; Olson is from Albert Einstein College of Medicine.) But because these workers were, for the most part, quiet, methodical, and independent, they did not belong to the paleontological clique that the press was so fond of quoting.

This is not to say that the discovery of WT 17K did not have an unsettling effect on the field. It did. Family trees were redrawn to accommodate the Black Skull, which was generally regarded as intermediary between *Australopithecus afarensis* and the more recent robust australopithecines from East Africa. The problem was what, then, to do with the robust australopithecines from South Africa, as well as the gracile australopithecines. Numerous workers solved this problem by adding branches to their trees—by drawing various species of hominins that

FIGURE 6.3.
A cast of the Black Skull (KNM-WT 17000) from Kenya. This beautiful 2.5-million-year-old robust australopithecine overturned the Johanson and White hominin family tree and demonstrated the dangers of developing elaborate scenarios from insufficient data. (Photograph by Dean Falk.)

evolved in parallel through time. I was skeptical about such bushy hominin trees because they required an awful lot of coincidence. (After all, there's a limit to the notion of happy accident.)

Russell Tuttle was also skeptical about bushy trees:

Students. Teachers, and paleophiles, beware! A new era of taxonomic splitting is upon us. The splitomania, which recently reappeared in Miocene hominid classification, is also infesting the humanoid arena. . . . Several paleoanthropologists . . . now accept no fewer than five species of australopithecines: *Australopithecus afarensis, Australopithecus africanus, Australopithecus robustus, Australopithecus crassidens,* and *Australopithecus boisei.* And we should not be surprised if the recently discovered "black skull" (KNM-WT 17000) and certain other eastern African specimens get dubbed a sixth species (*Australopithecus aethiopicus*) instead of being lumped with an existing species of robust australopithecines. . . .[19]

And get dubbed it did! Furthermore, since Tuttle made the above observation in 1988, numerous other species of australopithecines (*Australopithecus anamensis, Australopithecus bahrelghazali, Australopithecus garhi*) as well as entirely new genera of early presumed hominins (*Sahelanthropus, Orrorin, Ardipithecus,* and *Kenyanthropus*) have been named.[20] The overall result is paleoconfusion. As noted, they can't *all* be on the line leading to *Homo sapiens,* as most discoverers propose for their individual fossils. There are, however, some workers who discount such bushiness at the base of hominin evolution. Alan Walker, for example, comments that "I think there's no strong evidence that there's anything more than one evolving hominid from 6 million years to 2.5 million years."[20] (The problem here, however, is the implication that robust australopithecines [specifically KNM-WT 17000] popped up out of nowhere 2.5 million years ago, which seems unlikely.) Tim White is also skeptical of so much bushiness in the early part of the hominin record, but still maintains that all of *his* fossils are on the line leading to *Homo sapiens.* White thus postulates that the mysterious *Ardipithecus ramidus* (see below) led to *Australopithecus anamensis* (the only fossil in this sequence that he did not help name), which led to *Australopithecus afarensis,* which led to *Australopithecus garhi* that White and his colleague propose as "a candidate ancestor for early *Homo.*"[21]

Despite his own proclivity for naming new hominin taxa, White observes that "many of today's paleoanthropologists herald each new fossil as evidence of ancient hominid biodiversity," noting that this is a "peculiar form of politically correct paleoanthropology."[22] As an example, White claims that diagnostic features used to name the new taxon *Kenyanthropus platyops* (represented by skull KNM-ER 4000)[23] did not really exist in life but, instead, are due to postmortem distortion of the fossil. If so, White suggests that, rather than being a valid taxon, *K. plat-yops* might really be an early variant of his own species, *A. afarensis*. For gravy, White "formalized" this concept with a scientific-sounding term for the distortion process, "expanding matrix distortion (EMD)."[22]

I have no idea whether or not *K. platyops* is distinct enough to warrant a new genus, as Meave Leakey and her colleagues believe.[23] But I do know this: although Leakey described distortion in the KNM-ER 4000 skull, she also noted that its face was better preserved, and this part of the skull contains important diagnostic features. Furthermore, the skull was fossilized in two main parts, which removed much of the guess-work that ordinarily goes into reconstructing hominin skulls. Equally important, the new genus was named according to the international rules of nomenclature, with a detailed description of the skull and how it differs from those of other hominin taxa. This was done in *Nature* in 2001,[23] relatively soon after the skull was discovered (1999). Because *Kenyanthropus platyops* was named and meticulously described in a timely fashion in an internationally visible journal, the scientific community now has the necessary information for beginning the process of assessing its role during hominin evolution.

Waiting for *Ardipithecus*, Waiting for Godot

Not so for the naming of *Ardipithecus ramidus*, although it started out all right. In 1994, White and his colleagues named a new species of australopithecine from Aramis, Ethiopia, and as fitting, they did so in *Nature*.[24] The species was named *Australopithecus ramidus*. White and his colleagues suggested that their approximately 4.4-million-year-old species represented "a long-sought potential root species" for hominins ("ramid" is the word for root in the Afar language). Most of the evidence was dental, much of it appearing chimpanzeelike. The evidence for bipedalism (a prerequisite for being hominin instead of ape) rested on a questionable interpretation of a scrap of the bottom of one skull. This was a dramatic find and the field was abuzz with rumors that, although he was claiming these fossils were ancestral to humans, perhaps White had found the first fossil chimpanzee.

In the *Nature* article, reference was made to the "anticipated recovery at Aramis of additional postcranial remains, particularly those of the lower limb and hip" that might further elucidate the nature of this new species. And, indeed, less than four months later (on January 13, 1995), White and his colleagues announced that they had found a collection of *A. ramidus* bones embedded in a rock matrix not far from the site of the first discovery. Less than four months after that (on May 4, 1995) an extraordinary note occurred in *Nature*. In a "corrigendum" that occupied less than half a page,[25] White, Suwa, and Asfaw changed the genus name for *ramidus* from *Australopithecus* to *Ardipithecus,* and did so with little discussion and without describing any of the additional fossils. Hello *Ardipithecus ramidus!* Although this is decidedly *not* the way new genera should be named, the editors at *Nature* declined to publish correspondence about the violation of the *International Code of Zoological Nomenclature*[5] that would have set the record straight, at least on that score.

But what about that cache of fossils announced before the corrigendum appeared in 1995, which is purported to include "skull, vertebrae, ribs, pelvis, arm, wrist, hand, leg, ankle, [and] foot" bones from a single skeleton?[26] Although it has been more than nine years since the first of these bones was discovered,[20] they have yet to be described. White says the description will soon be out, however, and that it is a skeleton worth waiting for, calling it a "phenomenal individual" that will be the "Rosetta stone for understanding bipedalism."[27] As the field awaits details of *Ardipithecus,* rumors abound. Is White about to disclose that this genus was not bipedal, after all, and then attempt to redefine *the* criterion for being hominin on the basis of dental rather than locomotor features? Has he waited too long to publish his findings, which are now susceptible to being upstaged by new contenders for the "root" hominin like *Orrorin* and *Sahelanthropus* (discussed in chapter 4)? Enquiring minds want to know, and I hope it won't be another decade before we find out!

Functional Morphology versus Cladistic Analyses

At this point, it may be illuminating to consider the method that most paleontologists use to construct their trees, namely cladistic analysis. Cladists judge the degree of evolutionary closeness of two species by the number of specialized (derived) features that they have in common. The greater the number of shared derived traits, the closer the evolutionary relationship. However, shared traits that are not specialized (primitive traits) cannot be used to assess evolutionary closeness. For example, both gracile and robust australopithecines have five fingers on each hand and backbones, but these shared primitive traits cannot be used to assess the evolutionary relationship of the hominins. Lots of mammals have these features. On the other hand, both kinds of australopithecines have feet and shortened pelvic bones that are specialized for bipedalism, and these derived features (plus others) link them together as bipedal hominins who most likely inherited their shared specializations from a common ancestor.

The cladistic method is governed by a very formal set of rules. For instance, one mustn't count each trait that is part of a functional complex separately (correlated features count once, as a package). Otherwise, too much weight might be given to a single part of the body, such as a tooth that has changed in numerous small ways in conjunction with a particular diet. (Unfortunately, paleoanthropologists frequently violate this rule.) Workers sometimes disagree on whether or not a given trait is derived or primitive, which, needless to say, can be problematical for constructing family trees.

However, the biggest problem with the cladistic method has to do with the list of traits that each worker selects for analysis. In order for the analysis to work, one must assume that any given trait list is a balanced representation of all of the independently derived features that characterize the species under consideration. I believe that truly representative (or statistically stratified) trait lists are a rarity in hominin paleontology. One's tree is only as good as one's trait list, and too often (unconsciously or otherwise) workers come up with trait lists that result in the very trees that they have been pushing all along—a sort of designer cladistics. Given these reservations about the applications of the cladistic method, I do not find it surprising that the field of hominin paleontology can be unsettled by the discovery of one new skull.

Although derived and primitive states can be recognized for venous sinuses and other related features, these traits are not proper subjects for cladistic analysis because they are components of one functional complex that is involved with draining blood from the head (that is, the traits are correlated, which is a no-no). However, this does not mean that the features are without evolutionary significance. On the contrary, an effort can be made to understand the evolution of cranial blood flow as a system, and to examine its changes from a functional point of view. This is the approach that Conroy and I took. Although our method incorporated recognition of derived and primitive character states, it differed from cladistic analysis in that independently derived features were not enumerated and weighed in an effort to arrive at a most probable phylogeny.

In a 1986 article about the cladistic method, Randal Skelton and his associates from the University of California at Davis compiled and compared numerous trait lists (and their resulting trees) that had been constructed by numerous paleontologists.[28] They concluded that the most probable tree had *Australopithecus afarensis* giving rise to gracile australopithecines who evolved into robust australopithecines, on the one hand, and *Homo habilis* on the other. The possibility of *Australopithecus afarensis* giving rise directly to robust australopithecines was barely mentioned and then was shown to be unsupported by the brunt of the cladistic studies. Then came the surprising robust Black Skull, looking like a probable offspring of Hadar early hominins—just as the functional morphological approach to cranial blood flow had predicted. Despite this turn of events, however, the growing vascular evidence is still rejected by some workers.

Australopithecus afarensis: A Species in Question

Because of the Black Skull, few researchers today continue to believe that gracile australopithecines evolved into robust australopithecines. Even though the 1979 Johanson and White taxonomic scheme has now been abandoned, some new trees retain a limb with gracile australopithecines leading to South African robust australopithecines and add another totally separate branch with *Australopithecus afarensis* giving rise to East African robust australopithecines—"splitomania," as Russ Tuttle calls it.

In the introduction to the volume from the 1987 international workshop on robust australopithecines, Clark Howell, of the University of California at Berkeley, states that, with respect to *Australopithecus afarensis:*

consensus seemed to emerge that this was not only a valid taxon . . .
but that a single species was represented by the large Hadar Formation sample, and that the species hypodigm certainly included both
the Laetoli and Hadar samples (as long maintained by D. C. Johanson
and T. D. White, in particular).[29]

I participated in this workshop, and this was not the view I expressed.
Nor was it the view of a number of workers who did not participate in
the workshop. For example, Senut and Tardieu's studies of elbows and
knees suggested to them that both *Homo* and *Australopithecus* were represented in the Hadar material (Lucy falling with the australopithecines). Zihlman also concluded that the amount of variation seen in
Australopithecus afarensis was too extensive to be accounted for by sex
differences alone and that more than one species was therefore represented in this taxon. Sounding the same theme at ground zero, Tuttle
said that the Hadar foot bones and the Laetoli footprints were from
different critters (with the Laetoli tracks appearing to be those of *Homo*).

And the evidence from cranial blood flow? This is problematic when
it comes to the question of how many species are really contained in
Australopithecus afarensis. Kimbel scored one Laetoli specimen as lacking an enlarged O/M sinus. If he is right, then Laetoli differs from all of
the six scorable Hadar fossils (or seven, if you count Kimbel's scoring of
Lucy). This is consistent with the suggestion that Laetoli and Hadar do
not belong in the same species (in which case *Australopithecus afarensis*
needs to be redefined).

The Hadar material itself is another story. All of the scorable crania
have robust-like O/M sinuses, and it is therefore reasonable to suggest
that they gave rise to or shared a common ancestor with robust australopithecines. (Unfortunately, it is difficult to score Lucy for this feature
because most of the appropriate part of her skull is missing.) The bottom line on all this is that things don't look good for *Australopithecus
afarensis*. Minimally, this "species" seems to contain ancestors of robust
australopithecines and (at Laetoli) gracile australopithecines and/or
Homo. Lucy's supposed maternity of *Homo* is therefore in deep jeop-
ardy.

For Lucy to remain the mother of *Homo,* she must have a legitimate
heir. And that is just what Johanson and his colleagues claim to have

found at Olduvai Gorge in 1986. Reader, I'll spare you the gossip about how Johanson came to work at Olduvai Gorge after Mary Leakey's retirement from that wonderful site. Nor will I dwell on the ancient conflict between Richard Leakey and Donald Johanson. You can read about those details and more recent paleo infighting in other books. What I want to address here is not gossip, but rather the evidence that pertains to Lucy's so-called child. To do that, we must first consider the criteria for distinguishing early *Homo* from australopithecines, as well as another spectacular find from East Africa, called the Turkana Boy (or Strapping Youth, WT 15000).

Earliest *Homo*

There wasn't much to go on when *Homo habilis* was named by Louis Leakey and his colleagues in 1964.[30] The name *Homo habilis* ("handy man") was chosen because Leakey thought he had found the true maker of primitive stone Olduwan tools that had been found in the same general neighborhood and credited to robust australopithecines ("Zinj") discovered five years earlier at Olduvai Gorge. Although a number of skulls from Olduvai Gorge in Tanzania formed the basis for naming *Homo habilis*, they were all distorted or fragmentary. However, their cranial capacities averaged about 650 cm^3, considerably larger than the average for robust australopithecines. Was it not reasonable to think that the brainier new species had produced the associated tools?

Besides having a larger brain, *Homo habilis* also appeared to have larger front teeth (compared with the back teeth) than australopithecines. Nevertheless, the dental characteristics of *Homo habilis* overlapped a good deal with those of gracile australopithecines from South Africa (who, the reader will recall, also had relatively large front teeth compared with robust australopithecines). This led many workers to reject the notion that the Olduvai specimens represented a new species. Instead, they suggested that Leakey's so-called *Homo habilis* was simply a more recent, larger-brained, thicker-skulled, and smaller-faced East African version of gracile australopithecine. The future did not look good for *Homo habilis*. Could the new species withstand future tests by evidence?

FIGURE 6.4.
A nearly two-million-year-old hominin skull (KNM-ER 1470) from
Kenya that some workers now place in *Australopithecus rudolfensis*.
(Photograph by John Reader, copyright 1992/Science Photo Library.)

The first tests came from the Omo region of Ethiopia and Lake Tur-kana in Kenya and, at the time, it seemed that *Homo habilis* held up beautifully. For example, in 1972 the KNM-ER 1470 skull was found on the east side of Lake Turkana and attributed to *Homo habilis*, as were numerous other specimens from the same region in Kenya. Now known to be just younger than two million years, this specimen had an even larger cranial capacity of about 775 cm³. In addition to its large brain, the teeth, skull, and face were thought to distinguish this hom-inin from australopithecines. Unlike the endocasts of australopithe-cines, the endocast of ER 1470 appeared humanlike in parts of its fron-tal lobe. Further, because of the form of its left frontal lobe, Phillip Tobias and I independently concluded that the group to which ER 1470 belonged may have been capable of some rudimentary form of speech.

I have always thought it odd that, while robust australopithecines had been identified in both South and East Africa, gracile australopithecines (*Australopithecus africanus*) were recognized only from South Africa. Thus, the early suggestion by some that the *Homo habilis* specimens identified at Olduvai Gorge in 1964 may simply have been more re-cently evolved descendants of gracile australopithecines seemed reason-able. Although it was not accepted by many workers at the time, this initial interpretation of the Olduvai specimens has now gained credibil-ity. One reason for this is a 1992 landmark paper in which Bernard Wood (from George Washington University) suggested that KNM-ER 1470 and some other specimens from Kenya differed too much from the Olduvai specimens to be included in the same species.[31] Consequently, Wood removed ER 1470 and its look-alikes from *Homo habilis* and placed them in a different species (*Homo rudolfensis*).

But musical hominins does not stop there! The Olduvai hominins (*Homo habilis sensu stricto*) looked like australopithecines, at least from the neck down (that is, with relatively apelike limb proportions), and it is possible that future discoveries will confirm that *H. rudolfensis* did too. Wood and his colleague, Mark Collard, have now taken another dra-matic step by removing both *habilis* and *rudolfensis* from the genus *Homo* and placing them in *Australopithecus*. They did this because the dentitions, body sizes and shapes, and presumed locomotor patterns that combined bipedalism with proficient climbing suggested that both species differed profoundly from *Homo*.[32] But if *habilis sensu stricto* and *rudolfensis* are really australopithecines, where are the first representatives of *Homo*?

WT 15000: *Homo erectus*—Early, Tall, and African!

One of the most complete early hominin skeletons ever found was discovered ten years after Lucy came to light. In the summer of 1984, Richard Leakey and Alan Walker excavated this marvelous specimen from the base of a thorn tree that happened to be using the skull as a flower pot. The hominin was recovered from the west side of Lake Turkana in Kenya and assigned the museum number KNM-WT 15000 (Kenya National Museums, West Turkana 15000).[33] Dated at 1.6 million years (other fossils that are grouped with it go back to about 1.78 mya), WT 15000 is an almost complete skeleton of a twelve-year-old boy. Because of its teeth and skull shape, WT 15000 was initially interpreted as an early African version of the Asian *Homo erectus*. Although some have preferred to recognize this specimen as a member of another species, *Homo ergaster,* the tide has now turned back to the original designation and interpretation.[34]

Clearly, WT 15000 was an extremely important discovery. It also turned out to be very surprising. By twelve years of age, the *Homo erectus* boy had already grown to be five feet, five inches tall; as an adult, he would probably have reached a height of at least six feet. Other fragmentary fossils confirm that early *Homo erectus* individuals were much taller than anyone had dreamed possible. It is also noteworthy that, unlike earlier hominins such as long-armed Lucy, the arms and legs of WT 15000 were proportioned like those of modern people. Until the discovery of this specimen, paleoanthroplogists regarded the tall stature of modern humans as a recent event that resulted partially from environmental causes, such as good nutrition. The lad from Lake Turkana shows us that at least some groups of humans have been tall since the time of earliest-known *Homo erectus*. So much for the long-held notion that our ancestors were smaller than we are.

FIGURE 6.5.
This dazzling skeleton (KNM-WT 15000) is from a young *Homo erectus* boy that lived around 1.6 million years ago and, had he grown up, would have been at least six feet tall.

Now we can look at Lucy's so-called child from Olduvai Gorge. And look we should. After all, Johanson and his colleagues implied that this important 1.8-million-year-old partial skeleton, OH 62 (Olduvai Hominin 62), provided the test by evidence that confirmed Lucy as the mother of *Homo*.[35] Johanson's approach to OH 62 was divided: He used its head to make the claim that the specimen belonged to an early species of *Homo*, and the rest of its body to show that it was a descendant of Lucy. Ergo, Lucy gave rise to *Homo*.

Let's begin at the top. OH 62 falls short in the head category. It consists mostly of the palate, jaws (mainly upper), fragments of teeth, and a tiny bit of the lower face. Very little of the cranial vault is represented, too little for cranial capacity to be estimated. This is unfortunate since brain size and skull shape are features that help distinguish australopithecines from early fossils of *Homo* such as KNM-WT 15000 that are acknowledged to be on the line leading to humans. But what about the ever-important teeth? Johanson and his colleagues estimated anterior/posterior dental proportions and found that they were too large to represent a robust australopithecine, but were at the low end of the range for *Homo*. Clearly, OH 62 cannot be viewed as distinct from gracile australopithecines on the basis of traditional criteria related to teeth and braincase. (Although Johanson and his associates said that none of the special features of robust or gracile australopithecine faces were seen in the face of OH 62, this claim is difficult to assess because most of its face is missing.)

Below the neck, Johanson compared 1.8-million-year-old OH 62 from Tanzania with 3.2-million-year-old Lucy from Ethiopia. The reader will recall that Lucy was petite and had long arms. Well, OH 62 was even more petite and had even longer arms, and Johanson found "striking anatomical and proportional similarities" between the two fossils. Although it was not possible to estimate cranial capacity for OH 62, Johanson suggested that

> small individuals of *Australopithecus* and *Homo habilis* were differentiated by cranial capacity but not by body size. This reinforces the view that encephalization in the terminal Pliocene played a key role in hominid evolution.[36]

In other words, OH 62's capacity would have been large if it could have been measured (because this specimen was presumed to be *Homo*). And since body size was so small in OH 62, relative brain size ("encephalization") had therefore evolved by the time of OH 62. Clearly, this reasoning was circular.

Then, there was the thorny problem of WT 15000, the *Homo erectus* boy who lived next door (in Kenya) a mere 200,000 years after OH 62. He would have grown to be six or more feet tall and his arms were proportioned like yours and mine. And little, long-armed OH 62 (who was approximately three feet, three inches tall) was supposed to have been his ancestor. To me, and to others,[31, 32] this seems unlikely.

In sum, the brunt of current evidence strengthens my earlier suggestion that there had been a mix-up at the hospital and that OH 62 was an East African australopithecine (perhaps *Australopithecus habilis*) rather than a direct ancestor of early *Homo*. If so, and if Lucy gave rise to OH 62 as Johanson suggested, then we had best look elsewhere for an unequivocal ancestor for *Homo*. Meanwhile, what is interesting about OH 62 is its long arms. They suggest to me that australopithecines slept in tree nests right to the end. Brainier *Homo* found other places to camp out. Places that were on the ground. And in the sun.

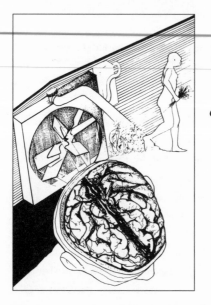

CRANIAL RADIATORS AND EVOLUTIONARY CACTI

The 1986 discovery of the Black Skull, a 2.5-million-year-old robust australopithecine from Kenya, completely upset the field of hominin systematics. This spectacular find showed that earlier efforts to interpret
various features of fossilized teeth and bones had led to erroneous conclusions about the overall pattern of hominin evolution. Today, consensus about the hominin family tree is still elusive. The present chaos
in hominin paleontology is partially due to the fact that cladists have
placed too much emphasis on user-designed lists of specialized traits.
The flip side of this coin is that not enough consideration has been given
to the evolution on whole, integrated organisms. For example, it is unlikely that hominins were weeded out of gene pools because of isolated

glitches on their teeth or bones. Or that our evolutionary history simply entailed changes in limb proportions or relative sizes of teeth. Rather, as populations of early hominins interacted with particular environments, each individual lived or died depending on how well his or her unique, complex, multifaceted being held up. In this sense, whole, integrated physiological systems provided important foci for evolutionary pressures.

My experience in the Red Cave taught me that I had been a Pollyanna to expect that paleoanthropologists would objectively consider new and compelling evidence that gored sacred cows. Instead, Holloway relentlessly questioned my research on hominin brain evolution, and the field sat back impassively watching the lobs and volleys of the controversy for twenty years. I was therefore delighted when I was able to shift away from australopithecine endocasts, toward an apparently less-controversial research topic, cranial blood flow.

Paleontologists should have been thrilled when a whopping big feature (an enlarged O/M sinus) showed up on all of the scorable Hadar fossils. And they should have been dying of curiosity about its possible functional significance. This did not turn out to be the case, however. If my venture into the Red Cave left me somewhat cynical about the field, the preliminary evidence regarding cranial blood flow showed me that the evolution of integrated physiological systems could no longer be ignored in paleontological research.

The nice thing about doing research is that it keeps building on itself. Solutions to much-struggled-over problems inevitably raise new questions. Just follow your nose and you'll never be idle. That is how it went with the topic of cranial blood flow. I followed my nose right into a major mystery of hominin brain evolution: Why did brain size increase rapidly in the genus *Homo* well over a million years *after* bipedalism originated in early hominins? What accounted for this mosaic evolution whereby the feet went first? How do we explain the breech birth of our genus?

The solution that Glenn Conroy and I proposed to explain the function of O/M sinuses in certain groups of early hominins raised another question. If enlarged O/M sinuses were the product of selection for bipedalism in early hominins, as we claimed, why don't bipeds like ourselves have them in high frequencies? This was an important question

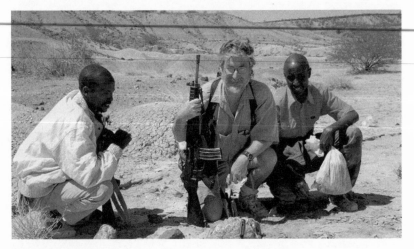

FIGURE 7.1.
Glenn Conroy of Washington University School of Medicine collaborated on research that formed the basis for understanding cranial radiators. (Photograph courtesy of Glenn Conroy.)

that required an answer. It was back to the drawing board and, eventually, back to Africa.

Conroy and I had already learned that when humans stand up, the blood leaving their skulls shifts away from the jugular veins and into the vertebral plexus of veins that surrounds their spinal cords. In fact, this information provided a major clue for understanding the function of enlarged O/M sinuses in early hominins. The question now became: How do living people deliver blood to their vertebral plexes of veins when they are upright, since their O/M sinuses are usually so small? The drawing board where I would first grapple with this question consisted of the gross anatomy laboratory (I was teaching human anatomy to medical students at the time) and, of course, the good old library.

The cadavers and the books both proved to be informative. Yes, the small O/M sinuses of humans are usually capable of delivering blood to the vertebral plexus of veins. However, humans have a whole network of numerous other little pathways that also direct blood to the vertebral plexus of veins. In other words, robust australopithecines and the Hadar early hominins had *one* enlarged route that could shift blood to the vertebral plexus when they stood up, but modern people have a more diverse, complicated network of small veins that carry out this function. Two different groups of bipedal hominins (one old, one new), two distinct ways to drain blood from the skull. Different systems of cranial blood flow had evolved in different groups.

It sounded good, but could this hypothesis be tested? Because of one saving grace in the hominin fossil record, it could. That saving grace? A few of the many little veins that contribute to cranial blood flow in living people go through holes (foramina) in the skull. These particular veins are called emissary veins and they have names like mastoid (near the back of the ear) and parietal (at the top rear of the skull) emissary veins. Emissary foramina don't exist for most cranial blood veins, of course, but the few that do exist provide a glimpse into the entire system (a kind of window). Best of all, although the tissue that composes veins disintegrates after death, the foramina through which emissary veins travel are often preserved in fossilized skulls.

It seemed to me that one could investigate the evolution of cranial blood flow by determining the percentages of emissary foramina in ape skulls and in the hominin fossil record up to, and including, cranial remains of living people. This procedure has the advantage of combining information from both living and extinct species. I decided to spend the summer of 1984 counting these little holes in skulls in museums in Africa and Europe.

And count holes, I did. Lots of holes in lots of specimens. Whole skulls were examined from fifty chimpanzees, fifty gorillas, and fifty modern humans. In addition, I scored every fossil cranial fragment I could get my hands on for gracile australopithecines, robust australopithecines, *Homo erectus,* archaic *Homo sapiens,* and Neandertals. For good measure, all of the relevant data that could be found in the literature were added to my data and included in my analysis.

Three features turned out to be especially informative: enlarged O/M sinuses and mastoid and parietal foramina.[1] African apes (representing the ancestral condition) had low frequencies for all three traits.[2] Robust australopithecines had low apelike frequencies for the two emissary foramina, but a 100 percent frequency for the O/M sinus.

Results for the lineage that presumably led from gracile australopithecines to *Homo sapiens* were more complicated, however. And more

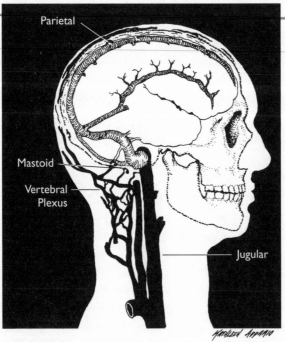

FIGURE 7.2.
The radiator network of veins is extensive. Small veins on the surface of
the skull enter the bone, within which they merge with other (diploic) veins.
These, in turn, communicate with the veins on the inside of the braincase
(meningeal veins) as well as the venous sinuses. A few components of the
radiator, known as emissary veins, penetrate clear through the skull via small
holes known as emissary foramina.

interesting. Frequencies for the O/M sinus were apelike for gracile australopithecines, then fluctuated in subsequently living hominins (never
getting above 50 percent), and finally were reduced to very low frequencies in modern populations. The overall trend in frequencies of
enlarged O/M sinuses in *Homo* was therefore toward reduction. Meanwhile, the frequencies for mastoid and parietal emissary foramina increased dramatically, especially in *Homo*. Interpreting these data as a
window into the entire system of cranial blood veins, it appeared that
increased frequencies of emissary veins were probably accompanied by
increased frequencies of other nontraceable blood vessels. It was a good
guess that the whole system of cranial blood vessels had undergone a

dramatic evolution, becoming more complex in the hominins leading to *Homo sapiens,* especially during the past two million years.

These findings were compatible with the conclusions that Conroy and I had published earlier regarding hominin systematics—two different lineages of hominins, two different systems for draining blood from the head when in an upright (bipedal) posture. The Hadar early hominins and robust australopithecines used one large O/M route to deliver blood to the vertebral plexus, whereas hominins leading from gracile australopithecines to contemporary *Homo sapiens* evolved a more complicated and widespread network of veins that served the same purpose.

With that, I thought I was done working on cranial blood flow. But I should have known better.

Of Car Radiators and Letters from France

It was an "aha" experience, if ever I've had one, and the weirdest combination of events led to it. First, the engine in my 1970 Mercedes needed major surgery. I took it to Walter Anwander (a whiz) in Lafayette, Indiana, who completely rebuilt the engine. One day, while enumerating the wonders beneath the hood (about which I definitely needed schooling), Walter pointed to the radiator and told me "the engine can only be as big as that can cool." I didn't think much about it at the time.

During the period when my car was in the shop, I received a letter (dated January 13, 1987) from Michel Cabanac, a French physiologist who is now at the School of Medicine at Laval University in Québec. He said that my publication on the evolution of emissary veins was of interest to his research team because they had been doing research on exactly the same veins. To my surprise, Cabanac's group had shown that the mastoid and parietal emissary veins help to cool the brain when people are overheated.

The brain is an exquisitely heat-sensitive organ. According to the noted vascular physiologist, Mary Ann Baker:

A rise of only four or five degrees C above normal begins to disturb brain functions. For example, high fevers in children are sometimes accompanied by convulsions; these are manifestations of the abnormal functioning of the nerve cells of the overheated brain. Indeed, it may be that the temperature of the brain is the single most important factor limiting the survival of man and other animals in hot environments.[3]

Cabanac and his colleague Heiner Brinnel (of the Hôpital de l'Arbresle, France) wanted to know how the human brain keeps cool when everything else heats up, such as occurs during intense physical exercise. Accordingly, they studied the relationship between different temperature states and the direction of blood flow in cranial veins (which lack valves) by carrying out intriguing physiological experiments on six healthy adult men.[4] To achieve the cold state (hypothermia), the subjects occupied a turbulent climatic chamber set at 0°C for half an hour. Their blood vessels constricted, they shivered, and their oral temperature dropped to 36.3°C ± 0.05°. To attain the heated condition (hyperthermia), the men pedaled on a cycle for twenty to thirty minutes, by which time they were sweating profusely and had an oral temperature of 37.6°C ± 0.18°.

In the minutes following cold exposure or exercise, the direction of blood flow was recorded for the parietal and mastoid emissary veins. This was done by placing an instrument called a Doppler probe directly on the scalp at the point where the vein passes through the cranium. (Four of the men were conveniently bald.) The results were startling. In cold subjects, blood flow was slow and flowed out from the cranium, that is, from the brain to the skin. In overheated subjects, however, blood rapidly drained from the skin *into* the braincase. Further, these findings were identical to those determined earlier for a third emissary vein, the ophthalmic vein of the face. Thus, when subjects became overheated, blood flow reversed direction in all three of these emissary veins. Consequently, blood that had been cooled by evaporation from the sweating face and scalp was delivered into the braincase.

Whereas I had merely speculated that the mastoid and parietal emissary veins provided the windows into a wider, more complicated network of cranial veins, Cabanac and Brinnel had actually demonstrated this to be the case. They noted that innumerable, microscopic emissary veins exist in humans and that the network of veins found within the bones of the skull itself (diploid veins) opens both externally and internally. By gently massaging the outside surface of the skullcap from a fresh cadaver, Cabanac and Brinnel showed that blood is capable of flowing through this entire network of emissary and diploic veins from the outside to the inside of the cranium.

The three relatively large emissary veins that were used to record direction of blood flow are located at dispersed points throughout the network of cranial veins—at the face (ophthalmic), the back of the ear (mastoid), and the top, back part of the skull (parietal). Cabanac and Brinnel therefore took these three veins to be representative of the wider network and concluded that when blood flows into the braincase in the ophthalmic, mastoid, and parietal veins, it also flows inward in the innumerable other tiny veins that comprise the cranial network. Apparently, cool blood from the entire surface of the human head participates in cooling the brain—but only when a person is overheated. Physiologists call this phenomenon "selective brain cooling." Although other experimental evidence supported Cabanac and Brinnel's original paper, whether or not an extensive net of veins that can support selective brain cooling in humans actually existed remained surprisingly controversial. At least until 1996, that is, when Wolfgang Zenker and Stefan Kubik unequivocally demonstrated its existence.[5] (To view the extensive network of veins that comprise the human radiator, visit my website [www.anthro.fsu.edu] and click on "Research," "Braindance," then "Theories.") Just like my car, the brain has a radiator!

You can see these cranial radiators at work in any gymnasium. Take where I now work out, in Tallahassee, Florida. Every Saturday I take a cardioblast class. The class begins with a moderately paced warm-up. Everybody stays cool. Most people are not even wearing headbands. The warm-up is followed by 45–50 minutes of nonstop, high-impact aerobics (done to music). After a while, small sweat spots start to appear on torsos (whole-body cooling has kicked in). Further into the hour, sweat marks get bigger. Headbands go on. By about the forty-five minute mark, even the teacher has put on a headband. Near the end of the high-impact portion of the class, cranial radiators are in full throttle, causing faces to flush as surface vessels dilate and assimilate the cooling effects of evaporation. Some heads are actually dripping. In vessels of a dozen bouncing crania, cooled surface blood flows inward to soothe exhilarated brains. These people are ready for pump class!

Cabanac's letter had a profound influence on me. In a key portion, he wrote:

> It is possible that emissary veins were developed for the defense of brain temperature. Brain size has increased with bipedalism. The brain's thermolytic (cooling) needs have increased with its increasing size. . . . This hypothesis does not contradict yours but might complement it. I would be interested in hearing from you.

Cabanac enclosed reprints of his scientific articles with his letter. I read them right away and should have seen their implications immediately, but it took three days for the light bulb to go on.

The impact of Cabanac's research hit me in the middle of the night, when I awoke thinking something to the extent of: "Holy moly! Cabanac's work might be the key for understanding why bipedalism preceded the major increase in brain size." There was only one thing to do. I got up, got dressed, and went to my lab to plot hominin cranial capacities against the data for emissary veins. It turned out to be worth the trip.

It was beautiful. For the past two million years, the increase in frequencies of emissary foramina kept *exact* pace with the increase in brain size in *Homo*. Clearly, the brain and the veins had evolved relatively rapidly and together. I saw that Cabanac's letter was right and that I had unwittingly charted the evolution of a radiator for the brain in my earlier work on emissary foramina. As Anwander had said about my car, the engine can only be as big as the radiator can cool. Apparently, the same is true for heat-sensitive brains.

But the engine, or brain, and the radiator increased in only one lineage of hominins—that leading to *Homo*. Why? And what about bipedalism and gravity? If the above reasoning is correct, heat stress (or thermoregulation) would have been a key factor in the evolution, and possibly the origin, of *Homo*. As it turns out, there is plenty of speculation, and even some evidence, that suggests just that.

Hot Times on the Savanna

The apes that gave rise to the CA around five to seven million years ago were presumably already semierect or preadapted for bipedalism because of their primate ancestry. Like living pygmy chimpanzees, they would have been capable of spurts of bipedalism on the ground or even in the trees. But the shift to full bipedal locomotion would take some time. And during this process, vascular systems would be reshaped through natural selection because of the changed hydrostatic pressures associated with erect posture. Whatever else was demanded of the cranial veins, they had to be able, by hook or by crook, to sustain delivery of blood to the vertebral plexus of veins. Further, because of gravity, this would be true forever after, for all hominins, in all types of environments.

Apparently, robust australopithecines kept cool throughout their evolution. Their ancestors from Hadar had curved finger and toe bones that were handy for hanging in the shady trees growing in Hadar's evergreen bushland habitat. According to Elisabeth Vrba of Yale University, the more recent robust australopithecines from East Africa also lived in wooded areas near water. (Unfortunately, the environments occupied by South African robust australopithecines are, for various reasons, difficult to assess.) Further, all robust australopithecines were probably vegetarians, just as Robinson suggested years ago. No need for them to chase down animals during the heat of the day! They had it made in the shade. Except, of course, for the fact that their brains never got very big, and they eventually became extinct.

It's another story for gracile australopithecines, however. Although it has recently become clear that the earliest known hominins lived in woodlands rather than savannas, by two million years ago their gracile australopithecine descendants (and early *Homo* for that matter) were occupying more open habitats. Both the teeth and cranial vascular systems show that gracile australopithecines were completely different from robust australopithecines. For example, of six scorable gracile australopithecines, only Taung had an O/M sinus system like that found in robust australopithecines. (And remember, Taung might actually have been an immature robust australopithecine.) Further, the data for emissary veins indicate that unlike robust australopithecines, gracile australopithecines had the beginnings of a floor plan for a radiator network of veins. These are excellent reasons for believing that by the time we pick up their fossil records, robust and gracile australopithecines had been separated for a relatively long time—long enough to evolve distinctly different systems for cranial blood flow.

But how did the division between robust and gracile australopithecines occur? These so-called speciation events generally happen when one subgroup of a population settles down somewhere else. If the new environment (which doesn't have to be far away) is different enough from the original environment and if the pioneers remain isolated from the original group, then the two groups will go their own evolutionary directions. Given enough time, the two populations will become more and more different, until, eventually, they are no longer able to interbreed with each other (if, that is, they were so inclined, which they probably wouldn't be anyway). At that point, speciation has occurred.

Now, I can think of no better way for a hominin to go somewhere else than to walk there. In fact, by its very nature, any new form of locomotion (be it bipedalism or airplanes) should open up new territory (niches) for more adventurous souls. Further, we know that a variety of patchy environments were available to hominins during the Plio-Pleistocene. It again appears that Robinson had it right: While robust australopithecines kept cool among the trees, at least some gracile australopithecines and their *Homo* descendants ventured afield on foot. Like savanna baboons, these hominins spent much of their waking hours away from the forests and woodlands, and on the hot African savanna. It was *there* that full-fledged bipedalism was refined.

And it was on the savanna that hominins experienced the double whammy of changed gravitational pressures on their vascular systems and heat stress on their whole bodies. Presumably, both sexes spent a good deal of time exploiting the scattered resources of open African grasslands that were subject to hot temperatures and intense solar radiation during the day. Many workers, including Zihlman and Cohn, have argued convincingly that sweat glands, reduced body hair, and dark skin evolved as a functional complex in response to the thermal stress associated with living on the African savanna.[6]

Pete Wheeler, as was discussed earlier, takes the topic of savanna-adapted hominin responses to thermal stress a step further. According to Wheeler, early hominins foraging in patchy habitats reduced their heat loads by postural means, that is, by engaging in increased amounts of bipedal locomotion, especially during the heat of the day, which reduced the amount of body surface exposed to direct hits of solar radiation. In other words, Wheeler sees bipedalism itself as an adaptive response to heat stress. His theory also incorporates ideas about the evolution of sweat glands, hair loss, and even body fat.

Whenever I read Wheeler's papers, I have a flashback to an experience that I had on the island of La Parguera, off the southwest coast of Puerto Rico. During the early 1980s, the island, which is uninhabited by people, provided a refuge for a large group of beautiful, strawberry blond Old World patas monkeys. In their native African habitats, patas monkeys are quadrupedal animals that live in open savanna grasslands. Although well known for being silent, extremely swift runners, patas monkeys frequently assume bipedal stances in the wild. Primatologists have traditionally attributed this proclivity for uprightness to sentinel behavior—for standing up to look out (over the high grass) for predators.

When I visited La Parguera, it was extremely hot. So much so that I could barely function. During the middle of the day, I positioned myself (and a good water supply) on a shaded observation deck that overlooked a large corral containing dozens of patas monkeys. The corral was encircled by high corrugated metal sheeting and, unfortunately, there were no trees within it to shade the monkeys. Although I had read about sentinel behavior in patas monkeys, I was amazed at the amount of bipedalism I saw that day. At the same time, I guessed that the monkeys might be trying to see over the tops of the metal enclosure, although it did seem odd because the sides were much too high to allow that. Years later, after reading Wheeler's work, I now suspect that the monkeys were standing up simply because they were more comfortable absorbing less sunshine. (Incidentally, I also think it was inhumane to place the monkeys in such a horrid situation.)

The Radiator Hypothesis in a Nutshell

Put all this information together and you have the radiator hypothesis of hominin brain evolution. The hypothesis explains why bipedalism preceded the increase in brain size in *Homo* and why brain size never got very big in australopithecines. Beginning with the latter, brain size never got greater than 600 cm³ because an organism's ability to cool its cranial blood places a limiting factor, or constraint, on its brain size. Australopithecines simply did not have vascular systems that were able to regulate temperature in larger brains. Although robust australopithecines evolved a dramatic, enlarged O/M sinus that delivered blood from the cranium, this system was not connected with a cooling net of veins that could function as a radiator for an enlarging brain. Thus, brain size remained relatively conservative in this group of hominins.

Bipedalism in early gracile australopithecines preceded the takeoff in brain size in their descendants, *Homo,* for two reasons. First, because of the constraints of gravity, bipedalism necessitated a rearrangement in cranial blood vessels. (Since this was also true for robust australopithecines, it was a necessary but not sufficient condition for the subsequent evolution in brain size.) Second, bipedalism allowed the descendants of gracile australopithecines to "go over there" to thermally stressful habitats. And if Wheeler is right, thermally stressful habitats themselves may have contributed to an increase in the frequency of bipedal behavior. (This is a cyclical, yet logical, notion.) Thus, the vascular systems of the gracile australopithecines that gave rise to *Homo* became modified in response to both gravitational and temperature pressures associated with refinement of bipedalism on the savanna. One result was the beginnings of a cranial radiator system of veins in gracile australopithecines that could help cool the brain under conditions of intense exercise. More important, once in place, this system was modifiable. It, therefore, released thermal constraints that had previously kept brain size in check. The engine (brain) could and did get bigger in *Homo,* but only after *Homo's* australopithecine ancestors had refined bipedalism in a savanna environment that facilitated development of a prototype radiator. That is why the feet went first.

A Fair Hearing for the Radiator Hypothesis

As discussed earlier, my work with Conroy on cranial blood flow was all but ignored by hominin paleontologists. Further, because the initial blood flow evidence was so dramatic, I was pretty sure it would have been widely discussed if our research had supported rather than refuted the (then) generally accepted taxonomic scheme of hominin evolution. Having now formulated the radiator hypothesis, I was faced with a problem: Given the politics of paleoanthropology, how would I ever get this new, more complicated idea discussed? And what good is a hypothesis if it's not discussed?

I knew that for the radiator hypothesis to get a fair hearing, it should be put in a forum where it would be criticized by a number of experts who were knowledgeable about various scientific aspects of the hypothesis, not just by paleontologists with old trees (and reputations) to protect. I therefore decided to submit my paper as a "target article" to the journal *Behavioral and Brain Sciences*. If accepted there, it would be not only published but also subjected to open peer commentary from many experts, including circulatory physiologists, comparative neuroanatomists, psychologists, neurophysiologists, anthropologists, and paleoanthropologists. They would be tough critics, but I would have the opportunity to respond to their commentaries. Further, my response would be published with the target article and open peer commentaries.

My main motivation for going the target-article route was that I knew the radiator hypothesis would benefit from, and be strengthened by, the cross-fertilization process entailed in open peer criticism. I also knew that paleoanthropologists would no longer be able to ignore the blood-flow evidence if the radiator hypothesis survived intense scrutiny from a variety of scientists, including vascular physiologists.

The radiator hypothesis did survive open peer review. Most of the reviewers were critical but constructive. Many brought new ideas and information to the discussion. Some even suggested interesting new research projects related to the theory. Thanks to *Behavioral and Brain Sciences,* the radiator hypothesis is out and has generated much discussion, as new ideas should.

Not all of the commentators were helpful in their assessments, however. Consider the comment of William Kimbel: "Falk plunges into pure speculation, propping up a shallow hypothesis with a cartoon-like adaptationist narrative." And Ralph Holloway said:

At this level of speculation, I could easily assert that as the Pliocene progressed and aridity increased, the distances between shade trees increased and hominins developed bipedalism so that they could stand in the shade during midday more easily, thus reducing the risk of hyperthermia, inadvertently leaving the hands free to make sombreros.

Although these two comments were not constructive, they illustrate better than I can describe the depth of emotion that pervades paleoanthropology.

My Cactus

As Tuttle noted, the age of "splitomania" had begun in earnest some fifteen years ago. Today, it is more fashionable than ever for paleoanthropologists to envision bushy hominin family trees that have lots of branches. A different picture emerges, however, if one ceases to focus exclusively on cladistic analyses of specialized features and, instead, considers the evolution of whole, integrated physiological systems. Using the latter approach, details of the circulatory, locomotor, and nervous systems suggest that the overall pattern of hominin evolution was relatively sleek, rather than bushy. The prickly pear cactus (*Opuntia*) has large flattened pads instead of branches and thus provides a good model for this trimmer view of hominin evolution.

The cactus included here incorporates a number of exciting new discoveries, particularly in the pads representing the earliest parts of the hominin record. Because workers have been so cavalier about proliferating new species (often declared to be on the line leading to *Homo sapiens*), the only way to arrive at a reasonable evolutionary overview is to deemphasize species and, instead, focus on broader, more inclusive taxonomic levels such as genera (which contain one or more species). My cactus does just this, while remaining compatible with the radiator hypothesis. Thus, by about 2.5 million years ago hominins had branched into at least two genera, *Paranthropus* (robust australopithecines) and *Australopithecus* (gracile australopithecines). It cannot be determined exactly when or from whence *Homo* budded off, although most workers (the discoverers of *Orrorin* being notable exceptions) believe it was from the *Australopithecus* pad of the cactus, and that it happened before 1.8 million years ago. Furthermore, one can see from the cactus that the coexistence of late-living gracile australopithecines with

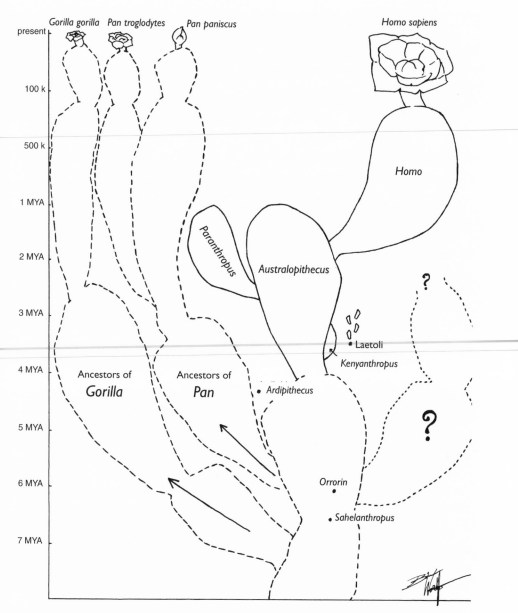

FIGURE 7.3.

Instead of an evolutionary tree that illustrates hypothetical relationships of species, this evolutionary cactus is constructed from pads that represent genera. The three pads that are outlined with solid lines (*Paranthropus, Australopithecus,* and *Homo*) are represented by good fossil records. Dashes indicate less substantive or (in the case of *Gorilla* and *Pan*) empty fossil records.

Homo does not preclude gracile australopithecines from having given rise to *Homo*. In other words, like branches of a plant, populations of hominins can continue to evolve (grow) after other populations have budded off.

The earliest-known robust australopithecines appeared about 2.5 million years ago, and may have originated at some unspecified earlier time from gracile australopithecines like those from Hadar, which had enlarged O/M sinuses and lived in wooded habitats. Over time, *Paranthropus* eventually branched out to South as well as East Africa. As far as can be determined, all of the populations on this pad of the cactus were characterized by 100 percent frequency of enlarged occipital/marginal sinuses. At least some robust australopithecines are believed to have lived in habitats that included trees and, presumably, shade. Further, their teeth reveal that all robust australopithecines were highly vegetarian. Thus, evidence related to blood flow, teeth, and habitat suggests that, rather than trotting out in the open after game and other resources as some of their contemporaries are thought to have done, the *Paranthropus* pad of the cactus, indeed, represents a distinct group of hominins that went about their business under relatively comfortable thermal conditions.

I believe that the physical differences between South and East African robust australopithecines existed because the two forms lived in, and became adapted to, different geographical regions. This should not be a surprising concept, since it is one that applies to human variation in the world today: Because all living people belong to the same species, *Homo sapiens,* many of the physical differences that distinguish different populations are due to geographical variation. Presumably, enough contact and crossbreeding occurred between robust australopithecines living in the different regions to keep these hominins appearing generally similar to each other (that is, within the same genus).

The 3.6-million-year-old footprints that appear next to the cactus are from Laetoli, Tanzania. Scraps of jaws and teeth were also recovered at Laetoli and, as the reader will recall, Johanson and White placed the Laetoli remains together with those from Hadar, Ethiopia, in the species *Australopithecus afarensis.* Since Laetoli's habitat was characterized by open savanna vegetation, and its climate was more arid than Lucy's home (Hadar), this group of hominins seems to have gotten more sunlight than *A. afarensis* (and robust australopithecines).

To review, I have separated Laetoli from Hadar for three reasons: First, certain teeth from Laetoli are significantly larger than their counterparts from Hadar. (However, since Laetoli is perhaps half a million years older than Hadar, this evidence could be interpreted as simply indicating evolutionary reduction in size of dentition within one lineage.) Second, Tuttle has argued that the footprints from Laetoli were made by feet that were more modern than those represented by the fossilized foot bones from Hadar. Specifically, Tuttle claims that the curved foot bones from Hadar (good for hanging out in trees) could not have made the humanlike prints from Laetoli. Tuttle's analysis does not wash well with authorities whose evolutionary schemes are being called into question, but I find the anatomical evidence that he marshals convincing. Third, the only skull fragment from Laetoli to be assessed for the enlarged O/M sinus that is found in 100 percent of seven scorable specimens from Hadar and 100 percent of the ten scorable robust australopithecines[7] from South and East Africa was L.H.-21, and this Laetoli specimen was found to lack the feature in question. For these three reasons, I show the Laetoli footprints tiptoeing alongside the cactus, possibly leading to *Homo*! (Tiptoeing "over there" to forage and scavenge for food in thermally stressful new environments.)

It is generally acknowledged that the gracile australopithecines who were the direct ancestors of *Homo* probably made their living foraging for food or scavenging for meat in hot, patchy savanna habitats. During the course of their evolution, the physiological mechanisms associated with bipedalism became more and more refined. Hair was lost, skin became dark, and subcutaneous fat and sweat glands developed in order to regulate body temperature in new, thermally demanding habitats. The radiator network of cranial veins also began to develop in conjunction with a brain that was steadily increasing in size. Had this not been the case, the terminal pad of the cactus belonging to *Homo* might never have produced the blossoms that represent humanity as we know it today.

That's it for the well-known pads of the cactus. What's new with this cactus are the older, newly named genera whose interpretations lack consensus. Thus, *Sahelanthropus* has been interpreted variously as ancestral to *Homo* or to gorillas, *Orrorin* as being the forerunner of *Homo* or of chimpanzees, and *Ardipithecus* as giving rise to *Australopithecus* or to chimpanzees. Although their discoverers scoff at the possibility of their alleged hominins being fossil chimpanzees or gorillas, it would be very exciting if one or more of them actually were because, so far, the two African great apes completely lack direct fossil records.

The *Homo* Pad of the Cactus

And what an interesting pad it is. A dazzling representative of *Homo erectus* (*ergaster* to some), WT 15000, showed up rather abruptly 1.6 million years ago in Kenya. As discussed earlier, what was especially surprising about this youth was his remarkable stature and humanlike body proportions. It was also noted that certain specimens that had previously been assigned to early *Homo* such as OH 62 (*habilis*) and the 1.9-million-year-old skull ER 1470 (*rudolfensis*) are now considered by some to be *Australopithecus*. It seems that this might, indeed, be the case. If so, it strengthens the argument that *erectus* was the first species of *Homo* to diverge from *Australopithecus* at some point prior to 1.8 million years ago.

It has also been widely presumed that ape-proportioned australopithecines were sticks-in-the-mud, while long-legged members of early *Homo* eventually migrated from Africa and thus became the first hominins to live in other parts of the world. When *Braindance* was first published, the scientific community believed that this initial migration occurred no earlier than one million years ago. However, thanks to revised dates for some *Homo erectus* specimens from Java, plus some surprisingly old discoveries from China and Eurasia, a new consensus has emerged that hominins began to exit Africa around two million years ago.

What is even more interesting is that questions are currently being raised about whether *Australopithecus* might not have been the hominin to initiate the exodus from Africa, rather than *Homo erectus*. Since australopithecines have never been recognized outside of Africa, such a finding would constitute a significant paradigm shift. The spark for this hypothesis comes from a 1.75-million-year-old Eurasian site in Georgia known as Dmanisi.[8] Because hominin skulls from this site share features with WT 15000, they have been classified as *Homo erectus*. However, the specimens also share numerous features with *Australopithecus*, and are associated with relatively primitive Oldowan-like stone tools that, traditionally, have been attributed to australopithecines. For example, one skull (D2700) has thin brow ridges that slope upward above the eyes and a cranial capacity of about 600 cm^3, which is substantially smaller than those for other identified *Homo erectus* specimens. The bottom line is that the Dmanisi fossils are not from Africa, are extremely old for Eurasia, and appear to be morphologically transitional between *Australopithecus* and *Homo erectus*. What is sorely needed, however, are some leg bones to go along with the skulls. Was the Dmanisi population short-legged and ape-proportioned like australopithecines, or were they long-legged and tall like the *Homo erectus* lad from Nariokotome? Hopefully, new discoveries will shed light on this question, the answer to which will be crucial for understanding the dynamics of early hominin migration from Africa and, perhaps, even something about the refinement of bipedalism.

The record for *Homo erectus* goes back nearly two million years. Some paleoanthropologists say its evolution must have been an abrupt, punctuated event because this species seems to appear rather suddenly in the fossil record. The fact is, however, that we don't know exactly when, where, or how quickly *Homo erectus* evolved from australopithecine stock. We do know that, once it appeared, *Homo erectus* traveled far but remained one species for a long time. This is confirmed by an exciting new skull from Ethiopia known as "Daka" that shares features with both African (for example, the Nariokotome youth) and Asian *Homo erectus* specimens, leading its discoverers to conclude that this species had colonized much of the world by one million years ago without yet giving rise to other species of *Homo*.[9]

From one million years forward, however, the fossil record becomes very confused because of splitters' attribution of numerous fossils to new species of *Homo*. As noted by Glenn Conroy, some workers go so far as to recognize a half-dozen coexisting species of early *Homo*, which is too many for such a relatively large mammal.[10] Whatever the number of other species of *Homo* that eventually evolved, *erectus* lasted until at least 300,000 years ago, and some workers believe that relic populations may even have lived in Java as recently as 37,000 years ago![11]

During its long evolution, brain size of *Homo erectus* increased from around 800 cm³ to 1250 cm³, and its skull became long, low, and thick. Despite its relatively modern-looking body proportions, a fleshed out *Homo erectus* would probably look odd to us with its receding forehead, big front teeth, extremely thick neck, and huge brow ridges over the eyes (with bushy eyebrows?).

But what was *Homo erectus* doing during all this time? Well, making a variety of stone tools for one thing. These included choppers, hand axes, cleavers, scrapers, spheroids, and projectile points. However, this tool kit did not evolve as much over time as *Homo erectus'* physique. As one might expect, tools were used not only for gathering plant food, but also for hunting. In fact, *Homo erectus* was the first big-game hunter, and some of his brethren may have even managed to drive a herd of elephants into a swamp at one site in Spain. Evidently, the first true hunter preferred his meat cooked, since the first signs of the deliberate use of fire are also associated with this species. With the hearth goes the home, and it appears that *Homo erectus* lived in huts as well as caves.

Lest we credit this particular hominin with too much civility, we should note one or two areas in which he lacked refinement. Where there are signs of huts (in France), there are also indications that even adults of the species thought nothing of going to the bathroom inside the home. Apparently, toilet training is a relatively recent concept. Moreover, the remains of certain fossilized skulls indicate that *Homo erectus* may have had the unsavory habit of eating his neighbors. This latter interpretation is based partly on existing casts and records for the important *Homo erectus* specimens known as Peking Man. (Unfortunately, the original fossils were lost when the United States declared war against Japan in 1941, and an effort was made to move the Chinese specimens from Beijing [then Peking] to the United States for safekeeping.)

Several hundred thousand years ago, *Homo erectus* evolved into early (archaic) *Homo sapiens,* which eventually gave rise to completely modern-looking people (*Homo sapiens sapiens*) that appeared in Europe around forty thousand years ago. Consequently, the fossil record from this duration is confused with transitional specimens that can be classified as either advanced *Homo erectus* or primitive *Homo sapiens*. Geographical variation is also a factor in this confusion, since these hominins lived in and became adapted to different environments in Africa, Europe, and Asia. Recently, Tim White and his colleagues described three crania from Herto, Ethiopia, that date to approximately 155,000 years ago.[12] The authors suggest that these specimens appear morphologically to be direct descendants of the *Homo erectus* population represented by the one-million-year-old Daka specimens and that, in turn, they are the oldest specimens known to date that are directly ancestral to anatomically modern humans. Because their morphology still contains some *Homo erectus* features, the authors place the Herto specimens in a new subspecies of *Homo sapiens* (*Homo sapiens idaltu*), rather than placing them squarely in *Homo sapiens sapiens*. If this interpretation is correct, these newly discovered fossils confirm that, in addition to giving rise to the first *Homo erectus* specimens that colonized the rest of the work, Africa may later have been the home of the first completely modern humans—which brings us to the much-debated Eve hypothesis.

African Eve

In the late 1980s, molecular evidence based on comparative studies of mitochondrial DNA (which is located outside of the nuclei of cells, and is inherited solely through the maternal line) suggested to some molecular anthropologists that all living people are descended from one woman (dubbed "Eve") who lived in Africa around 200,000 years ago. Presumably, a small group of early *Homo sapiens* that included Eve's female descendants migrated from Africa no later than 100,000 years ago, colonized the world, and thoroughly outcompeted the other hominins who already lived there. However, if the Eve (or "out-of-Africa") hypothesis is true it means that much of the known fossil record represents individuals who became extinct without leaving offspring, which seems counterintuitive to many critics.

A number of paleoanthropologists such as Milford Wolpoff of the University of Michigan, therefore, reject the Eve hypothesis, which they say is based on false assumptions about the mutation rate of mitochondrial DNA, as well as on a disregard for mitochondrial DNA's possible role as a subject for natural selection. They also believe that if it were properly calibrated, the mitochondrial clock would be shown to actually measure the migration of *Homo erectus* out of Africa (now thought to have occurred some two million years ago), rather than the more recent dispersal of *Homo sapiens*. Paleoanthropologists who reject the Eve hypothesis believe that *Homo sapiens* emerged simultaneously in various parts of the world, known as the multiregional hypothesis. According to C. Loring Brace, also from the University of Michigan, the one trend that characterized the simultaneous transformation of earlier hominins into modern humans was reduction in robusticity of bones and teeth. He attributes the simultaneous emergence of *Homo* in various regions to reduced selection for large (strong) bodies and teeth that occurred in conjunction with the rapid spread of hunting and culinary technology.[13]

Since the Eve hypothesis was first proposed, numerous attempts have been made to resolve the issues surrounding the timing and origin of anatomically modern people by carrying out other molecular studies, not only on mitochondrial DNA but also on nuclear DNA including portions of the X and Y chromosomes. Many of these studies seem to support the Eve hypothesis and the notion that her group and their descendants totally replaced all other hominins when they migrated from Africa. In fact, until recently this seems to have been the majority view.

As it turns out, a seminal study published by Alan Templeton of Washington University in 2002 strongly suggests that this view is wrong.[14] Instead of focusing on one molecule or piece of genetic material as most molecular studies have done, Templeton statistically analyzed numerous published evolutionary trees based on Y chromosomes, X chromosomes, genetic regions of other nuclear chromosomes, and mitochrondrial DNA. His methods allowed him to infer both historical events such as range expansions and recurrent events such as gene flow between populations. In the final analysis, Templeton arrived at a single, internally consistent model for human evolution (see figure 7.4).

Templeton's model accepts the fossil evidence (discussed above) that *Homo* started in Africa and migrated about 1.7 million years ago. His analysis strongly suggests that a major out-of-Africa expansion occurred later, between 840,000 and 420,000 years ago, in which migrants interbred with, rather than replaced, hominins elsewhere. A still more recent out-of-Africa expansion took place between 150,000 and 80,000 years ago (when Eve's group would have migrated) and was also charac-

FIGURE 7.4.

An important study by Alan Templeton (see reference 14, chapter 7) shows that hominins left Africa "again and again," as shown in this figure, which is modified after his illustration of the major migrations he identified. Templeton's findings also strike a blow against the Eve hypothesis of total replacement.

terized by interbreeding rather than replacement. After that, *Homo sapiens* became a frequent traveler who eventually colonized most parts of the world, and traveled in multiple directions in the process. Templeton did not set out to confirm any particular hypothesis, and his study is convincing. His analysis confirms the special role of Africa for human evolution, but strongly rejects the notion that Eve's relatives replaced all other hominins. Templeton's study is tremendously important, and I am at a loss to explain why it has not made a major impact on the field in the nearly year and a half since it was published. In a nutshell (to quote Templeton[14]):

> African and Eurasian populations were linked by recurrent gene flow, certainly over the last half a million years, and probably longer. Overlaid upon this gene-flow trellis are occasional major movements out of Africa and out of Asia that enhanced gene interchange through interbreeding. More recently, population expansions acted to extend the geographical range of the human species and to establish additional areas linked by gene flow. This model emphasizes that genetic interchange among human populations, facilitated both by gene flow and range expansions coupled with interbreeding, has been a major force in shaping the human species and its spatial pattern of genetic diversity. . . . The current spatial and frequency heterogeneity in "modern" traits undercuts the idea of a global replacement of an "archaic" type by a "modern" type but is consistent with a trait-based evolution of humans that is allowed under expansion with interbreeding.

Homo sapiens

In general, *Homo sapiens sapiens* has a more graceful appearance than earlier species. The brain size is larger, with a cranial capacity that averages around 1350 cm³. And the expanded braincase is accompanied by a rounder skull, higher forehead, and more vertical face than seen in *Homo erectus*. In keeping with the graceful skull, teeth and jaws are relatively small, and bones of the arms and legs are less thick than those of earlier hominins. And what, among all this dramatic change, is the hallmark of *Homo sapiens*? Is it the big brain? No. This distinction goes to the chin, of all things, which became prominent in association with a vertical face.

One group of fossil *Homo sapiens* may have been sadly misunderstood. This is the Neandertals, who lived between 125,000 and 36,000 years ago (although a large sample of hominins discovered in the Atapuerca Mountains in Spain that are around 300,000 years old appear to have been their ancestors). Contrary to the general rule, this species of *Homo* was not graceful looking. Instead, Neandertals had big faces, large noses, protruding jaws, and thick limb bones. These so-called classic Neandertals lived in Europe and the Middle East during extremely cold glacial times, and their physical features were probably adapted for just such cold environments, as experts such as Loring Brace have painstakingly pointed out. Nevertheless, primarily because of their chunky appearance, some physical anthropologists still will not accord Neandertals status as a direct ancestor of *Homo sapiens*. Today, the extent to which Neandertals contributed genetically to *Homo sapiens* is hotly debated. One view, expressed by Christopher Stringer of the British Museum of Natural History and Rainer Grün of the University of Cambridge, is that the replacement of Neandertals by modern *Homo sapiens*, "was not an overnight process." Instead, "the real fate of the Neandertals may well have been gradual displacement to more marginal and less favorable environments." The authors conclude, "Neandertals probably went out with a whimper, not a bang."[15]

Poor Neandertals. They have traditionally been viewed as brutes. At various times, they have been improperly accused of being stooped over, stupid, and even incapable of walking properly on the bottoms of their feet. Today, there are still some workers who maintain that Neandertals could not produce the full range of speech sounds. Is this fair? Not when one considers the cultural evidence, it isn't. Neandertal stone tools, particularly flake tools, were more varied and sophisticated than those of their predecessors. The earliest known deliberate burials are associated with Neandertals, and these were often accompanied by rituals such as surrounding the deceased with animal horns or covering the grave with flowers. Various sites have yielded suggestions of bear cults or hunting rituals that included the use of red ochre. Like *Homo erectus*, Neandertals sometimes ate their neighbors. In short, even if Neandertals appeared a little less refined than other groups of hominins, they seemed to have a relatively advanced culture. They also had the largest average cranial capacity on record, exceeding even that of modern humans.

About forty thousand years ago the weather warmed and, as if out of the blue, archaeological evidence generally associated with modern humans like ourselves appeared in Western Europe. Nobody is quite sure whence came *Homo sapiens sapiens,* otherwise known as Cro-Magnon, or what the relationship of this subspecies was to earlier living Neandertals. What is known, however, is that these humans underwent an incredible cultural revolution—one that was so dramatic that science writer John Pfeiffer has called it a creative explosion.[16] During this last part of the Old Stone Age, tools were more complicated, better designed, and made from a variety of materials, including stone, bone, teeth, wood, and antler. Hunting was still an important way of life and reindeer had become a highly preferred meat, although fishing had also come into its own. For the fist time, artistic expression is well represented in the fossil record. Many materials were engraved with artistic designs, and personal ornaments were valued by these people. It is during this time that the famous cave art appeared, as well as little figurines of humans and animals. By thirty thousand years ago the female Venuses, which some take to be mother-goddesses, were prevalent. Finally, apparently having inherited the wanderlust of early *Homo, Homo sapiens* colonized Australia by (or before) fifty thousand years ago and crossed the Bering land bridge into North America at some point after that, perhaps as recently as twenty thousand years ago.

We are at the tip of the cactus and, although it may seem incredible, for all practical purposes one species of primate has taken over the world. I believe that *Homo sapiens* was able to do this because of the evolution of the brain that occurred during the past two million years. I also think that brain size would not have increased as it did in *Homo* if our australopithecine ancestors had not begun to develop a radiator network of cranial veins that could evolve with and cool an enlarging brain. I call what happened to the internal organization of the brain as it increased in size in *Homo* the "braindance."

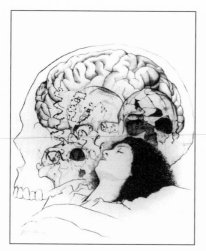

BRAINDANCE

The braindance has been a lively, even jazzy, affair. In a little less than two million years, brain size doubled in *Homo,* from around 650 cm³ to 1350 cm³. Since only a small portion of *Homo*'s newfound larger brains were tied to increasing body size, the braindance has not been a mere byproduct of selection for bigger bodies. Something else has been going on. And that something was unprecedented in the evolutionary histories of other mammals.

That's not to say that some of the dance's steps aren't familiar. They are. As brain size increased in *Homo,* neurons enlarged and became more widely spaced. But this is a general rule for the evolution of larger brains. The cerebral cortex also became more convoluted as brain size increased. This, too, is expected. Furthermore, no new structures have been found in human brains. As described in the introduction, in tap dance, a shift in the emphasis within certain combinations of steps completely changes the feel of a routine. Thus, the sequence of steps may be identical for two routines but because of different emphases, the resulting dance is not. (In fact, performing the same routines with different emphases is a standard warm-up exercise for tap classes.) As is true for tap and other forms of dance, it is the overall choreography of the braindance that's unique, not its individual steps.

While increasingly large brains catapulted *Homo* into the future, subtle neurological shifts influenced the three themes discussed earlier: frontal lobes, association cortex, and brain lateralization. As expected for an enlarging brain, the cerebral cortex of *Homo* became more convoluted. But this particular dance routine had two emphases, one on the prefrontal cortex and the other on posterior association areas. For it is precisely these two regions of the brain that became especially convoluted during the evolution of *Homo*.[1]

We know that the ancestors of early *Homo* had brains that were already lateralized to some extent. Nevertheless, it is likely that shifts occurred in the timing of developmental events of *Homo*'s two hemispheres, and that these shifts resulted in increased brain lateralization. For example, there is some evidence that right hemispheres of humans develop sulci before left hemispheres do. This accords with the fact that the part of Broca's speech area that has been identified as a structural region underlying speech (on the left) appears to be denser and larger than its counterpart in the right hemisphere.[2] The anatomical complexity of Broca's area has been attributed to its development after that of the comparable region in the right hemisphere (at a time when the end branches of neurons form and when related language functions are developing).

The work of Stanley Glick and his colleagues on lateralization of neurochemicals in animals ranging from rodents to humans is crucial for understanding another level of the braindance. Presumably, as new motor repertoires associated with behaviors such as language were favored by natural selection, the receptor sites for certain neurochemicals (such as dopamine) shifted subtly in the brain, with some becoming more asymmetrically distributed between right and left hemispheres. As happens in a warm-up exercise for tap class, slight changes in emphases during neurological development accompanied the ongoing evolution from primatelike calls to full-blown speech.

The basic stuff of hominin brain evolution probably had to do with the timing of specific events during neurological development. Insight into this has been offered by Barbara Finlay and Richard Darlington of Cornell University, who suggest that the order and timing in which neurons in specific parts of the brain are generated during development are key to understanding brain enlargement and evolution.[3] As a result of these processes, subtle shifts occurred in at least two related areas: the distribution of receptor sites for neurochemicals and the connectivity of neurons. The steps were familiar, but the timing of events changed the overall dance. As the brain skyrocketed to three times its expected size, other shifts occurred in its overall floor plan. Extra amounts of cerebral cortex appeared in prefrontal areas (where ambition lives and ideas are held online) and posterior association regions (where everything is put together).

But the evolution of the brain of *Homo* didn't just happen of its own accord. The shifts in neurochemicals, anatomy of neurons, and so on provided only the underlying mechanics (or steps) of the braindance. The real cause of this lively jig rests with the behaviors of early *Homo* that were targeted by natural selection. Therein lies the prime mover of human brain evolution.

And the radiator network of veins: What was its role? Certainly not that of a prime mover. Rather, the radiator was a prime releaser. Think of it this way: You've got a frisky puppy and your neighborhood has a very strict leash law. Every day you and your puppy pass numerous other dogs that are being properly walked by their owners. There are no strays running loose. Your dog is a rambunctious thing who periodically hears or smells something interesting and strains vigorously to take off; however, your trusty leash keeps him in check. One day, the two of you are calmly walking down the street. For some reason, you let go of the leash. At first, Fido does not notice and just keeps going at his normal pace. Suddenly, he perceives something interesting and takes off. What caused him to run away? Your dropping the leash? No. That merely released him so he could take off. The real cause was the "something interesting" that Fido perceived. Like the dropping of the leash, the radiator network of veins merely permitted brain size to increase in *Homo*. We're going to have to look at what went on during the past two million years to see why it did.

Since the time of Darwin, there have been many speculations about possible prime movers of human brain evolution. Some of these have been rather fanciful. Among the nominees are warfare, work, language, tool production, throwing, and hunting. As one might surmise from this list, more credit for stimulating brain evolution has traditionally been given activities typically pursued by males than by females. Fortunately, this bias has been corrected now that many of the investigators whose work influences paleoanthropology are female. (Some of the women whose research has direct implications for understanding evolution are Leslie Aiello, Este Armstrong, Barbara Finlay, the late Beatrix Gardner, Kathleen Gibson, Lori Hager, Melissa Hines, Doreen Kimura, Meave Leakey, Marjorie LeMay, Sue Savage-Rumbaugh, Denise Schmandt-Besserat, Katrin Schaefer, Margaret Shoniger, Katrina Semendeferi, Brigitte Senut, Pat Shipman, Holly Smith, Elisabeth Vrba, Adrienne Zihlman, and Betty Zimmerberg. Darwin never had it so good! This is not to say that there aren't lots of wonderful men in the field. There are.)

Despite all the speculation about prime movers, there seems to have been resistance to the simple possibility that brain size increased in association with selection for general intelligence. Although it is true that brain size correlates to a small degree with intelligence within men and, separately, within women,[4] this resistance is puzzling for several reasons. First, as Harry Jerison (of the University of California at Los Angeles) has shown, relative brain size increased a bit during the independent evolution of many groups of mammals. Since increased relative brain size among nonhuman primates has been shown to be related to increased curiosity, intelligence may well have been an important factor during nonhuman primate and (by extension) mammalian evolution.

It is also easy to envision the adaptive advantage of intelligence in its multifaceted sense (which is the best way to go, since intelligence is a notoriously difficult concept to define). Hominins that (a) stayed alive, and (b) bred successfully would have been targets of natural selection. Presumably, many aspects of intelligence would have facilitated such selection. For example, numerous workers have suggested that social intelligence was strongly selected for because socially skilled hominins would have had differential access to food and mates. Similarly, selection for the comprehension and production of speech would also have benefited the early possessors of these gifts. Left-hemisphere time se-

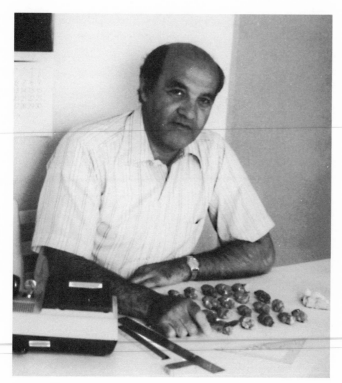

FIGURE 8.1.
Harry Jerison with an array of endocasts. A leading expert on the brain and intelligence, Jerison showed that brain size increased somewhat during the independent evolution of many groups of mammals. (Photograph courtesy of H. Jerison.)

quencing would have been honed with the refinement of language skills, and such selection may even have facilitated development of the perception of time itself.[5]

With the latter would have come a concept of death (and burial of the dead), the ability to worry about the future (for example, to fantasize escape routes), and a tendency for looking both ways when crossing the ravine (or street). Surely these behaviors were and are adaptive. Humans are speculative, language bearing, and fretful to a degree that exceeds nonhuman primates, including our closest cousin, the chimpanzee. It is time to view these aspects of mind within an evolutionary framework. I suggest that better information processing (which would have facilitated not only language evolution but also general intelligence) was the prime mover of brain evolution in *Homo*. That's what Mother Nature went for, once the brain *could* get bigger.

Through a Mirror Darkly

Remove part of a person's prefrontal cortex and the person loses ambition, the ability to plan ahead, and, yes even his or her worries. In this respect, the "me" (or sense of self) lives in the prefrontal cortex. Psychologist Gordon Gallup has shown that chimpanzees and orangutans recognize themselves in mirrors. Like humans, then, they seem to have a sense of "me." Gallup's research (some of it with Jack Maser of the National Institute of Mental Health) suggests that information processing regarding self probably intensified along with increased brain size in *Homo*.[6]

Gallup defines mind (I would probably call it social intelligence) as the ability (1) to "reflect on one's own thoughts and emotions (i.e., to be aware of being aware)" and (2) "to use this capacity as a basis for inferring the experience of others." Although it is a little difficult to investigate the first ability in apes, some ingenious experiments have clearly demonstrated that chimpanzees are capable of the second. In one of the first recorded examples, the late Wolfgang Kohler placed a chimpanzee named Chica in a room with two sticks that could be fitted together to obtain a fruit bait.[7] When it was clear that Chica was not going to solve the problem, Kohler gave the two sticks to Sultan, a chimpanzee who was watching the experiment from outside the cage. Sultan fitted the two sticks together and, rather than using them to acquire the fruit himself, pushed the sticks toward Chica. Kohler concluded that Sultan saw "the task to be carried out, from the standpoint of the other animal." Since Kohler's classic work, numerous investigations have confirmed that chimpanzees, like humans, make presumptions about the mental life of others.

However, only humans have evolved social intelligence to the point where they infer the mentality of deities. As Maser and Gallup say:

God, as the ultimate attribution, is a natural extension of our ability to reflect on our own mental states. We typically use these reflections as a model for presuming the mental life of others, but a logical extension of that capacity is to use these reflections to infer the mentality of a theistic entity.[8]

In other words, only humans have the cognitive capacity to conceive of a God, and Maser and Gallup see a sense of self as a necessary but not sufficient condition for this capacity.

Why, then, do humans conceive of a God when, presumably, other animals do not? I think it is because humans have relatively large, time-binding, worrying, planning-ahead prefrontal cortices. As Maser and Gallup point out, once one becomes aware of (a) the self's existence, and (b) death in others, one's own inevitable death becomes a source of concern. Thus, "death is a major motivational component forcing into use our cognitive capacity to conceive of God."[9] Religion (the great comforter) provides an adaptive means by which our species copes with the existential terror that derives from better information processing by our evolved frontal lobes. (Suicide would be an example of a maladaptive way to cope with such terror.)

Maser and Gallup have done nothing less than identify a basic behavioral complex that seems dependent on higher cognitive abilities facilitated by an expanded prefrontal cortex. From a paleoneurological perspective, it is significant that religion appears exclusively and universally in humans. But what of the fossil record? When do the concepts of death and an afterlife first appear? Although a precise answer may never be determined, the fossil record does provide some upper limits for the appearance of religious behaviors.

Certainly big-brained but beleaguered Neandertals had some sort of religion. As far as we know, they were the first hominins to bury their dead. Times were cold and the earth was frozen hard. Consequently, Neandertals often buried their dead in small graves, with corpses in flexed or semiflexed positions. Despite the practicality of their burials, by fifty thousand years ago some Neandertal graves had become quite spectacular. For instance, analysis of pollen deposits from Shanidar Cave in northeastern Iraq indicates that the grave of an adult male may have been covered with an assortment of colorful flowers.

From our Western perspective, we might be tempted to view other examples of Neandertal's treatment of the dead as ghoulish. For example, there's the lad from a shallow grave in Teshik-Tash, Russia, whose remains were surrounded by numerous pairs of goat horns. An equally intriguing find emerged with the discovery of a cave that had been closed for many thousands of years in Monte Cicero, Italy. Within the cave, a Neandertal skull was found resting bottom up in the middle of a circle of rocks. The base of the skull was broken away as if the brains had been deliberately removed.[10] Nor was this the first sign of a possible cannibalistic ceremony in the fossil record! Perhaps as long ago as half a million years, *Homo erectus* had acquired the unsavory habit of breaking into the braincases of his dead brethren.

Although the reader may flinch at the suggestion that cannibalism indicates higher cognitive abilities, historical records indicate that cannibalisms practiced by *Homo sapiens* in the late nineteenth and first half of the twentieth centuries served ceremonial more that nutritive purposes. Admittedly, because of their sensationalism, reports of cannibalism are murky and difficult to interpret. Nevertheless, several points of agreement do emerge from the literature regarding the eating of human flesh among Australian aboriginals from a tropical rain forest environment: Cannibalism was a relatively rare event. But when it did occur, women and children were eaten more often than men. And as one might expect, the victims usually came from other tribes. Furthermore, women or boys seem to have been prohibited from witnessing cannibal feasts. In fact, it is the practice of cannibalism exclusively by adult males that is most suggestive of a ceremonial significance:

> [I]n 1940 . . . (when a man was deliberately killed for excessive sexual misconduct), it was necessary that a man drink the blood of a cannibalistic victim before he could attain the status of a *gubi* ("wise man" or "doctor"); it was also reported that anyone who had persistently broken the social code might be killed by senior men of the tribe, the flesh eaten, and the blood offered to younger men to drink.[11]

We, of course, have no way of knowing what *Homo erectus* thought about death or a possible afterlife. We do know, however, that there are a large number of *Homo erectus* skullcaps that look as though they have been deliberately opened. Too many, I think, to be mere coincidence. If *Homo erectus* did practice cannibalism, it could have been for any number of reasons documented in historical times. These include intertribal warfare, personal revenge, punishment, or rituals associated with rites of passage, such as birth, formal entrance into manhood, marriage, or death. Or perhaps *Homo erectus* simply ate the brains of his victims to assimilate their powers. We'll never know for sure. But one thing is certain. Unless the numerous faceless, bottomless skullcaps from Java and China occurred coincidentally by pure, dumb luck, *Homo erectus* did have a concept of death. And that's not bad information processing for some 1,000 cm³ of brains.

Language: "The Rolls-Royce of Brain Adaptations"

But there are earlier signs of better information processing in the fossil record. For one thing, knapping experiments with stone tools by Nicholas Toth of Indiana University indicated that a little less than two million years ago at least some African hominins (perhaps *Homo erectus*) were already right-handed. If so, the subtle shifts toward greater brain lateralization were well underway by the time hominins left Africa.

Harry Jerison calls language the "Rolls-Royce of brain adaptations." I think he is right, for this particular kind of information processing is a luxury item, afforded no species other than our own. Noble machines like the Rolls are not invented overnight. Their splendor is honed over generations, and not without some pride. The fossil record indicates to me, if not to others, that language's manufacture has also had a long and proud duration.

Some of my colleagues would disagree. They think the capacity to make symbols originated in *Homo sapiens* and that this capacity did not emerge as fully reflective language until the appearance of the gorgeous cave art, sculpture, fishing technology, and personal adornment that characterized the Upper Paleolithic, some thirty-five thousand years ago. Although it is true that the cultural products of earlier *Homo* are dowdy by comparison, a sudden appearance of something as universal and complex as language does not feel right. That is not to say that early *Homo* had full-blown language. Of course not. But they were, at least, in the dance hall, and the band was tuning up for the beginnings of language.

The beginnings of language. Now there's the crux. Since primates either have language or they don't, how do we conceive of the beginnings of language? What was the first language, the *Ur*-language, like?

And if the first glimmerings of language had begun by two million years ago, what accounts for its long evolution? Although these questions may seem impossible to answer at first, the dazzling research of one woman offers strong clues for understanding the origins of language.

The Evolution of Writing

Presumably, the first manifestations of language were spoken. This presents something of a problem to those who grapple with language origins. If only there were such a thing as a fossilized remnant of the *Ur*-language or a magic CD of speech utterances that occurred in early *Homo*! All is not lost, however, because the evolution of the ability to record speech, or writing, did leave an archaeological record. Although writing did not appear until around fifty-five hundred years ago,[12] I believe archaeologist Denise Schmandt-Besserat's delineation of the prior stages that led to writing is instructive for understanding the earlier evolution of spoken language.[13, 14]

Schmandt-Besserat, of the University of Texas at Austin, did a remarkable thing. While working in archaeological collections from sites ranging from Turkey and Palestine to Syria and Iran (that is, throughout the Fertile Crescent), she noticed that little clay objects kept popping up. Nobody had paid much attention to them and, consequently, they were cataloged under different categories in different collections. Thus, one archaeologist's game pieces were another's phallic symbols, amulets, or sling missiles. Schmandt-Besserat found this very curious, so she began a systematic investigation of these little objects. And what a gold mine her research turned out to be! From seemingly insignificant bits of little clay, Schmandt-Besserat's findings blossomed into a clear exposition of the origins and evolution of writing.[14]

As Schmandt-Besserat has shown, writing derived from earlier record keeping that was invented for very practical reasons. By five thousand years ago, metallurgy and food production had resulted in the world's first civilizations, such as those developed by the Sumerians of Mesopotamia. Trade was in full flourish, and accurate record keeping had already been invented to keep track of exchanges of livestock and other goods. Obviously, accurate counting was crucial for these records, and counting was one of the earliest precursors of writing.

FIGURE 8.2.
Denise Schmandt-Besserat. From seemingly insignificant little bits of clay, her findings have blossomed into a clear exposition of the origins and evolution of writing. (Photograph courtesy of D. Schmandt-Besserat.)

The earliest-known artifacts connected with simple counting are bones upon which sightings of the moon are thought to have been recorded as individual notches. These lunar calendars have been found in caves in the Middle East that were inhabited between twelve thousand and seventeen thousand years ago, and in Abri Blanchard, France, as long ago as thirty thousand years. However, concrete counting whereby one-to-one counting is fused with specific indentification of the thing being counted did not appear until about ten thousand years ago. That's where Schmandt-Besserat's bits of clay come in.

Each clay object turned out to be a token. These tokens appeared in a variety of shapes, and each shape stood for a different unit of goods. Thus, three animals could be recorded with three cylinders, three measures of grain could be recorded with three spheres, and so on. For the next five thousand years, tokens spread throughout the Middle East, and eventually there appeared new and more complicated tokens to represent merchandise associated with an increasingly complex urban economy.

According to Schmandt-Besserat, Sumerian accountants were responsible for three cognitive leaps that occurred by five thousand years ago: First, three-dimensional tokens were replaced by two-dimensional pictographs that could be inscribed on tablets with styluses. Second, shapes that had previously denoted measures of grain were impressed on tablets as specific numerals (wedge = 1; circle = 10), so that counting was no longer one-to-one. Thus were abstract numbers invented.

Before five thousand years ago, the only written works were ledgers of accountants with lists of names and quantities of goods. A third cognitive leap led to profound changes in the nature of writing: Two-dimensional pictographs were used phonetically to record the sounds of proper names and then, later, other words. To use Schmandt-Besserat's example, if a syllable in a name sounded like the Sumerian word for "oil," the slashed oval symbol for "oil" might be used in the person's name, even if the idea of oil played no role in the origin of the name. This was the beginning of phonetic writing that ultimately led to the Phoenician alphabet by thirty-five hundred years ago.

Implications for the Evolution of Speech

Can Schmandt-Besserat's lucid analysis of the evolution of writing tell us anything about whether or not speech had a long evolution prior to the origin of writing? I believe it can. It is instructive that it took up to seven thousand years for abstract clay tokens representing animals to occur after realistic images of a bull and deer first appeared at the entrance of Beldibi Cave in Turkey. It took another five thousand years for humans to make the cognitive leaps from tokens to two-dimensional pictographs, numerals, and phonemes and another fifteen hundred years to establish a phonetic alphabet. Even though its domain was visual and, therefore, easily recordable, writing had a long evolution.

Think of how much more difficult the evolution of information technology (to use Schmandt-Besserat's term) would have been in an unrecordable auditory domain than in the visual domain! Human memory would have exerted greater constraints on cultural transmission of new speech technology than on new writing technology that could be remembered in clay. Even though human speech can encode information about shape, quantity, and sound much more rapidly than writing can, the latter has its advantages. As any student will attest, it is best to prepare for examinations by studying written notes and texts rather than by relying on one's memory of lectures—to quote the old saying, "out of sight, out of mind"—and it was no doubt for this reason that writing was eventually invented.

Presumably, there were cognitive leaps associated with the evolution of speech, just as there were for the evolution of writing. Were leaps of speech necessarily invented many times over because of the frailty of human memory? If so, did this slow down the whole process, so that cognitive leaps that occurred during the emergence and evolution of speech were incorporated more slowly into language than were the later leaps associated with writing?

And what about the first words? As the first renderings in clay were realistic rather than abstract, were the first words imitative (or onomatopoeic)? If it took seven thousand years to get from realistic images of cattle to abstract clay-token cows, how much longer would it have taken to get from a realistic sound for cow (perhaps a "moo") to an unseen and unrecorded, yet conventionally accepted, abstract word for cow? It seems that if visible writing had a long evolution, then that of its predecessor, unseen speech, must have been much, much longer. It is therefore reasonable to attribute the increase in cranial capacity that occurred in *Homo* to prolonged selection for better information processing that included a hefty dose of speech. After all, such an honor is only befitting the Rolls-Royce of brain adaptations!

The Art Scene

Between thirty-five thousand and ten thousand years ago, a prehistoric artistic revolution occurred in Europe. During this period, known as the Upper Paleolithic, Cro-Magnon painters, sculptors, and craftsmen created thousands upon thousands of works, ranging from spectacular cave paintings to wonderful little engraved figurines. Some of my colleagues, as has been noted, believe that the sudden appearance of Upper Paleolithic art coincided with the emergence of language in *Homo sapiens*. Since I reject this notion in favor of the one outlined above, what does account for the Upper Paleolithic art scene?

First of all, the view that language did not occur until the appearance

FIGURE 8.3.
Examples of engravings and sculpture from the Upper Paleolithic in Europe. (Image #39686; photograph by Lee Boltin; American Museum of Natural History Library.)

of art is a materialistic interpretation that is typical of our Western culture. (It is also understandable that such a position has its advocates, given that archaeologists, at least, are particularly interested in material culture.) There is also an underlying fallacy that paintings and sculpture provide direct evidence for language skills. However, research on brain lateralization shows that this is not the case. Great works of art (including music) pack a satisfying emotional wallop precisely because they largely spring from (and appeal to) right-hemisphere spatial, intuitive, and holistic processes. In fact, artists include more left-handers than does the population at large. So, if anything, the Upper Paleolithic artistic explosion reveals more about the state of the right hemisphere than it does about the language-bearing left hemisphere. (However, since the two hemispheres do work together, one could still argue indirectly that right-hemisphere accomplishments would be mirrored by increased left-hemisphere skills.)

The earliest-known art consists mostly of vulvas and parts of animals engraved on blocks of limestone, and these two themes—sex and food—were emphasized throughout the Upper Paleolithic. I think this tells us a good deal about Cro-Magnon culture. So-called Venus figurines were found from France to Russia. These small, stylized sculptures are simply wonderful.[15] With small heads and tapered lower legs, they stand there naked, demurely looking down. The thighs, hips, stomach, and breasts are enormous, and their arms are often missing or resting meekly on the breasts. Some of the Venuses are knock-kneed, which adds to their charm. Facial features are usually not explicit, but the hair is often elaborate. Venus figurines are frequently associated with domestic sites and are widely interpreted as fertility goddesses. (I sometimes wonder if they might not be somewhat classier versions of modern-day kitchen witches.) One is tempted to assume that Venuses represented the idealized feminine body build in Upper Paleolithic times. The models for these little statues had definitely been well fed, a clear advertisement for the hunting skills of their providers.

This brings us to food, the second theme. There were plenty of animals to hunt, including reindeer (a favorite dish), bison, aurochs, ibex, horses, and mammoth. Pictures of animals were engraved on bones, and animal sculptures were carved on weapons such as spear throwers. Beautifully colored animals were also painted in ocher, charcoal, and manganese on the walls of deep caverns that were often dangerous to reach. The French cave of Lascaux probably provides the most famous example of prehistoric cave art. Most of the paintings within its chambers are of animals, and many of these are larger than life. They portray exquisite details of anatomy and demonstrate a feel for movement.

What was the purpose of these galleries? Some anthropologists suggest that they were stages for initiation rituals or magic rites to insure successful hunts and continued fertility of the animals. Were these great caverns the domain of men more than women? After all, women are not the subjects of much cave art, although occasionally men are.

Science writer Roger Lewin has studied the art of Lascaux. His description provides a hint about the possible purpose of cave art:

> Finally, Marsal leads you to the shaft, site of Lascaux's most enigmatic and disturbing composition. Located just off the Apse, the shaft is reached through a trap door, which Marsal lifts with care and anticipation. A metal ladder takes you to the bottom of the twenty-six-foot-deep retreat. The flashlight beam sparkles on the white and yellow calcite crystals. And then the beam of light falls on an incredible scene.
>
> A great black bison stands poised for attack, its forelegs taut as a spring. Tail lashing. The animal has been desperately wounded, a barbed spear crosses its body and its entrails spill to the ground. A man has fallen in front of the bison, and is about to be gored. But, unlike the careful naturalistic representations that characterize most of Lascaux's images, this image appears crude and infantile—a stick-man with no life, wearing what might be a bird mask.[16]

Imagine coming upon such a scene by torchlight and without a modern ladder. Think of the drama! Perhaps Lascaux and the other Upper Paleolithic art caves were forerunners of modern books and television—the first theaters.

I have an acquaintance, Michael Zansky, who is a professional artist. He has been a painter since he was a child. Some years ago, he went to see an exhibit of Ice Age art at the American Museum of Natural History in New York City. "What did you think of it?" I asked him. "The moment I walked in and looked around, I knew they were just like us," he answered. I think Michael was right. From a neurological perspective, sophisticated information processing was well underway long before the Upper Paleolithic. Thus, the key to understanding the revolution in prehistoric art does not lie with the brain or language. Cro-Magnon was already there.

Perhaps the crucial factor for Upper Paleolithic art was the luxury of free time. Because of the abundance of game and plants, not everybody had to hunt or gather food. Some individuals could do other things. Furthermore, the glacial climate provided an incentive for spending extra

FIGURE 8.4.
Painting of a bison from the cave of Altamira in Spain. (Image #317637; photograph by Shane Bierwer; American Museum of Natural History Library.)

hours indoors. (Like a child coloring pictures on a rainy day.) Fortunately for posterity, at least some talented individuals chose to spend their time on artistic endeavors.

As with contemporary hunting-and-gathering societies, a clear division of labor probably existed in Cro-Magnon times, with men hunting and females and young children gathering plant food. As is also typical of these societies, males may indeed have staged special rituals or ceremonies away from the women and children. There is no doubt that hidden caves would have provided excellent stages for such rituals. Further, since women and animals were the main subjects of Upper Paleolithic art, some workers have suggested that the artists were primarily male. Although one cannot be sure, the suggestion seems plausible because adult males may have been more adept at reaching the hard-to-access inner caves that served as art galleries. In any event, there is no denying that Upper Paleolithic art was breathtaking. However, rather than being some kind of cognitive pinnacle, I believe that it simply represents one aesthetic component of the ongoing braindance.

Not that information processing slowed down during the Upper Paleolithic. Oh, no. By the time the Upper Paleolithic began, *Homo sapiens*
had already migrated to Australia and would soon colonize the Ameri-
cas. With the spread of humans over the globe, speech diversified into
regional dialects, and these evolved into distinct languages and, eventually, generations of daughter languages. Meanwhile, back in the Fertile
Crescent (as Schmandt-Besserat so eloquently showed), realistic depic-
tions led eventually to abstract tokens and, later, to the breakthrough
concepts of numbers, a phonetic alphabet, and writing. From there, information processing has sped along.

And it keeps getting better. Now that the telephone, radio, and television have been invented, our species is engaged in other revolutions in
information processing. In 1975, I punched my dissertation data onto
computer cards by hand. Today, I can walk into my office, turn on my
computer and crunch numbers to my heart's content or, for fun, check
my e-mail to see what's up with Adrienne Zihlman at Santa Cruz or
Scooter in St. Louis. Or, perhaps, Stevan Harnad (former editor of the
journal *Behavioral and Brain Sciences*) will have an e-mail discussion
cooking about some aspect of neuroscience that I'll want to join.
(Harnad calls this skywriting.) Once I've collected the gossip and other
tidbits from my friends, I'll do some research on the web (can't find
something? then "Google it"), access and print journal articles I need
from the library, or work on correspondence or a paper. Need a graph or
some art work? My machine can handle that, too. If you had told me
twenty-five years ago that computers with these capabilities would be
standard equipment for today's academics, I would have accused you of
dreaming.

My generation learned to use computers as young adults, which is
not a particularly good age for learning second languages. The easiest
way to learn a second language, such as French or Spanish, and to end
up with a perfect accent while you're at it, is to be exposed to the language at a very young age (preferably before puberty). This thought
crosses my mind every time I see one of my more computer-literate
colleagues working at a terminal with a toddler on his or her lap. That

kid is going to understand computers, and so will many of the seven-year-olds one sees walking around with portable videogames.

If computers seem cold or artificial, another revolution has occurred in information processing at a more organic level. This is the Human Genome Project, of course. The goal of this project was to determine the exact sequences of thousands of genes that reside on the forty-six human chromosomes, a monumental task that is essentially completed. The resulting genetic map has already dramatically increased our knowledge of genes involved in human disease. The DNA of medically important genes may now be decoded, and the resulting information used to genetically engineer tools for diagnosis and treatment. (This has already happened for some genes, such as that for cystic fibrosis.) This project has been so enormous that it had to be divided among different research centers (a hunk of a chromosome here, decode a particular gene there). It has also been expensive, with costs of hundreds of millions of dollars. Was it worth it? You bet your life, which could literally be extended by results from the Genome Project.

But there's a darker side to our Western version of the braindance. Vast populations of human beings press relentlessly on the earth's surface at the very time that genetic engineers are racing to develop technology that will dramatically increase lifespan. Unless population-management policies are soon initiated and successfully employed at a global level, the crunch is going to get much, much worse. Yet a conservative, vocal, and politically active segment of the population of the United States has successfully opposed population-management programs (family planning, choices concerning gestation and the right to die) both domestically and abroad. This is an example of the braindance gone awry. It represents a short-sighted desire to impose particular religious/moral codes on others and, as such, is a frightening distortion of the prefrontal ability to conceive of a God. In the long run, it would be better if our species used its evolved frontal lobes to plan for the future of an earthly world.

As the reader well knows, better information processing has resulted in other threats to our species. Biomedical engineering has yielded horrible biological weapons, not just medical breakthroughs. *Homo sapiens'* relatively new innovations for harnessing energy and synthesizing materials mercilessly batter the global environment and reduce the biodiversity that is crucial for our continued existence, even as these activities make our lives more convenient (and purveyors of the desired resources wealthier).[17] Finally, despite the dismantling of the "cold war," there's still the "Big Nuclear One" to worry about. And what a sad ending for the braindance that would be.

The Emotional Brain

Children must be taught to monitor their behavior in order to get along with others. Thus, a significant aspect of growing up in human society entails learning to "think before you act" or, more technically, to exert cortical control over impulses and emotions. At times, often under the wrong circumstances, the delicate balance between reason and emotion is subject to disruption. And that, as we all know, is when people lose control.

Reason meets emotion in a phylogenetically old part of the brain known as the limbic system. This system is located in a series of structures on the lower and inside surfaces of the cerebral hemispheres, and its primary concerns are emotions, memory, and—to a smaller degree in humans—smell. The limbic system receives and sends information via fibers to highly integrated association cortices and also has connections with gut-level visceral circuits. One limbic structure, the hippocampus, is particularly important for activating the storage and retrieval of memories. Thus, an important limbic function is to label incoming cognitive (higher) information in light of input from an emotional (gut) level—with varying degrees of positive or negative valence. Another function is to archive some of these sensations in memory, depending on the quality of their emotional labels. The limbic system also sends information about emotional states such as fear or aggression to the cortex, which can then take action.

In the past, many researchers believed that the limbic system was primitive and that human emotions, therefore, remained static during the course of evolution. Este Armstrong, however, has shown that the limbic system played an important role during hominin evolution.[18] For one thing, once scaling factors are taken into account, the size of the human limbic system is as large as that of nonhuman primates. As the brain enlarged during hominin evolution, so did its limbic system. Within this system, however, olfactory structures are reduced in humans relative to other primates. On the other hand, there are more neurons than expected in another limbic structure of humans, the anterior thalamic nucleus (which helps bring emotional information into consciousness).

The latter finding by Armstrong and her colleagues is particularly interesting because, for reasons that remain mysterious, a similar trend for more anterior thalamic neurons correlates with single-male (that is, monogamous and harem) but not multimale (polygynous) mating patterns in nonhuman primates. This discovery led Armstrong to conclude that the integration of learning and memory states with emotions may be set somewhat differently in primates living in different social organizations. Other researchers, working on a variety of primate species, have confirmed the role of the limbic system for maintaining social order. Damage to limbic structures has been shown to alter dominance hierarchies and severely disrupt grooming, sexual, maternal, and other social behaviors.

Whatever its social functions, the limbic system must also have had an important role during the evolution of information processing in *Homo*. According to Armstrong:

> An enlarged limbic system strategically placed to receive a maximal amount of information from the association cortex enables a cultural adaptation by giving symbols access to the limbic system that is equal to that of information derived from sensory systems. This ability in turn permits the individual to focus attention upon arbitrary symbols, to have those symbols satisfy basic desires, and to sustain continuing symbolic/cultural behaviors.[18]

Despite this aspect of the braindance, we must not lose sight of the fact that our evolved limbic systems are delicately veneered on a basic primate brain. Chimpanzees are not very good at controlling their feelings, and inside each one of us there is a chimpanzee screaming to get out. The bottom line is that the issue of cortical control of emotional impulses is likely to be decisive for our species.

chapter 9

BRAINWAR

Say say oh enemy
Come out and fight with me
And bring your bull dogs three
Climb up my pricker tree
Slide down my razor blade
Into my dungeon door
And we'll be jolly enemies
Forever more more more
—1990s school-yard clapping song[1]
(sung to the tune "Say Say Oh Playmate")

There are cycles (or fads) in schools of thought regarding human nature. Books such as Konrad Lorenz's *On Aggression* and Robert Ardrey's *The Territorial Imperative* represent a viewpoint that received popular acclaim in the 1960s and early 1970s. According to these authors, intraspecies violence and warfare shows that humans have an aggressive internal drive that evolved to protect overexploitation of natural resources. Contemporary humans are seen as having inherited a proclivity for sexual competition and territoriality.

Though the public loved their ideas, Lorenz and Ardrey were severely criticized by academics for being too deterministic and biological. Cross-cultural anthropological data were brought to bear on the question of innate human aggression. After all, hadn't Margaret Mead shown that different primitive human societies varied dramatically in their propensity for violence, with some cultures such as the Arapesh of New Guinea being gentle to the point of sweetness? And isn't it true that pristine foraging (hunting and gathering) societies, such as the Kalahari San (or !Kung) who live in Africa, are peaceful souls who in some ways mirror the human condition as it existed through most of evolution? Surely, then, it must be modern living with its technology, crowding, and other cultural stresses that is responsible for the violence we see in the world today.

And what of violence in our nonhuman primate relatives, the Old World monkeys and apes? According to the traditional cultural deterministic point of view, there is nothing to worry about there. Although nonhuman primates engage in aggressive interactions, they certainly do not kill each other the way humans do. Furthermore, despite being extremely clever, apes were not thought to hunt or even to have a taste for meat. Thus, social scientists traditionally interpreted both cute chimpanzees and "noble savages" as evidence that "man's inhumanity to man" is a product of nurture rather than nature.

But the tide has turned. It's now acknowledged that Mead's gentle Arapesh men were required to commit murder in order to be initiated into adulthood and other pristine societies like the !Kung had surprisingly high homicide rates. As for our cuddly cousins, the Old World monkeys and apes that are most closely related to humans are now known to be extremely competitive, status conscious, and aggressive in their dominance interactions. In particular, numerous reports document that males of the best-known chimpanzee species not only eat meat and hunt, but are even prone toward cannibalism, group violence, and killing each other to settle dominance disputes. Clearly, the traditional sweetness-and-light view of human nature needs to be reassessed.

Dominance Hierarchies: The Baboon Model

I still vividly recall one lecture that I attended as a graduate student in the early 1970s. It was on baboon behavior, and I left the classroom with a worldview different from the one I held when I entered. Any biological anthropologist of my generation will have heard a version of that same riveting lecture; consequently, its content has left an indelible mark on our discipline.

We learned that certain baboons live in open grasslands (or savannas) that provide environmental conditions that were then believed to be similar to those experienced by our earliest ancestors. Because of an assortment of predators, it is dangerous out there on the African savanna. The saving grace of baboons is their tightly knit social organization. The baboon troop is organized around a hierarchy of adult males who provide protection as the troop wanders in its daily search for food and trees to sleep in. These males are characterized by a very specific pecking order or dominance hierarchy in which each individual knows his exact place with respect to every other adult male. (From then on, primatologists just assign them numbers.)

How do primatologists ascertain the ranks of male baboons? Essentially, they keep track of which animals receive preferential treatment and who takes part in and wins the most disputes. Dominant baboons receive more than their fair share of food, water, and sexually receptive females. They control troop movements and are the first to defend its members in the face of danger. Females, especially those with young, stay close to dominant males.

Subordinate baboons, including females, show submissive body language toward dominant monkeys. This includes facial gestures (such as, looking away, smacking the lips, or jerking the head), presenting the hindquarters (which is similar to the gesture made by sexually receptive females who are inviting copulation), and grooming of dominant monkeys' coats. The dominance hierarchy is continually being tested, as individuals monitor their own positions within it and try to displace others in higher positions by picking fights or through other dominance interactions. Thus, hierarchies change over time as animals gain or lose dominance or simply disappear. Anyway, you get the picture. It's a jungle out there. At least for males.

And what are the females doing? According to the 1970s model, females do not have dominance hierarchies. Rather, a female's status changes according to her state of sexual receptivity and whether or not she is a mother of a young infant. Unlike human females, baboon females periodically go into a hormonal state known as estrus and will mate only during this time. Visual and probably olfactory cues clearly identify estrous females who are, well, popular with the males. At the beginning of her estrous cycle, a female mates with less-dominant males, but at the peak of estrus, when she ovulates and can conceive, she is more likely to mate with dominant monkeys, including the alpha male.

Sexually receptive females are accorded higher status (at least by primatologists) than females who aren't as sought after. A female also gets high marks for having a newborn or very young infant. Why? Again, it is a question of being the focus of social attention. Adults of both sexes in the troop are keenly interested in youngsters and seek their company—accompanied by the mother's presence. There you have it. Female baboons depend on their mates and offspring for their status—at least according to the theory that held sway thirty years ago. (But then, think about how a woman's status was measured thirty years ago.) Thus was born the baboon model for speculating about social organization during the earliest part of human evolution.

At the time I first heard about savanna baboons, what crystallized in my thinking was not an understanding of our ancestors' behavior. Rather, what struck me was that the model seemed to adequately explain much of the behavior of another group of higher primates—modern humans! Remember, I was in a classroom at that time and American universities are wonderful places to observe dominance interactions.

Whether one is a graduate student or a faculty member, it's a jungle in academia. At each level of the university (department, college or school, university), decision-making is dominated by a central core of (mostly) males. Students and faculty have designated ranks and the name of the game is to ascend in the hierarchy. Academics, therefore, continually vie for resources and compete with each other for rank. Testing of the dominance hierarchy is actually institutionalized in a tenure system. We have even outbabooned baboons on one point. Our retired alpha males need not lose their dominance. Universities can bestow them with an honorary rank: professor emeritus.

By collecting and analyzing biological and behavioral information, much of it within the framework of evolutionary psychology, primatologists have recently rectified a good deal of the male bias that was inherent in the classic baboon model as well as in earlier studies of other primate species. Where once the roles of female primates were written off as passive (or ignored altogether), contemporary workers have used updated field techniques during the past twenty-five years to gather evidence that sheds new light on sex roles in various species of primate. So, say good-bye to the unassertive, noncompetitive, and unintelligent female!

Recent studies of apes and Old World monkeys, including baboons, reverse many of the earlier stereotypes about female behavior.[2] Both sexes of some monkeys are motivated to seek status, and females can be quite skillful at manipulating the social environment toward that end. In some species, dominant females bear more healthy offspring than submissive females; they use their status to gain resources needed to reproduce rather than employing the male strategy of using status to acquire mates. Females may even use sexual assertiveness (read promiscuity) to stimulate more males to help care for the offspring they might have fathered.[3]

Because of female choice (a term straight out of evolutionary psychology) females may also have a broader role than previously believed in determining whose offspring they conceive. Thus, a good friend rather than the alpha male may impregnate an estrous female. Studies of chimpanzees show that females have a more highly developed sense of adventure (wanderlust) than their male conspecifics do, and they appear to be more experienced users of tools for activities like nut-cracking or insect-collecting. However, as adventurous and manipulative as female chimpanzees are, it is the males who do most of the hunting. And the killing.

Chimpicide

Jane Goodall's remarkable research at the Gombe National Park in Tanzania has revolutionized our understanding of chimpanzee behavior. These apes, with whom we shared a common ancestor some five to seven million years ago, can no longer be thought of as sweet-natured or peaceful. In fact, Goodall's observations show that they can be every bit as violent as modern, stressed out, technologically inclined people.[4]

Chimpanzees like to hunt and eat meat. They prey on a variety of animals including bushpig, rodents, bushbuck, and, of course, other primates. Favorite primate foods include red colobus monkeys and baboons. Upon occasion, chimpanzees will kill and eat other chimpanzees, and anecdotal reports suggest that they have even been known to kill human infants. Although a single chimpanzee may hunt on his or her own, hunting is usually a group activity that involves mostly males.

Chimpanzees are skilled at cooperative hunting. Before starting to hunt monkeys, they often spend time on the ground gazing up into the trees at potential prey. According to Goodall, it seems as if they are assessing suitable victims and their possible escape routes. Just before beginning a hunt, chimpanzees utter grunts or squeaks, and grin and embrace each other. Although they become excited at the prospect of hunting, chimpanzees can be stealthy, quiet, and incredibly persistent as they surround their prey and prevent it from escaping.

Monkey mothers with clinging infants are often the targets of hunts. If a baboon or colobus mother screams, the males of her social group may come to her aid and attack the marauding chimps. This tactic is frequently successful, allowing the mother and infant to get away. At other times, however, there are no nearby males to defend the victims. More often than not, the chimpanzees will snatch the infant from the mother. Several adult males may then tear the victim's body apart and eat it. Although most victims die quickly, Goodall reports that one ten-month-old baboon infant was eaten by only one adult male and was still alive and calling feebly, forty minutes after its capture. (After an infant has been killed, its mother sometimes remains nearby while the prey is being eaten. Consequently, she may herself become a victim.)

Meat is a highly prized food for which chimpanzees intensively compete or beg. Once a kill has been distributed, meat is eaten slowly, as if it is being savored. If the prey is small, a chimpanzee begins by biting open the top of its skull, sucking its blood, and then consuming its brain. In other instances, the skull may be enlarged around the entrance for the spinal cord and fingers then inserted to scoop out the brain, which chimpanzees apparently view as a delicacy.

However, chimpanzees do not just hunt for a good meal. They seem to enjoy hunting for its own sake, as is indicated by the following passage from Goodall:

> On three occasions individuals who were already in possession of meat nevertheless hunted again, successfully. Once, as Figan sat feeding on an infant he had snatched from its mother he intently watched other chimpanzees who were still hunting. Suddenly he handed his entire carcass to Humphrey (who had been begging), joined the hunt, and caught a second monkey—which he then ate. Humphrey once made a kill while still holding a large piece of meat in one hand; and Sherry, holding in his mouth the remains of an infant that he had killed and partially eaten, captured an adult female (its mother) when she ran toward him (avoiding another hunter).[5]

Surprisingly, the aggression that chimpanzees show during hunting of other species is nothing compared with what they are capable of doing to each other! This is especially true of males, who invest an enormous amount of aggression in settling rank-related affairs. Nevertheless, chimpanzees resolve most of their disputes by threats rather than by actual fighting. However, when fighting does break out over male status, it can be vicious and even lethal—especially if it concerns access to estrous females.

A group of chimpanzees studied intensively by Frans de Waal (of Emory University), at the Arnhem Zoo in the Netherlands, provides a case in point. In his book *Peacemaking Among Prim..tes,* de Waal describes the fragile hierarchy between three males, Yeroen, Luit, and Nikkie.[6] At one point, Nikkie was the alpha male, but Yeroen was the most successful at mating. In effect, then, they were both the group's leaders. Then Nikkie and Luit formed a sort of coalition that was successful in reducing Yeroen's mating opportunities. Despite this, Nikkie received help from Yeroen that was necessary if he was to remain dominant over Luit. Although he was the alpha male, Nikkie tolerated matings by Luit,

FIGURE 9.1.
Meat is a highly prized food for which chimpanzees intensively compete. Here, one consumes a bushbuck carcass, while another looks on. (Photograph courtesy of Curt Busse.)

FIGURE 9.2.

One male chimp grooms another (foreground) immediately after they tried unsuccessfully to gain possession of the carcass from the chimp in the background. Both males are screaming in apparent frustration and excitement over the proximity of meat. (Photograph courtesy of Curt Busse.)

and this served to increase the tensions between Yeroen and Nikkie. An uneasy triangle, indeed. Then the hierarchy changed as a result of an unobserved fight that occurred in the night cage of the three males. Luit had become alpha male overnight.

Sadly, Luit's period of dominance, in which "peace and playfulness reigned," was to be a brief one. He died as the result of another unobserved fight that occurred with Nikkie and Yeroen in the night cage. As de Waal describes it, the males' night cage turned red with blood. By the time the staff arrived for work, the chimpanzees had apparently reconciled. Further:

> Luit made strong efforts to stay with the other males, which was quite remarkable in view of what they had done to him. . . . Luit had many deep gashes on his head, flanks, back around the anus, and in the scrotum. His feet in particular were badly injured (from one foot a toe was missing, from the other foot several toes). He also had sustained bites in his hands (several nails were missing). The most gruesome discovery was that he had lost both testicles. All the missing body parts were later found on the cage floor. Closer inspection, on the operating table, of Luit's scrotal sac revealed that, contrary to our expectation, it had not been ripped open. Instead, there were a number of relatively small holes. It was unclear how the testicles had come out.[7]

I do not mean to imply that chimpanzees are violent all the time. According to de Waal, when the Arnhem males had a stable hierarchy, violence was minimized. De Waal also stresses that peacemaking behavior is as deeply ingrained in chimpanzees as aggression is. Thus, chimpanzees engage in a variety of reconciliation and appeasement gestures that offset the tendency toward aggression. Under normal circumstances, submissive gestures such as extending a hand, presenting, or whimpering are often sufficient to preclude or end an attack. At other times, making-up behavior between rival chimpanzee males can be more subtle, as the following account by de Waal suggests:

> Yeroen, for example, would feign interest in a small object to break the tension and attract his adversary. He would suddenly discover something in the grass and hoot loudly, looking in all directions. A number of chimpanzees, including his adversary, would rush to the spot. Soon others would lose interest and leave, while the two male rivals would

stay. They would make excited sounds as they sniffed and handled the discovery, focusing all their attention on it. While doing so, their heads and shoulders would touch. After a few minutes the two would calm down and start grooming each other. The object, which I was never able to identify, would be forgotten.[8]

If social tensions are high, however, peacemaking mechanisms can fail. The violent interactions between the three Arnhem Zoo males were over relative status and access to sexually receptive females. As Goodall has documented, these are also issues for male chimpanzees that live in the wild. Despite parallels in the political concerns of chimpanzees living in social groups both in zoos and in the wild, it is reasonable to ask whether the violence directed toward Luit might not have been unnaturally ferocious, or even aberrant, because of artificial (zoo) living conditions.

Goodall's work, alas, shows that this does not appear to be the case. Incredible as it may seem, wild chimpanzees are capable of delivering at least as much (if not more) violence to their conspecifics as Luit received from Yeroen and Nikkie. In fact, under one set of circumstances, namely attacks on strangers from neighboring communities, the level of aggression is so high that Goodall regards it as a special form of attack.

Us versus Them: Male Patrols

Groups of male chimpanzees regularly go on excursions or patrols to monitor the peripheral parts of their range for enemy neighbors. Although they may be accompanied by estrous females who happen to be traveling with them at the time, patrolling is essentially a male activity. Patrolling chimpanzees are cautious and unusually silent, and they avoid stepping on dry leaves or rustling the vegetation. The reaction of chimpanzees upon hearing the enemy depends on how many strangers appear to be nearby. If it sounds as if they are outnumbered, the patrols may retreat silently. However, when the two parties appear to be of similar size, members of both sides display in wild outbursts of vocalizing, throwing, and drumming. Frequently, these challenges end with the two parties withdrawing noisily to their respective core areas.

But woe to the chimpanzee who is caught traveling alone or with an infant because, as Goodall puts it, chimpanzees appear to have "an inherent dislike or 'hatred' of strangers." Repeated observations by Goodall's assistants have documented the manner in which patrolling males assault their male and female victims: The attacks were gang attacks of long duration. In all of the incidents, the strangers were held to the ground by some chimpanzees, while others hit, bit, stamped upon, and pounded the victims. The strangers were also dragged about. Although the victims eventually gave up and crouched or lay passively, the attacks continued until the victims were completely immobilized, if not dead. Significantly, the field assistants who observed these attacks believed that the chimpanzees were trying to kill their victims. On several occasions, the aggressors later returned to the scenes of the violence to search for or inspect the bodies of their victims.

In her impressive volume, Goodall meticulously documents a series of aggressive interactions that led to the complete annihilation of one chimpanzee community (the Kahama) by males from another (the Kasakela). What does she make of this? Goodall believes that chimpanzees should be considered territorial, although she notes that they differ in some ways from classically territorial animals. For example, rather than simply chasing trespassers out of their territories, chimpanzees create opportunities for encountering strangers by patrolling peripheral areas about once every four days. Furthermore, adult males behave as if they *like* aggressive encounters. The violence of their hostility toward neighbors and the fact that they will make raids into the core areas of other communities also distinguishes chimpanzees from other territorial animals. In other words, chimpanzees are not just territorial. When it comes to strangers, they seem almost to have a bloodlust. Goodall stops short of attributing warfare to chimpanzees, reasoning that language, which would be necessary, is absent. I'm not so sure. Although their aggression is not corticalized with verbal strategies or modified weapons, it seems to me that our chimpanzee cousins do a chillingly efficient job of waging war. And I, for one, believe that the common ancestor (CA) of chimpanzees and humans is probably responsible for the human taste for warfare.[9]

FIGURE 9.3.
Kasakela chimpanzees on patrol. (Photograph copyright Curt Busse, 2002.)

Homicide

As mentioned earlier, many social anthropologists argue against a biological or evolutionary basis for human violence. Instead, they extol the gentle nature of modern people who live in simple nonintensive foraging/horticultural societies (sometimes called bands), and they make the claim that these societies reflect social organization as it prevailed during most of hominin evolution. This level of organization is frequently described as egalitarian, because male status is de-emphasized, and sharing and crosscutting ties with other groups are encouraged. In other words, the norms of cooperation and communal sharing are said to be extremely strong in these relatively simple societies. Thus, according to Bruce Knauft of Emory University, the !Kung of southern Africa are known as "harmless people," the Semai from Malaya as "nonviolent people," the Waorani of Ecuador as a "tribe where harmony rules," and Inuit relations are described as "never in anger."[10]

Knauft's own research is on the Gebusi, a small, opportunistic hunting and foraging/horticultural society that lives in lowland New Guinea. Knauft describes male social life among the Gebusi as markedly devoid of hierarchical relationships and rivalry. In this peaceloving society, diffuse friendship and camaraderie are the stated norms, and anger is viewed as antisocial and threatening to communal sociality. Yet, despite their apparent gentleness, the homicide rate among the Gebusi is one of the highest ever reported for any society!

According to Knauft, homicide among the Gebusi is primarily a male activity. Almost two-thirds of middle-aged men from two communities have committed homicide, "including some who were among the least assertive and aggressive even by Gebusi standards."[11] Of nearly four hundred deaths surveyed, about one-third were homicides. Although a certain number of deaths (less than 10 percent) occur in bow-and-arrow encounters between Gebusi from different settlements, the most frequent context for homicide is the killing of a man or woman for allegedly being a sorcerer who caused the sickness and death of another person.

Knauft believes that few Gebusi actually practice sorcery; nevertheless, when someone becomes ill and dies, his or her death is frequently attributed to a male or female sorcerer. Aggressive or assertive individuals are likely targets for such accusations. An accused individual must undergo public divinations and is subject to a swift, violent death if found guilty. As Knauft points out, Gebusi violence thus acts as a strong leveling mechanism that discourages the emergence of assertiveness and reinforces the norms of sociality and sharing.

But what is Gebusi homicide really about? Knauft's careful analysis reveals an answer, of which the Gebusi themselves are apparently unaware: Violence is ultimately about male control of women. For example, the killing of sorcerers is statistically correlated with lack of reciprocity in exchange of sisters for marriage. Significantly, Knauft notes that other gentle societies such as the !Kung, Central Inuit, and Semai also engage in extreme violence in disputes over female sexuality. Although simple societies may lack the resources (including leadership) for waging much in the way of war, lethal violence is no stranger. As de Waal documented for the chimpanzees at the Arnhem Zoo, tensions over heterosexual access frequently erupt between human males living in simple societies.

Knauft used his data for the Gebusi to test a controversial hypothesis regarding violence. A basic tenet of evolutionary psychology is that animals, including humans, behave in ways that maximize their reproductive fitness, either through producing offspring themselves or by facilitating reproduction in relatives such as siblings or cousins. According to this hypothesis, humans should avoid killing their relatives. Also, if violence is adaptive, one would expect those who commit homicide to leave more offspring than other people. And, indeed, the hypothesis was confirmed for at least one group of people when Napoleon Chagnon (from the University of California at Santa Barbara) found that killers from a South American tribe (the Yanomamo) have more than twice as many wives and three times as many children as nonkillers. However, Knauft's data failed to confirm the hypothesis. In fact, contrary to expectations of evolutionary psychology, Knauft found a statistically significant correlation between homicide and genealogical relatedness (that is, Gebusi tend to kill their relatives)!

Knauft's work on the Gebusi is extremely important and has received a good deal of attention. Unfortunately, debate on the social implications of the Gebusi data has been prevalent in the discussions about his research and this has clouded understanding of its *biological* significance. In fact, Knauft himself emphasizes the interrelationship of cultural, ecological, and sociological constraints on Gebusi violence, but he seems to have thrown biology out with sociobiology.

The extreme violence practiced by the Gebusi and other seemingly gentle societies supports the contention that aggression is a basic component of human nature that emerges in some form, regardless of the explicit cultural constraints on violence. This conclusion is strengthened by the fact that, universally, males apparently kill each other over (among other issues) heterosexual access. Furthermore, the fact that Gebusi men are prone to killing their own sisters as a means of taking vengeance on their brothers-in-law does not negate the general validity of explanations of violence that are grounded in evolutionary psychology.

It matters not a whit, of course, whether there is or is not a human (or chimpanzee) gene for homicide. What does matter is that men the world round are predisposed toward lethal aggression. Furthermore, the assertion that violence is strictly culturally determined is not going to change things.[12] Just as chimpanzee males cheerfully patrol the periphery looking for rumbles, so do human males. And these males usually call themselves "civilized."

Murder in Detroit

Nonmilitaristic lethal violence is not a product just of simple human societies, as Martin Daly and Margo Wilson (both of McMaster University) document thoroughly in their fascinating book, *Homicide (Foundations of Human Behavior)*.[13] Homicides occur in all cultures. Among industrialized nations, homicides are particularly frequent in the United States, where there are approximately sixty per day. As with the Gebusi, it is enlightening to see who kills whom within civilized societies and why. Daly and Wilson's approach to this question incorporates biology and the framework within which they formulate their conclusions is informed by evolutionary psychology.

I asked several colleagues to guess what the most prevalent relationship is between murderers and their victims in the United States. Their answers varied. One said "relatives," and another said "strangers, because I think most would have to do with theft or robberies." Another (newly wed) suggested "domestic violence between husbands and wives." In fact, the answer is quite different from any of the above, and very interesting.

In keeping with the hypothesis of violence that draws from evolutionary psychology, few Americans kill relatives who share their genes. Of 509 homicides in Detroit surveyed by Daly and Wilson, only 6 percent involved blood kin. Upon further analysis, the Detroit data proved to be typical for American homicides. Thus, "blood relationships are much less lethal than other intimate relationships."[14]

The main cause of lethal violence wherever homicide rates are high, including the United States, is trivial altercations between males. Swift, violent death can result from amazingly minor disputes over such issues as a parking space, access to a pool table, or a macho barroom boast. Although these proximate causes seem incredibly insignificant, Daly and Wilson offer a perceptive analysis that makes sense of these homicides:

> In most social milieus, a man's reputation depends in part upon the maintenance of a credible threat of violence. Conflicts of interest are endemic to society, and one's interests are likely to be violated by competitors unless those competitors are *deterred*. Effective deterrence is a matter of convincing our rivals that any attempt to advance their interests at our expense will lead to such severe penalties that the competitive gambit will end up a net loss which should never have been undertaken.[15]

Although Daly and Wilson conclude that machismo behavior probably increased reproductive fitness during most of human history, they think its utility has been mitigated in modern societies, where states have assumed a monopoly on the "legitimate" use of violence.

Daly and Wilson concluded their book by noting that homicide rates have fallen in historical times in most state societies. They added that twentieth-century humans may have a better chance of dying peacefully in bed than did their hominin predecessors. But then the authors probably did not know about a U.S. military plan called "Treetop."

Just as male chimpanzees love to patrol their borders, so do human males (sometimes with the help of females). The difference is that men, with their fancy neocortices and language, provide rationalizations for why they patrol. Thus, civilized humans patrol in the name of loved ones, or country, or freedom, or God's will, or—my favorite—peace. But patrol they do. When chimpanzees find an unfortunate stranger, the marauding group holds their victim to the ground and attacks him or her with their hands and feet and teeth. They do not stop until the victim is completely incapacitated or dead. Because of their evolved brains, men have been able to replace extremities and teeth with technologically advanced weapons that are both convenient and ruthlessly lethal. And because of their chimpanzeelike natures, they cannot resist these and other military endeavors.

Take, for example, Americans. They have invested heavily in the patrol.[16] In 1982, a secret agency called the Defense Mobilization Planning Systems Agency was created and instructed to report to then–Vice President Bush. By the time (the first) Bush assumed the presidency in 1989, more than $3 billion had been spent to upgrade the command, control, and communications technology associated with the U.S. strategy for surviving a nuclear attack. That strategy was known in "militarese" as COG, short for "continuity of government." And what a plan it was.

At the time, the COG plan for what happens to government officials in the event of a nuclear attack was known as "Treetop." According to this plan, the president would be evacuated from the White House (assuming that's where he was) by helicopter. He would probably fly directly to a National Emergency Airborne Command Post, known then as "kneecap." There were four kneecaps, or Boeing 747s, in the early 1990s that had been customized with specialized telecommunications equipment. One was kept flying at all times, and another was always waiting at Andrews Air Force Base, less than ten minutes from the White House. With midair refueling, the "kneecap" could serve as an airborne command post, from which the president would be able to direct military and civilian operations.

The president could also take up residence in the well-provisioned Mount Weather command bunker in Virginia or in one of the approximately fifty fallout-resistant command bunkers that have apparently been equipped to act as emergency White Houses. To diminish the chances of sustaining direct hits, these bunkers are secretly located across the United States. One underground bunker whose location is not so secret is Raven Rock, near Camp David, Maryland. During the nuclear holocaust, its lucky inhabitants would be able to enjoy a racquet-ball court, chapel, laundry, medical clinic, and a barber shop. (Now that's what I call optimism.)

Who were the lucky residents of American fallout-resistant bunkers going to be? First of all, there would be the president and a dominance hierarchy of seventeen government officials who are designated (in serial order) as his potential successors. Then, there were forty-six key Pentagon officials who would be airlifted to the relative safety of the bunkers, any time, day or night. Another 248 relief specialists and senior Pentagon officials may have joined them, but only during working hours. In all, the plan was for more than one thousand military and political officials to be evacuated.

If all of this sounds as if the military intended to protect itself in the case of Armageddon, that is far from the stated rational for "Treetop." Former President Reagan, for instance, believed that a nuclear war would be winnable, but only if government leaders survived. Furthermore, there is the added notion that government leaders must survive in order to halt the aggression and to help civilians.

But these noble motives weaken somewhat when one examines the highly sensitive issue of what the United States chooses to target with its own nuclear weapons. As of 1989, the United States was reported to be drastically changing its strategy for fighting a nuclear war with the former Soviet Union.[17] A plan called the Strategic Integrated Operations Plan (or SIOP-7), called for development of devastating weapons that could penetrate the deepest military bunkers, thereby removing Soviet leadership shortly after the onset of conflict. In order to facilitate this goal the United States would have planted remote sensing devices inside Soviet territory. Critics of SIOP-7 pointed out that such tactics might "upset the fragile balance of terror," and increase the chances of an inadvertent launch of nuclear missiles by nervous Soviet Union leaders operating under siege constraints. They also noted that the elimination of the USSR's leadership would have left no one to halt the Soviet side of the conflict.

The dramatic upheaval and eventual demise of the former Soviet Union created a quandary for U.S. military experts. In 2003, officials remained uncertain about who controls the former Soviet arsenal of thousands of nuclear weapons. As long ago as February 1990, Senator Sam Nunn (a Democrat from Georgia) called for a fail-safe review of the mechanisms for ensuring nuclear safeguards.[18] It was Nunn's hope that the Pentagon would reverse its long-standing objections to new technology that would allow U.S. missiles to be called back (or destroyed) after they had been launched. He also suggested that it would be prudent to share such fail-safe technology with the former Soviet Union. The most amazing revelation associated with Nunn's proposal was that senior American military officials were apparently resistant to calls for further nuclear safeguards.

These facts represent bits and pieces about (usually) secret American military operations that were gleaned by the media more than a decade ago. What about now? I can no longer find information about "Treetop" or "kneecap" on the web. I have learned, however, that a Presidential Decision Directive (called PDD-67) was issued in 1998 that replaced earlier directives regarding COG, although the text of this directive (or a White House Factsheet summarizing its provisions) appears not to have been released to the public.

My scientific journals are more forthcoming. Two recent pieces in *Science* reveal that, on the heels of the war in Iraq and September 11th, 2001, our government is in the process of reshaping its nuclear arsenal.[19] The White House intends to reactivate the underground nuclear test range in Nevada and is accelerating research on low-yield "mini-nukes" including "bunker busters" that can target objects that are buried as well as those on the surface. The House and Senate have supported requests for millions of dollars to explore such concepts. Not to be outdone, the Russian government has warned that the renewed nuclear program in the United States could trigger a space-based arms race, and is in the process of funneling money into defense research to develop comparable weapons.[19] So much for the end of the cold war.

An even more amazing story that appeared in my other favorite journal, *Nature,* gives new meaning to the title of this chapter.[20] In 2002, $24 million of the basic research budget of the U.S. Defense Advanced Research Projects Agency (DARPA) was allocated to research on interfacing brain and machines. The ultimate goal of this research is to insert electrodes into the brains of military personnel that will permit them to control weapons through thought! Although it sounds like science fiction, research on animals suggests that, one day, human thoughts will, indeed, be able to kill.

Despite the paucity of public information, the overwhelming impression one receives is that military leaders take pride in what they do. Indeed, the rapprochement between the United States and the Soviet Union (not to mention the reunification of Germany) threatened long-standing positions of military interests worldwide. Whether disarmament is ever achievable is another, deeper question that goes to the heart of our views of our species and our apparent predilection for aggressive behavior. Ominously, at least one widely respected scientist, British astronomer Martin Rees, thinks there is a 50 percent probability that our species will become extinct by the end of this century.[21]

Although the cerebral cortex may be evolved in humans, the limbic system still divides the universe into us and them. Men will patrol their borders. And more. Like Goodall's chimpanzees, human beings are reluctant neither to penetrate the territories of others nor to use lethal force against strangers. The contributions of the human neocortex are in the areas of weaponry and verbal strategy, and can also be found in the fact that men frequently do violence to others in the name of religion.

One may choose to believe that the parallels between aggressive behavior in ourselves and chimpanzees are just coincidence. It does not matter. Whatever the mix between biological and cultural factors, human beings are aggressive, territorial primates who, resources permitting, venerate their dominance hierarchies within, and seek the thrill of patrolling the periphery without. Although males usually engage in these activities, it is entire societies that support them. In simplest terms, human behavior suggests that, without a "them" to worry about, the "us" would be most unfulfilled.[22]

The Last Dance?

Two million years of natural selection for better information processing has given our species a marvelous brain. Because of its size and wiring and delicate balance of neurochemicals, humans pursue wonderful activities—like worrying about whether or not the cosmos has an origin or trying to find a still larger prime number. People weep at sad movies, write poetry, and laugh uproariously at funny jokes. They listen to music, paint murals, and are capable of seeing the solution to a problem in an intuitive flash. They also make the best damned tap dancers. And all because of the braindance.

But our lovely cortices are veneered over a brain that is constructed according to a basic primate floorplan. The limbic system looms, ever in the background, and our males (and sometimes females) cannot keep themselves from patrolling the borders. Society has encouraged them, of course, by supporting development of what may soon become a global nuclear "Fright Machine" that is not fail-safe against the wrong leader hearing doomsday instructions from the Almighty, at the wrong time. Although the cortical mechanisms for controlling aggression are part of the neurological package that we inherited from our hominin ancestors, our species must vigilantly exercise those controls over our natural primate tendencies to engage in potentially catastrophic dominance interactions. We, therefore, must question which one will ultimately win out—the braindance, or the brainwar. Events that have ensued since September 11, 2001, make this question, posed more than ten years ago in the first edition of this book, all the more ominous.

In her chapter on territoriality, Jane Goodall says of the chimpanzee:

> If ever he develops the power of language—and, as we have seen, he stands close to that threshold, too—might he not push open the door and wage war with the best of us?[23]

In my opinion, he has developed language and (to quote the immortal Pogo) "he is us." All things considered, since *Homo sapiens* appears to have a strong predilection for potentially catastrophic aggression, perhaps the best we can hope for is that our species continues to exert control over its limbic impulses.

Then, at least, we stand a chance of being jolly enemies *forever more more more.*

REFERENCES

Introduction

1. The term "hominids" was used in the first edition of *Braindance*. Because this term is now interpreted by numerous (but not all) workers to include the African apes as well as humans and their earlier relatives, this edition uses the more restrictive term "hominins," which is understood by everyone to include only the non-ape branch of the family.

Chapter 1. Foraging in the Red Cave

1. R. Dart, *Adventures with the Missing Link* (New York: Random House, 1959).

2. Ibid., 10.

3. R. A. Dart, "*Australopithecus africanus:* The man-ape of South Africa," *Nature* 115 (1925):195–99.

4. J. T. Robinson, "Adaptive radiation in the australopithecines and the origin of man," in F. C. Howell and F. Bourlieve, eds., *African Ecology and Human Evolution* (Chicago: Aldine, 1963), 385–416.

5. G. Findlay, *Dr. Robert Broom, F.R.S.: Palaeontologist and Physician/1866–1951* (Cape Town: A.A. Balkema, 1972).

6. This idea has been eloquently elaborated by R. A. Foley and P. C. Lee in "Finite social space, evolutionary pathways, and reconstructing hominid behavior," *Science* 243 (1989):901–6.

7. This suggestion was presented by several workers who attended the International Workshop on the Evolutionary History of the Robust Australopithecines, at the State University of New York, Stony Brook, March 27–April 2, 1987. See also F. Grine, ed., *The Evolutionary History of "Robust" Australopithecines* (New York: Aldine de Gruyter, 1989).

8. R. L. Susman, "Hand of *Paranthropus robustus* from Member I, Swartkrans: Fossil evidence for tool behavior," *Science* 233 (1989):781–84. Susman analyzed several finger bones from a South African site named Swarkrans, dated to 1.8

million years ago. He believes the bones are those of robust australopithecines and that they indicate the hand of this early hominin was capable of making tools, "possibly for plant procurement and processing." In keeping with this, Susman concludes that lack of tool behavior was not responsible for the extinction of robust australopithecines and, further, that the acquisition of tools was not responsible for the emergence of *Homo*. Even more tantalizing is the somewhat oblique suggestion that robust australopithecines may have used fire for cooking, protection against predators, or warmth, in C. K. Brain and A. Sillen, "Evidence from the Swartkrans cave for the earliest use of fire," *Nature* 336 (1988):464–66. The problem with this interpretation is that *Homo* was at Swartkrans too and it is not known if one or both hominins used fire.

9. In hindsight, these reservations were unfounded (and unfair) in the case of South Africa. I've since learned that some curators, such as Bob Brain of the Transvaal Museum, are fastidious about never excluding qualified workers from their collections. In fact, my career in fossil hominins would never have gotten off the ground without the access to African fossils that was kindly extended to me by Bob Brain, Elisabeth Vrba, Phillip Tobias, and Richard Leakey. The present curator, Francis Thackeray, carries on this tradition.

10. In a letter dated January 16, 1991, Bob Brain informed me that the Red Cave is no more! Most of the research departments of the Transvaal Museum have now moved to a new building behind the museum. According to Brain, the hominin fossils "are now housed in another strongroom which is still a bit sterile but which, it is hoped, will acquire some atmosphere before long. Our new Curator of Palaeontology is Dr. Francis Thackeray and he will be attending to the aesthetics of a new hominid cavern." Dr. Thackeray continues as curator in 2004.

11. During hominin evolution, the lunate sulcus was pushed toward the back by expansion of the parietal association cortex, which is concerned with higher integrative functions.

12. The line of reasoning used by Holloway here is a logical error that is called resorting to higher authority or the *argumentum ad verecundiam*.

13. R. L. Holloway, "Revisiting the South African Taung australopithecine endocast: The position of the lunate sulcus as determined by the stereoplotting technique," *American Journal of Physical Anthropology* 56 (1981):43–58; see pp. 50–51.

14. R. L. Holloway, "The role of human social behavior in the evolution of the brain," Forty-third James Arthur Lecture (New York: The American Museum of Natural History, 1975), 11–12.

15. R. L. Holloway, "Revisiting the South African Taung australopithecine endocast: The position of the lunate sulcus as determined by the stereoplotting technique." *American Journal of Physical Anthropology* 56 (1981):43–58; see p. 49.

16. D. Falk, "Apples, oranges, and the lunate sulcus," *American Journal of Physical Anthropology* 67 (1985):313–15; see p. 315.

17. D. Falk, "Hadar AL 162-28 endocast as evidence that brain enlargement preceded cortical reorganization in hominin evolution," *Nature* 313 (1985):45–47.

18. R. L. Holloway, "Cerebral brain endocast pattern of *Australopithecus afarensis* hominid," *Nature* 303 (1983):420–22.

Chapter 2. Taung Goes to St. Louis—and Beyond

1. Thank you, NIH (R01 NS 24904).

2. H. Jerison's book *Evolution of the Brain and Intelligence* (New York: Academic Press, 1973) is a classic. For a discussion of its impact on the field, see the festschrift in Jerison's honor: *Evolutionary Anatomy of the Primate Cerebral Cortex* (D. Falk and K. Gibson, eds., Cambridge University Press, 2001).

3. For details see D. Falk, C. Hildebolt, and M. W. Vannier, "Reassessment of the Taung early hominid from a neurological perspective," *Journal of Human Evolution* 18 (1989):485–92.

4. K. Zilles, E. Armstrong, A. Schleicher, and H. Kretschmann, "The human pattern of gyrification in the cerebral cortex," *Anatomy and Embryology* 179 (1988):173–79.

5. See E. Armstrong, K. Zilles, M. Curtis, and A. Schleicher, "Cortical folding, the lunate sulcus, and the evolution of the human brain," *Journal of Human Evolution* 20 (1991):341–48; H. J. Jerison, "Fossil evidence on the evolution of the neocortex," in E. G. Jones and A. Peters, eds., *Cerebral Cortex*, vol. 8A (New York: Plenum Press, 1990), 285–309.

6. The Barcelona conference was titled "L'evolucio del cervell i l'origen de la parla humana," and it took place on November 8–9, 2001 at the Museu de la Ciencia de la Fundacio "la Caixa."

7. Some of our preliminary findings are described in A. Gibbons, "Hot spots of brain evolution," *Science* 296 (2002):837.

8. This preliminary observation was initially made in my laboratory using tried and true eyeballing of endocasts combined with simple caliper measurements in collaboration with two wonderful graduate students, John Redmond Jr. and John Guyer. The study then expanded to incorporate the expertise of an international team. For details see D. Falk, J. C. Redmond, J. Guyer, G. C. Conroy, W. Recheis, G. W. Weber and H. Seidler, "Early hominid brain evolution: a new look at old endocasts," *Journal of Human Evolution* 38 (2000):695–717.

9. See B. Wood, "Origin and evolution of the genus *Homo*," *Nature* 355 (1992):783–90.

Chapter 3. Chimp Brain, Human Brain

1. Much of this information is from E. S. Savage-Rumbaugh and D. Rumbaugh, "The emergence of language," in K. R. Gibson and T. Ingold, eds., *Tools, Language and Cognition in Human Evolution* (Cambridge: Cambridge University Press, 1993), 86–108. This paper was presented at the Wenner-Gren International Symposium on Tools, Language and Intelligence: Evolutionary Implications, Cascais, Portugal (1990), and some of Sue Savage-Rumbaugh's comments at the symposium are also included.

2. J. P. Taglialatela, S. Savage-Rumbaugh, and L. A. Baker, "Vocal production by a language-competent *Pan paniscus,*" *International Journal of Primatology* 24 (2003):1–17.

3. Drs. Gibson and Boesch were both participants in the Wenner-Gren symposium noted above.

4. I thank Sue Savage-Rumbaugh for providing me a copy in 2002 of the video of Panbanisha and Kanzi playing the piano while making music with Peter Gabriel and his colleagues.

5. The illustration was modified after W. Penfield and T. Rasmussen, *The Cerebral Cortex of Man* (New York: Hafner, 1968.)

6. The homunculus is based on my modification of Penfield's classic maps. It is greatly simplified and over generalized. In order to maintain continuity, some artistic license has been taken. For example, the tongue is shown protruding from the mouth, rather than as a separate structure located beneath the face representation. In reality, there are multiple representations for certain parts of the body, such as the hand, and sensory and motor areas overlap and differ more from each other than is apparent from this illustration. The relative sizes of body parts also differ a bit from person to person.

7. For details, see K. Zilles, E. Armstrong, A. Schleicher, and H. J. Kretschmann, "The human pattern of gyrification in the cerebral cortex," *Anatomy and Embryology* 179 (1988):173–79.

8. P. S. Goldman-Rakic, "Circuitry of primate prefrontal cortex and regulation of behavior by representational memory," in V. B. Mountcastle, F. Plum, and S. R. Geiger, *Handbook of Physiology—The Nervous System* V (Bethesda, Md.: American Physiological Society, 1987), 373–417.

9. Ibid., 374.

10. K. Semendeferi, A. Lu, N. Schenker and H. Damasio, "Humans and great apes share a large frontal cortex," *Nature Neuroscience* 5 (2002):272–76.

11. Much of this section is gleaned from the classic textbook: E. C. Crosby, T. Humphrey, and E. W. Lauer, *Correlative Anatomy of the Nervous System* (New York: Macmillan, 1962). For more contemporary examples, see P. Rakic and W. Singer, eds., *Neurobiology of Neocortex* (New York: John Wiley and Sons, 1988); G. M. Edelman, W. E. Gall, and W. M. Cowan, eds., *Dynamic Aspects of Neocortical Function* (New York: John Wiley and Sons, 1984).

12. Wernicke's area is defined differently by different workers. Although Wernicke did not include them in his classic definition, Brodmann's area 39 (angular gyrus) and area 40 (supramarginal gyrus) are incorporated in Wernicke's area by many contemporary workers. This is probably appropriate since a lesion in area 39 leads to alexia (inability to read) and patients with damage to area 40 show a profound loss regarding the symbolism of language. For an entertaining discussion of the location of Wernicke's area, see J. E. Bogen and G. M. Bogen, "Wernicke's region—Where is it?" *Annals of New York Academy of Science* 280 (1976):834–43.

13. Positron emission tomographic (PET) studies reveal that semantic associations for words are processed in Brodmann's area 47 rather than in classic Broca's area (consisting of Brodmann's areas 44 and 45). Because of this, Petersen et al. suggested that classic Broca's area is not related to language-specific output programming but, instead, has general motor function. See S. E. Petersen, P. T. Fox, M. I. Posner, M. Mintum, and M. E. Raichle, "Positron emission tomographic studies of the cortical anatomy of single-word processing," *Nature* 331 (1988): 585–89.

14. A. Kendon, "Gesticulation and speech: Two aspects of the process of utterance," in M. R. Key, ed., *Nonverbal Communication and Language* (The Hague: Mouton, 1980), 207–27; see pp. 208–9.

15. Quotation is from pp. 44–45 of A. Kendon, "Human Gesture," in K. R. Gibson and T. Ingold, eds., *Tools, Language and Cognition in Human Evolution* (Cambridge: Cambridge University Press, 1993), 43–62.

16. S. Goldin-Meadow and H. Feldman, "The development of language-like communication without a language model," *Science* 197 (1977):401–3. S. Goldin-Meadow and C. Mylander, "Levels of structure in a language developed without a language model," in K. Gibson and A. Peterson, eds., *The Brain and Behavioral Development: Biosocial Dimensions* (New York: Aldine de Gruyter, 1989), 315–44.

Chapter 4. Of Family Trees, Darwin's Theory, and the Origins of Bipedalism

1. Specifically, changes in the frequencies of alternate kinds of genes cause generations to change over time. For example, if eye color were controlled by two types of the eye-color gene (one for brown and one for blue), a population in which 95 percent of the eye genes were the blue type would look considerably different than a population in which 95 percent were the brown type. Thus, although the ingredients would be the same within the two groups, the relative amounts of the different types of eye-color gene would cause the populations to appear generally different (but with overlap) as far as eye color goes. In this sense, evolution can be viewed simply as a change in gene frequencies over time.

2. So much for the lighter side of Malthus. What one doesn't read in most textbooks on evolutionary theory are Malthus's proposals for restraining human population growth in *An Essay on the Principle of Population* (New York: W. W. Norton, 1976.) He suggested that the poor were having too many children and that the laws that protected poor children from starvation (i.e., that gave them the right to parish assistance) should be abolished. He further proposed that the lower classes should be instructed that it would be immoral for a man to marry and bear children unless he knew he could support his family. If a poor man chose to marry anyway, "All parish assistance should be denied him; and he should be left to the uncertain support of private charity. He should be taught to know that the laws of nature, which are the laws of God, had doomed him and his family to suffer for disobeying their repeated admonitions; that he had no claim of right on society for the smallest portion of food" (135–36). This was controversial stuff even in Mal-

thus's day. Jonathan Swift's satirical *Modest Proposal for Preventing the Children of Poor People from being a Burden to their Parents or the Country* was perhaps the most famous retort to Malthus's essay. Swift wickedly suggested that Irish babies should be fattened to make food for the rich.

3. Some workers put the date of the CA at six or seven million years ago, others place it at four or five. For simplicity's sake, I accept five to seven million years ago as a reasonable approximation.

4. The arboreal theory was elaborated by Elliot Smith and F. Wood Jones early in the last century. See Jones's book *Arboreal Man* (London: E. Arnold, 1916). More recently, Matt Cartmill ("Rethinking primate origins," *Science* 184 [1974]:436–43) emphasized the importance of general primate adaptations for catching insects. His "bug-snatching" theory puts a new twist on the arboreal theory.

5. See A. Zihlman, "Pygmy chimps, people, and the pundits," *New Scientist*, 15 November 1984:39–40.

6. B. G. Richmond and D. S. Strait, "Evidence that humans evolved from a knuckle-walking ancestor," *Nature* 404 (2000):382–85. For a fuller review of knuckle-walking and the origins of bipedalism, see B. G. Richmond, D. R. Begun, and D. S. Strait, "Origin of human bipedalism: The knuckle-walking hypothesis revisited," *Yearbook of Physical Anthropology* 44 (2001):70–105.

7. Interestingly, the third great ape, the orangutan, is not a knuckle-walker. Orangutans are from Asia and more distantly related to humans than the gorilla or chimpanzee. They lack the bony signs of knuckle-walking for the simple reason that they rarely engage in it. In fact, orangutans spend as little time as possible on the ground. When they are on the ground, however, orangutans rest and move on their fists or palms rather than their knuckles. Although orangutans are not knuckle-walkers, it is extremely interesting that all three of the great apes ball their hands up in one way or another when moving on the ground. Perhaps this tendency was inherited from their common ancestor.

8. M. D. Leakey, "Pliocene footprints at Laetoli, northern Tanzania," *Antiquity* 52 (1978):133. See also M. D. Leakey and R. L. Hay, "Pliocene footprints in the Laetoli Beds at Laetoli, northern Tanzania," *Nature* 278 (1979):317–23.

9. R. H. Tuttle, "Kinesiological inferences and evolutionary implications from Laetoli bipedal trails G-1, G-2/3, and A," in M. D. Leakey and J. M. Harris, eds., *Laetoli, A. Pliocene Site in Northern Tanzania* (Oxford: Clarendon Press, 1987), 503–23.

10. Though controversial, Tuttle's work is so thorough and he has answered his critics so skillfully that he's convinced me that the toe bones that made the Laetoli impressions were probably flat rather than curved.

11. S. L. Washburn, "Tools and human evolution," *Scientific American* 203 (1960):63–75.

12. This notion of different parts of the body evolving at different rates is called "mosaic evolution."

13. In fact, Sherwood Washburn's name is linked with both theories.

14. A number of anthropologists now support this idea, which was suggested by S. Linton, "Woman the gatherer: Male bias in anthropology," in W. Jacobs, ed., *Women in Cross-Cultural Perspective* (Champaign-Urbana: University of Illinois Press, 1971), 9–21. For an up-to-date treatment of women in human evolution, read A. L. Zihlman, "Women's bodies, women's lives: An evolutionary perspective," in M. E. Morbeck, A. Galloway, and A. L. Zihlman, eds., *The Evolving Female* (Princeton: Princeton University Press, 1997), 185–97.

15. C. Boesch and H. Boesch, "Possible causes of sex differences in the use of natural hammers by wild chimpanzees," *Journal of Human Evolution* 13 (1984): 415–40.

16. P. Shipman, "Scavenging or hunting in early hominids: Theoretical framework and tests," *American Anthropologist* 88 (1986):27–43.

17. C. O. Lovejoy, "The origin of man," *Science* 211 (1981):341–50.

18. A. L. Zihlman, "Gathering stories for hunting human nature: A review essay," *Feminist Studies* 11 (1985):365–77.

19. Ibid., 374. On p. 346 of "The origin of man" (see reference 17, above), Lovejoy says, "Human females are continually sexually receptive (79)." Footnote 79 (p. 350) reads: "D. C. Johanson, personal communication."

20. N. M. Tanner, "Gathering by females: The chimpanzee model revisited and the gathering hypothesis," in W. G. Kinzey, ed., *The Evolution of Human Behavior: Primate Models* (State University of New York Press, 1987), 3–27; see pp. 14, 18.

21. J. Goodall, *The Chimpanzees of Gombe* (Cambridge: Belknap Press, 1986), 145.

22. Whenever I read about the large size of human penises compared with those of other mammals, I am transported back to an experience I had in 1979 while doing research at the Smithsonian. I entered a spacious room that contained various alcohol-preserved specimens and began to search the shelves for the primate brains. As I peered into one jar, I thought "that looks like a—no, it couldn't be." When I looked at the next jar, I thought "Why that also looks like a—Nooo." Along about the third jar, I realized that, indeed, I had happened upon a collection of preserved penises. I must admit that I then observed the entire collection with some awe. What marvelous variety there is in this most fundamental of animal appendages!

According to William G. Eberhard, a leading expert on animal genitalia in *Sexual Selection and Animal Genitalia* (Cambridge: Harvard University Press, 1985), the most likely selective factor explaining large penis size in humans is tactile stimulation of the female. Apparently, the cervix of the human female actually withdraws from the opening of the vagina during sexual arousal. However, sensory stimuli from a protruded glans of the human penis can trigger contraction of the female reproductive tract that results in sperm transport, thereby increasing the likelihood of conception. Thus, sexual selection by females for males that were adept at sexual stimulation may have been a contributing factor to large penis size in males.

23. A. R. E. Sinclair, M. D. Leakey, and M. Norton-Griffiths, "Migration and hominid bipedalism," *Nature* 324 (1987):307–8.

24. P. E. Wheeler, "Stand tall and stay cool," *New Scientist,* 12 May 1988:62–65.

25. P. E. Wheeler, "The loss of functional body hair in man: The influence of thermal environment, body form and bipedality." *Journal of Human Evolution* 14 (1985):23–28. Also see P. E. Wheeler, "The evolution of bipedality and loss of functional body hair in hominids," *Journal of Human Evolution* 13 (1984):91–98.

26. R. W. Wrangham, "The significance of African apes for reconstructing human social evolution," in *The Evolution of Human Behavior: Primate Models,* ed. W. G. Kinzey (State University of New York Press, 1987), 51–71.

27. See pp. 352–53 of D. Falk, *Primate Diversity* (New York: W. W. Norton, 2000).

28. G. Richards, "Freed hands or enslaved feet? A note on the behavioral implications of ground-dwelling bipedalism," *Journal of Human Evolution* 15 (1986): 143–50; see p. 146.

29. M. Brunet et al., "A new hominid from the upper Miocene of Chad, Central Africa," *Nature* 418 (2002):145–55.

30. M. H. Wolpoff, B. Senut, M. Pickford, and J. Hawks, "*Sahelanthropus* or '*Sahelpithecus*'?" *Nature* 419 (2002):581–82.

31. B. Senut, M. Pickford, D. Gommery, P. Mein, K. Cheboi, and Y. Coppens, "First hominid from the Miocene (Lukeino Formation, Kenya)," *Comptes Rendus de l'Academie de Sciences* 332 (2001):137–44.

Chapter 5. Boy Brain, Girl Brain

1. Sperry's Nobel Prize was shared with David Hubel and Torsten Wiesel, who did pioneering work on brain structures involved in the visual system.

2. R. W. Sperry, "Mental unity following surgical disconnection of the cerebral hemispheres," in *The Harvey Lecture Series,* vol. 62 (New York: Academic Press, 1968).

3. R. W. Sperry, "Consciousness, personal identity, and the divided brain," public lecture presented at the Smithsonian Institution, 1977. Also in D. F. Benson and E. Zaidel, eds., *The Dual Brain* (New York: The Guilford Press, 1985), 11–26; see p. 17.

4. For a review of these and other techniques, see S. Springer and G. Deutsch, *Left Brain, Right Brain* (New York: W. H. Freeman, 1998) and J. McGlone, "Sex differences in human brain asymmetry: A critical survey," *Behavioral and Brain Sciences* 3 (1980):215–63.

5. For reviews, see D. Falk, "Hominid brain evolution and the origins of music," in N. L. Wallin, B. Merker, and S. Brown, eds., *The Origins of Music* (Cambridge: MIT Press, 2000), 197–216; D. Falk, "Brain lateralization in primates and its evolution in hominids," *Yearbook of Physical Anthropology* 30 (1987):107–25.

6. As I prepare this edition of *Braindance,* a "target article" that will be published in *Behavioral and Brain Sciences* about the importance of motherese for prelinguistic evolution has just undergone international peer commentary. This

manuscript ("Prelinguistic evolution in early hominins: Whence motherese?") initially underwent more extensive refereeing than anything else that I have ever written, and I was surprised at the strength of some of the negative reviews from linguists. As discussed in my response to the commentaries ("The 'Putting the baby down' hypothesis: Bipedalism, babbling, and baby slings"), most (but not all) of the commentators now support the hypothesis that the way mothers universally speak to their babies (motherese) is not only important for language development in infants today, but was also important for the evolution of language in the first place.

7. For details, see N. Geschwind and A. M. Galaburda, *Cerebral Lateralization: Biological Mechanisms, Associations, and Pathology* (Cambridge: MIT Press, 1987).

8. J. E. Bogen, concluding overview in A. G. Reeves, ed., *Epilepsy and the Corpus Callosum* (New York: Plenum Press, 1985), 515–24; see p. 518.

9. S. M. Ferguson, M. Rayport, and W. S. Corrie, "Neuropsychiatric observations on behavioral consequences of corpus callosum section for seizure control," in Reeves (reference 8, chapter 5), 501–14; see p. 504.

10. For discussion, see Sperry (reference 3, chapter 5).

11. A number of studies report different lateralization patterns for musicians and nonmusicians, and there is some evidence that musically sophisticated listeners utilize their left hemispheres to recognize melody. This literature is reviewed in Falk (2000), "Hominid brain evolution and the origins of music," (reference 5, chapter 5).

12. Sperry, (reference 3, chapter 5), 23.

13. For a recent treatment of consciousness and the brain see J. Keenan, G. G. Gallup, and D. Falk, *The Face in the Mirror* (New York: Harper Collins, 2003).

14. J. Hyde, E. Fennema, and S. J. Lamon, "Gender differences in mathematics performance: A meta-analysis," *Psychological Bulletin* 107 (1990):139–55.

15. Reviewed in Falk (2000), "Hominid brain evolution and the origins of music," (reference 5, chapter 5).

16. This figure was provided courtesy of Roland Guay. For more information, see R. Guay and E. McDaniel, "Correlates of performance on spatial aptitude tests," Final Report, grant No. DAHC 19-77-G-0019 (Alexandria, Va.: U. S. Army Research Institute for the Behavior and Social Sciences, 1978). The answer to the task is B.

17. H. Pakkenberg and J. Voight, "Brain weight of the Danes," *Acta Anatomica* 56 (1964):297–307.

18. Detailed in D. Falk, N. Froese, D. Sade and B. Dudek, "Sex differences in brain/body relationships of rhesus monkeys and humans," *Journal of Human Evolution* 36 (1999):233–38. Some of the most important work in this area is reported in C. D. Ankney, "Sex differences in relative brain size: The mismeasure of woman, too?" *Intelligence* 16 (1992):329–36.

19. For further discussion of these differences, see D. Falk, "The evolution of sex differences in primate brains," in D. Falk and K. Gibson, eds., *Evolutionary*

Anatomy of the Primate Cerebral Cortex (Cambridge, Cambridge University Press, 2001), 98–112; "Brain evolution in females: An answer to Mr. Lovejoy," in L. D. Hager, ed., *Women in Human Evolution* (New York, Routledge, 1997), 114–36; and M. Hines, "Gonadal hormones and human cognitive development," in J. Balthazart, ed., *Hormones, Brains, and Behaviour, Comparative Physiology* 8 (1990):51–63. See also L. S. Allen, M. Hines, J. E. Shryne, and R. A. Gorski, "Two sexually dimorphic cell groups in the human brain," *The Journal of Neuroscience* 9 (1989):497–506. Various measurements of another area of the brain, the corpus callosum, have been reported to be larger in females than males, although these reports have been questioned by S. F. Witelson and D. L. Kigar, "Neuroanatomical aspects of hemisphere specialization in humans," in D. Ottoson, ed., *Duality and Unity of the Brain,* Proceedings of an International Symposium at the Wenner-Gren Center, Stockholm, May 29–31, 1986 (New York: Macmillan, 1987), 466–95.

20. R. C. Gur, B. I. Turetsky, M. Matsui, M. Yan, W. Bilker, P. Hughett, and R. E. Gur, "Sex differences in brain gray and white matter in healthy young adults: Correlations with cognitive performance," *The Journal of Neuroscience* 19 (1999): 4065–72.

21. J. McGlone (reference 4, chapter 5).

22. D. Kimura, "Sex differences in cerebral organization for speech and praxic functions," *Canadian Journal of Psychology* 37 (1983):19–35; D. Kimura and R. A. Harshman, "Sex differences in brain organization for verbal and nonverbal functions," *Progress in Brain Research* 61 (1984):423–41. See, however, another study that presents evidence against an intrahemispheric sex difference: A. Kertesz and T. Benke, "Sex equality in intrahemispheric language organization," *Brain and Language* 37 (1989):401–8.

23. For information about petalias see M. LeMay, "Morphological cerebral asymmetries of modern man, fossil man, and nonhuman primates," *Annals of the New York Academy of Sciences* 280 (1976):349–60; A. M. Galaburda, M. LeMay, T. L. Kemper, and N. Geschwind, "Right-left asymmetries in the brain," *Science* 199 (1978):852–56. LeMay's findings were confirmed by D. Bear, D. Schiff, J. Saver, M. Greenberg, and R. Freeman, "Quantitative analysis of cerebral asymmetries," *Archives of Neurology* 43 (1986):598–603. The finding of more reversals in the pattern of petalias for women by Bear and his colleagues is in keeping with still another study that reported more reversals for women from the normal pattern of a longer left temporal plane: J. A. Wada, R. Clark, and A. Hamm, "Cerebral hemisphere asymmetry in humans," *Archives of Neurology* 32 (1975):239–46.

24. Kimura and Hampson reported their findings at the November 1988 meeting of the Society for Neurosciences, in Toronto. See E. Hampson and D. Kimura, "Reciprocal effects of hormonal fluctuations on human motor and perceptual-spatial skills," *Behavioral Neuroscience* 102 (1988):456–59.

25. S. A. Berenbaum and M. Hines, "Early androgens are related to childhood sex-typed toy preferences," *Psychological Science* 3 (1992):203–6.

26. M. Hines, (reference 19, chapter 5), 51–63.

27. P. Flor-Henry, "Functional hemispheric asymmetry and psychopathology," *Integrated Psychiatry* 1 (1983):46–52.

28. D. Falk, L. Konigsberg, C. Helmkamp, J. Cheverud, M. Vannier, and C. Hildebolt, "Endocranial suture closure in rhesus macaques (*Macaca mulatta*)," *American Journal of Physical Anthropology* 80 (1989):417–28; L. Konigsberg, D. Falk, C. Hildebolt, M. Vannier, J. Cheverud, and C. Helmkamp, "External brain morphology in rhesus macaques (*Macaca mulatta*)," *Journal of Human Evolution* 19 (1990):269–84; A. Masters, D. Falk, and T. Gage, "Effects of age and gender on the location and orientation of the foramen magnum in rhesus macaques (*Macaca mulatta*)," *American Journal of Physical Anthropology* 86 (1991):75–80.

29. R. Weiss, "Women's skills linked to estrogen levels," *Science News* 134 (1988):341.

30. T. E. Robinson, J. B. Becker, D. M. Camp, and A. Mansour, "Variation in the pattern of behavioral and brain asymmetries due to sex differences," in S. D. Glick, ed., *Cerebral Lateralization in Nonhuman Species* (New York: Academic Press, 1985), 185–231; see p. 195.

31. Parts of this section were published in K. Gibson and T. Ingold, eds., *Tools, Language and Intelligence in Human Evolution,* (New York: Cambridge University Press, 1993).

32. S. J. Gaulin, R. W. FitzGerald, and M. S. Wartell, "Sex differences in spatial ability and activity in two vole species (*M. ochrogaster* and *M. pennsylvanicus*)," *Journal of Comparative Psychology* 104 (1990):88–93; S. J. C. Gaulin and R. W. FitzGerald, "Home-range size as a predictor of mating systems in *Microtus*," *Journal of Mammalogy* 69 (1988):311–19; "Sexual selection for spatial-learning ability," *Animal Behavior* 37 (1989):322–31.

33. F. Nottebohm, "Asymmetries in neural control of vocalization in the canary," in S. Harnad, R. Doty, L. Goldstein, J. Jaynes, and G. Krauthamer, eds., *Lateralization in the Nervous System* (New York: Academic Press, 1977), 23–44; "From bird song to neurogenesis," *Scientific American,* February 1989:74–79.

34. For discussion, see D. Falk, N. Froese, D. Sade, and B. Dudek, "Sex differences in brain/body relationships of rhesus monkeys and humans," *Journal of Human Evolution* 36 (1999):233–38. Other relevant work is reported in D. Falk, C. Hildebolt, J. Cheverud, M. Vannier, R. C. Helmkamp, and L. Konigsberg, "Cortical asymmetries in frontal lobes of rhesus monkeys (*Macaca mulatta*)," *Brain Research* 512 (1990):40–45.

35. T. Wynn, *The Evolution of Spatial Competence,* (Champaign-Urbana: University of Illinois Press, 1989).

36. Gotcha! Two things to remember: (1) Genes that are selected for in one sex are extremely likely to affect the other, and (2) there is a huge amount of "overlap" in the abilities of males and females.

1. D. C. Johanson, "Ethiopia yields first 'family' of early man," *National Geographic* 150 (1976):790–811.

2. D. C. Johanson and M. Taieb, "Plio-Pleistocene hominid discoveries in Hadar, Ethiopia," *Nature* 260 (1976):293–97.

3. Museum specimens are typically given identifications that indicate the museum and/or location where they were found. Thus, KNM-ER stands for Kenya National Museums, East Rudolf; KNM-WT indicates the same museum but a West Turkana site; and OH means Olduvai Hominin.

4. For information regarding climate and habitat at Hadar, see R. Bonnefille, A. Vincens, and G. Buchet, "Palynology, stratigraphy and paleoenvironment of a Pliocene hominid site (2.9–3.0 M.Y.) at Hadar, Ethiopia," *Palaeogeography, Palaeoclimatology, Palaeoecology* 60 (1987):249–81. For information about Laetoli, see R. Bonnefille and G. Riollet, "Palynological spectra from the upper Laetolil beds," in M. D. Leakey and J. M. Harris, eds., *Laetoli, A Pliocene Site in Northern Tanzania* (Oxford: Clarendon Press, 1987), 52–61.

5. *International Code of Zoological Nomenclature*, 2nd ed. (London: International Trust for Zoological Nomenclature, 1964). (There is now a fourth edition of the code, published in 2000, but the second edition was in use at the time *Australopithecus afarensis* was named.)

6. D. C. Johanson, T. D. White, and Y. Coppens, "A new species of the genus *Australopithecus* (Primates: Hominidae) from the Pliocene of eastern Africa," *Kirtlandia* 28 (1978):1–14; see p. 8.

7. N. T. Boaz, F. C. Howell, and M. L. McCrossin, "Faunal age of the Usno, Shungura B and Hadar Formations, Ethiopia," *Nature* 300 (1982):633–35.

8. D. C. Johanson and T. D. White, "A systematic assessment of early African hominids," *Science* 203 (1979):321–30.

9. For examples, see letters from M. H. Day, M. D. Leakey, and T. R. Olson; and from R. E. F. Leakey and A. Walker, "On the status of *Australopithecus afarensis*," *Science* 207 (1980):1102–3.

10. For a relatively recent tabulation of O/M sinuses see D. Falk, T. Gage, B. Dudek, and T. R. Olson, "Did more than one species of hominid coexist before 3.0 ma?: Evidence from blood and teeth," *Journal of Human Evolution* 29 (1995):591–600. To give credit where it is due, Tobias first described the O/M sinus system in robust australopithecines in his classic monograph on *Zinjanthropus*. See P. V. Tobias, *Olduvai Gorge*, vol. 2 (New York: Cambridge University Press, 1967). Holloway was the first to note that an O/M sinus system is also present in the Hadar fossil material in R. L. Holloway, "The endocast of the Omo juvenile L338y-6 hominid specimen," *American Journal of Physical Anthropology* 54 (1981):109–18.

11. H. Browning, "The confluence of dural venous sinuses," *American Journal of Anatomy* 93 (1953):307–29.

12. D. Johanson and J. Shreeve, *Lucy's Child* (New York: William Morrow, 1989), p. 117.

13. For example, Kimbel and White's discussion of O/M sinuses in W. H. Kimbel and T. D. White, "Variation, sexual dimorphism and the taxonomy of *Australopithecus*," in F. Grine, ed., *Evolutionary History of the "Robust" Australopithecines* (New York: Plenum Press, 1988), 175–92, consisted of the following: "Falk and Conroy's conclusions based on cranial venous flow patterns have been critically examined in other publications (Kimbel, 1984; Kimbel et al., 1985) and will not be addressed here" (p. 186).

Turning to the 1985 publication that they cite above, W. H. Kimbel, T. C. White, and D. C. Johanson, "Craniodental morphology of the hominids from Hadar and Laetoli: Evidence of '*Paranthropus*' and *Homo* in the mid-Pliocene for eastern Africa?" in E. Delson, ed., *Ancestors: The Hard Evidence* (New York: Alan R. Liss, 1985), 120–37, for their critical examination of the cranial blood flow evidence, we read: "Detailed discussions of venous drainage patterns and their value for hominid phylogeny reconstruction are available elsewhere (Falk and Conroy, 1983; Kimbel, 1984) and are therefore not reiterated here" (p. 36).

Finally, in the 1984 article they cite, Kimbel sums up the view from Johanson's camp but, contrary to the assertions quoted above, he does so without reference to or discussion of the evidence discussed by Conroy and me regarding cranial blood flow: W. H. Kimbel, "Variation in the pattern of cranial venous sinuses and hominid phylogeny," *American Journal of Physical Anthropology* 63 (1984):243–63.

14. Ibid., 243.

15. Johanson and Shreeve (reference 12, chapter 6), 122.

16. Actually, the specimen was discovered in 1985, but the discovery was not published until 1986 (see next reference).

17. A. Walker, R. E. Leakey, J. M. Harris, and F. H. Brown, "2.5-Myr *Australopithecus boisei* from west of Lake Turkana, Kenya," *Nature* 322 (1986):517–22.

18. See D. Falk, "Hominid evolution (letter)," *Science* 234 (1986):11.

19. For a wonderfully written review article, read R. H. Tuttle, "What's new in African paleoanthropology?" *Annual Review of Anthropology* 17 (1988):391–426; see p. 397.

20. Most of these taxa are discussed in A. Gibbons, "In search of the first hominids," *Science* 295 (2002):1214–19; (quote from Alan Walker on p. 1219).

21. B. Asfaw, T. White, O. Lovejoy, B. Latimer, S. Simpson, and G. Suwa, "*Australopithecus garhi:* A new species of early hominid from Ethiopia," *Science* 284 (1999):629–35.

22. T. White, "Early hominids—diversity or distortion?" *Science* 299 (2003): 1994–97 (quotations from p. 1994).

23. M. G. Leakey, F. Spoor, F. H. Brown, P. N. Gathogo, C. Kiarie, L. N. Leakey, and I. McDougall, "New hominin genus from eastern Africa shows diverse middle Pliocene lineages," *Nature* 410 (2001):433–40.

24. T. D. White, G. Suwa, and B. Asfaw, "*Australopithecus ramidus,* a new species of early hominid from Aramis, Ethiopia," *Nature* 371 (1994):306–12.

25. T. D. White, G. Suwa, and B. Asfaw, "Corrigendum *Australopithecus*

ramidus, a new species of early hominid from Aramis, Ethiopia," *Nature* 375 (1995):88.

26. C. Holden, "Another human ancestor steps out," *Science* 267 (1995):618.

27. Quotation from p. 1216 of reference 20 (this chapter).

28. R. R. Skelton, H. M. McHenry, and G. M. Drawhorn, "Phylogenetic analysis of early hominids," *Current Anthropology* 27 (1986):21–43.

29. F. C. Howell, foreword to *Evolutionary History of the "Robust" Australopithecines*, ed. F. Grine (New York: Aldine de Gruyter, 1988), xii.

30. L. S. B. Leakey, P. V. Tobias, and J. R. Napier, "A new species of the genus *Homo* from Olduvai Gorge," *Nature* 202 (1964):7–10.

31. B. Wood, "Origin and evolution of the genus *Homo*," *Nature* 355 (1992):783–90.

32. B. Wood and M. Collard, "The human genus," *Science* 284 (1999):65–71.

33. F. Brown, J. Harris, R. Leakey, and A. Walker, "Early *Homo erectus* skeleton from west Lake Turkana, Kenya," *Nature* 316 (1985):788–92.

34. B. Asfaw, W. H. Gilbert, Y. Beyene, W. K. Hart, P. R. Renne, G. WoldeGabriel, E. S. Vrba, and T. White, "Remains of *Homo erectus* from Bouri, Middle Awash, Ethiopia," *Nature* 416 (2002):317–20.

35. D. C. Johanson, F. T. Masao, G. G. Eck, T. D. White, R. C. Walter, W. H. Kimbel, B. Asfaw, P. Manega, P. Ndessokia, and G. Suwa, "New partial skeleton of *Homo habilis* from Olduvai Gorge, Tanzania," *Nature* 327 (1987):205–9.

36. Ibid., 209

Chapter 7. Cranial Radiators and Evolutionary Cacti

1. Whenever possible, presence or absence of the posterior condyloid, mastoid, occipital, and parietal foramina were determined. I also observed whether or not hypoglossal canals were single or divided and, of course, if an enlarged O/M sinus was present or absent. My raw data and analysis can be found in D. Falk, "Evolution of cranial blood drainage in hominids: Enlarged occipital/marginal sinuses and emissary foramina," *American Journal of Physical Anthropology* 70 (1986):311–24. For a relatively recent tabulation of O/M sinuses in larger samples of australopithecines see D. Falk, T. Gage, B. Dudek, and T. R. Olson, "Did more than one species of hominid coexist before 3.0 ma?: Evidence from blood and teeth," *Journal of Human Evolution* 29 (1995):591–600.

2. An earlier, stimulating study by G. I. Boyd showed that emissary foramina occurred in much lower frequencies in apes than in humans: "The emissary foramina of the cranium in man and the anthropoids," *Journal of Anatomy* 65 (1930):108–21. Boyd's study was influential in my decision to pursue emissary foramina in the hominin fossil record. Sometimes there's gold in old, nearly forgotten journal articles!

3. M. A. Baker, "A brain-cooling system in mammals," *Scientific American* 240 (1979):130–39; see p. 136.

4. M. Cabanac and H. Brinnel, "Blood flow in the emissary veins of the human head during hyperthermia," *European Journal of Applied Physiology* 54 (1985):172–76.

5. In response to my target article, several workers raised questions (in open peer commentary) about whether or not an extensive cranial radiator of veins really existed: D. Falk, "Brain evolution in *Homo:* The 'radiator' theory," *Behavioral and Brain Sciences* 13 (1990):333–81. For a landmark article that subsequently demonstrated the anatomical basis for selective brain cooling in humans (i.e., the radiator), see W. Zenker and S. Kubik, "Brain cooling in humans: anatomical considerations," *Anatomical Embryology* 193 (1996):1–13.

6. A. L. Zihlman and B. A. Cohn, "Responses of hominid skin to the savanna," *Suid-Afrikaase Tydskrif vir Wetenskap* 82 (1986):89–90; "The adaptive response of human skin to the savanna," *Human Evolution* 3 (1988):397–409.

7. Assertions continue to crop up that some newly discovered robust australopithecine skulls lack an enlarged O/M sinus. For example, this claim was made for a specimen from Konso, Ethiopia (see G. Suwa et al., "The first skull of *Australopithecus boisei*," *Nature* 389 [1997]:489–92). When I looked into the matter, however, I learned that the specimen lacked both sides of the part of the skull needed to score presence or absence of the O/M sinus. This is important because the sinus is often present on only one side. Specimens that do not have both sides of this region are therefore unscorable (unless, of course, they have the feature on the side that is present). Furthermore, because robust australopithecines can have both O/M and transverse/sigmoid venous drainage patterns, presence of the latter does *not* preclude the former, as some have asserted.

8. Variation that includes some australopithecine-like features is described for this material in A. Vekua et al., "A new skull of early *Homo* from Dmanisi, Georgia," *Science* 297 (2002):85–89; M. Balter and A. Gibbons, "Were 'little people' the first to venture out of Africa?" *Science* 297 (2002):26–27. See also L. Gabunia et al., "Earliest Pleistocene hominid cranial remains from Dmanisi, Republic of Georgia: Taxonomy, geological setting, and age," *Science* 288 (2000):1019–25; M. Balter and A. Gibbons, "A glimpse of humans' first journey out of Africa," *Science* 288 (2000):948–50.

9. See chapter 6, reference 34.

10. G. C. Conroy, "Speciosity in the early *Homo* lineage: Too many, too few, or just about right?" *Journal of Human Evolution* 43 (2002):759–66.

11. C. C. Swisher et al., "Latest *Homo erectus* of Java: Potential contemporaneity with *Homo sapiens* in southeast Asia," *Science* 274 (1996):1870–74.

12. T. White et al., "Pleistocene *Homo sapiens* from Middle Awash, Ethiopia," *Nature* 423 (2003):742–47.

13. The interested reader is referred to C. L. Brace, *The Stages of Human Evolution*, 5th ed. (Englewood Cliffs, N. J.: Prentice-Hall, 1995).

14. A. R. Templeton, "Out of Africa again and again," *Nature* 416 (2002):45–51; quotation from page 50.

15. C. B. Stringer and R. Grün, "Time for the last Neandertals," *Nature* 351 (1991):701–2.

16. J. E. Pfeiffer, *The Creative Explosion* (New York: Harper and Row, 1982). For a different view, see C. B. Stringer, "The emergence of modern humans," *Scientific American,* December 1990:98–104.

Chapter 8. Braindance

1. K. Zilles, E. Armstrong, A. Schleicher, and H. J. Kretschmann, "The human pattern of gyrification in the cerebral cortex," *Anatomy and Embryology* 179 (1988):173–79.

2. K. Amunts, A. Schleicher, U. Burgel, H. Mohlberg, H. B. M. Uylings, and K. Zilles, "Broca's region revisited: Cytoarchitecture and intersubject variability," *The Journal of Comparative Neurology* 412 (1999):319–41; A. B. Scheibel, L. A. Paul, I. Fried, A. B. Forsythe, U. Tomiyasu, A. Wechsler, A. Kao, and J. Slotnick, "Dendritic organization of the anterior speech area," *Experimental Neurology* 87 (1985):109–17.

3. B. L. Finlay and R. B. Darlington, "Linked regularities in the development and evolution of mammalian brains," *Science* 268 (1995):1578–84.

4. For a review of the relevant literature see D. Falk, "The evolution of sex differences in primate brains," in D. Falk and K. Gibson, eds., *Evolutionary Anatomy of the Primate Cerebral Cortex* (Cambridge: Cambridge University Press, 2001), 98–112.

5. My friend William Calvin has a somewhat different theory about the evolution of neurobiological sequencers, which he believes resulted from selection for throwing ability. Read his *A Brain For All Seasons* (Chicago: University of Chicago Press, 2002).

6. J. Keenan, G. G. Gallup, and D. Falk, *The Face in the Mirror* (New York: Harper Collins, 2003); J. D. Maser and G. G. Gallup, "Theism as a by-product of natural selection," *Journal of Religion* 70 (1990):515–32.

7. W. Kohler, *The Mentality of Apes* (London: Routledge and Kegan Paul, 1925; New York: Liveright, 1976), p. 145 of 1976 ed.

8. Maser and Gallup (reference 6, this chapter), 14.

9. Ibid., 19.

10. However, not everyone agrees with this interpretation, as shown by P. G. Bahn, "Eating people is wrong," *Nature* 348 (1990):395. In fact, interpretation of evidence that is theoretically associated with cannibalism in the fossil record is one of those controversial topics that has as many naysayers as advocates.

11. D. R. Harris, "Aboriginal subsistence in a tropical rain forest environment: food procurement, cannibalism, and population regulation in northeastern Australia," in M. Harris and E. B. Ross, eds., *Food and Evolution* (Philadelphia: Temple University Press, 1987), 357–85; see p. 372.

12. A. Lawler, "Writing gets a rewrite," *Science* 292 (2001):2418–20.

13. D. Falk, "Implications of the evolution of writing for the origin of language:

Can a paleoneurologist find happiness in the Neolithic?" Proceedings of NATO Advanced Study Institute, in B. Chiarelli, P. Lieberman, and J. Wind, eds., *The Origins of Human Language* (The Netherlands: Kluwer Academic Press, 1991).

14. D. Schmandt-Besserat, *How Writing Came About* (Austin: University of Texas Press, 1996); "Oneness, twoness, threeness; How ancient accountants invented numbers," *The Sciences* 20 (1987):44–48; "The earliest precursor of writing," *Scientific American* 238 (1978):51–59.

15. See also Alexander Marshack's discussion about Paleolithic art: "Hierarchical Evolution of the Human Capacity: The Paleolithic Evidence." Fifty-fourth James Arthur Lecture on the Evolution of the Human Brain (New York: American Museum of Natural History, 1985).

16. R. Lewin, *In the Age of Mankind* (Washington, D.C.: Smithsonian Books, 1988), 142–43.

17. The urgency of these issues is underscored in an important article by P. R. Ehrlich and E. O. Wilson (*Science* 253 [1991]:758–62): Almost 40 percent of all the food supply for all land animals and decomposers is "used, coopted, or forgone" because of *Homo sapiens*. This is causing an alarming rate of extinction of species that live on land. Furthermore, since the human population is expected to reach more than ten billion people by 2040, a five- to tenfold increase in global economic activity will be required to meet human needs. The authors conclude that "The indispensable strategy for saving our fellow living creatures and ourselves in the long run, is, as the evidence compellingly shows, to reduce the scale of human activities. The task of accomplishing this goal will involve a cooperative worldwide effort unprecedented in history. Unless humanity can move determinedly in that direction, all of the efforts now going into in situ conservation, will eventually lead nowhere, and our descendants' future will be at risk" (761).

18. E. Armstrong, "The limbic system and culture," *Human Nature* 2 (1991): 117–36; E. Armstrong, M. R. Clarke, E. M. Hill, "Relative size of the anterior thalamic nuclei differentiates anthropoids by social system," *Brain, Behavior and Evolution* 30 (1987):263–71.

Chapter 9. Brainwar

1. Provided by Lauren Gage, when she was six years old.

2. For an excellent treatment, see Meredith Small, ed., *Female Primates: Studies by Women Primatologists* (New York: Alan R. Liss, 1984). Jane Lancaster's introduction is especially insightful.

3. Sara Blaffer Hrdy is responsible for this idea. It is unfortunate that her work is frequently excluded from women's studies. Read *The Woman That Never Evolved: With a New Preface and Bibliographical Updates* (Cambridge: Harvard University Press, 1999).

4. Much of the information in this section is taken from Goodall's wonderful volume, *The Chimpanzees of Gombe, Patterns of Behavior* (Cambridge: Belknap Press, 1986).

5. Ibid., 272.

6. F. de Waal, *Peacemaking Among Primates* (Cambridge: Harvard University Press, 1989).

7. Ibid., 65–66.

8. Ibid., 238–39.

9. As I write this sentence, I hear a "yeah, but" from the cultural determinists! True, the other species of chimpanzee, the bonobo or pygmy chimpanzee, has been noted for its remarkable gentleness. However, as de Waal points out (reference 6, this chapter, p. 221), this same opinion prevailed about common chimpanzees until two decades ago. Compared to common chimpanzees, pygmy chimpanzees have barely been studied. Furthermore, de Waal notes that an astonishing number of bonobos lack fingers, toes, or hands, and he suggests that this may be linked with aggression.

10. B. M. Knauft, "Reconsidering violence in simple human societies," *Current Anthropology* 28 (1987):457–500.

11. Ibid., 466.

12. At the 1986 business meeting of the American Anthropological Association (AAA), members unanimously passed a proposed resolution endorsing the Seville Statement on Violence. The Seville Statement was drafted by a committee of scientists from various disciplines and nations at a meeting on May 16, 1986, sponsored by the Spanish National UNESCO Commission. The text of the AAA resolution reads in part:

> The propositions are: (1) It is scientifically incorrect to say that we have inherited a tendency to make war from our animal ancestors. (2) It is scientifically incorrect to say that war or any other violent behavior is genetically programmed into our human nature. (3) It is scientifically incorrect to say that in the course of human evolution there has been a selection for aggressive behavior more than for other kinds of behavior. (4) It is scientifically incorrect to say that humans have a "violent brain." (5) It is scientifically incorrect to say that war is caused by "instinct" or any other single motivation. The Statement on Violence concludes that humanity is not condemned to war by biology, but to the contrary, humanity is capable of investing in peace, as well as war.
>
> Because of widespread pessimism about the possibilities of reducing interpersonal violence and/or implementing nonviolent alternatives to war, the Statement on Violence merits wide circulation and discussion. Anthropologists and others are requested to reflect upon how they might use, or expand upon, the Statement on Violence in their various roles as teachers, researchers, consultants, and citizens.

Subsequently, the resolution was submitted to a mail ballot of the full AAA membership, where it passed. Although the resolution was clearly well intended, I voted against it because proposition 1 is probably false, and propositions 2 through 4 have not yet been tested sufficiently to permit specific statements about what is or is not scientifically incorrect. (Proposition 5, however, appears valid.)

However, as of 2004, the AAA resolution continues to reflect current thinking among social anthropologists, namely an abhorrence of the possibility that our species might be biologically predisposed to aggression. Of course, many biological anthropologists (including this one) suspect otherwise. If we are right, no amount of resolving or asserting is going to change matters. On the other hand, understanding and dealing directly with the truth might. Ironically, this paradigmatic difference between subdisciplines of anthropology has itself had a long history of stimulating aggressive and emotional academic exchanges. Although the topic of nature versus nurture is a touchy one for anthropologists and for other social scientists, it is, of course, based largely on a false dichotomy. For humans, there can be no nature without nurture, nor nurture without nature. Both are crucial, and it is just plain silly to argue otherwise.

13. M. Daly and M. Wilson, *Homicide (Foundations of Human Behavior)* (New York: Aldine de Gruyter, 1988).

14. Ibid., 24.

15. Ibid., 128.

16. Although this section reads like science fiction, it's not. Much of its content is taken from an August 7, 1989, *U.S. News and World Report* cover story, "America's Doomsday Project," by Stevan Emerson.

17. The information presented here is taken from an article by Robert C. Toth of the *Los Angeles Times,* published in the July 23, 1989, issue of the *Sunday Times Union,* Albany, N.Y.

18. This information is from a *Los Angeles Times* article published in the *Sunday Times Union,* Albany, N.Y., on February 11, 1990.

19. D. Malakoff, "New nukes revive old debate," *Science* 301 (2003):32–34; P. Webster, "Russia revives sagging research program," *Science* 301 (2003):34.

20. H. Hoag, "Remote control," *Nature* 423 (2003):797–98.

21. M. Rees, *Our Final Hour: A Scientist's Warning: How Terror, Error, and Environmental Disaster Threatens Humankind's Future in this Century—On Earth and Beyond* (New York: Basic Books, 2003).

22. The U.S. House of Representatives declined a wise investment when it voted to eliminate all funding for the search for extraterrestrial intelligence (SETI) from NASA's 1991 budget. Fortunately, these funds were subsequently restored. According to a report by Richard Kerr (*Nature* 249 [1990]:249–50), the technology now exists to develop an instrument that could monitor 20 million radio channels every second, and for a "relatively cheap price tag" at that. Although admittedly it's a long shot, confirmation of a "them" out there would not hurt the cause of terrestrial unification.

23. Goodall (reference 4, chapter 9), 534.

INDEX

Social behavior, 62, 63, 66, 71, 82, 96, 99, 116, 119
  australopithecines, 25
  baboons, 202–4
  CA (common ancestor), 98
  chimpanzees, 23, 84, 96, 163, 205, 209, 220
  gorillas, 96
  hominins, 21, 96
  See also Aggression, Body language, Grooming, Limbic system
Speech, evolution of. *See* Language
Sperry, Roger, 104–6, 110, 111
Split-brain. *See* Brain lateralization
Splitters/Splitomania, 16, 19, 138, 143, 166, 171
Sterkfontein fossils, 15, 16, 127
Strait, David, 85, 86
Stringer, Christopher, 177
Stuttering, 117
Sultan (chimpanzee), 184
Sumerians, 188, 190
Sweat glands/sweating, 96, 158, 159, 162, 163, 169
Sylvian fissure, 59, 61, 69

Taieb, Maurice, 129
Tanner, Nancy, 93–94
Tap dancing, 73–78
Tardieu, Christine, 137, 144
Taung
  apelike features, 3, 5, 15, 40, 44
  Australopithecus africanus, 13, 14
  child, 11, 13, 15, 20
  cranial capacity, 14
  CT scans, 15
  digital measurements, 40, 42–44
  endocast of, 5, 11, 29, 30, 31, 32–35, 40–41, 42–45, 48
  humanlike features, 3, 5, 11, 13, 14, 31–33, 44
  initial discovery, 11, 19
  lambdoid suture/lunate sulcus confusion, 31–35
  man-ape vs. ape-man, 13
  missing link, 11, 15
  O/M sinus of, 20, 133

Teeth. *See* Dentition
Temperature regulation
  brain, 26, 160
  thermoregulation, 96, 160
  whole-body cooling, 96
  See also Radiator hypothesis
Templeton, Alan, 174–76
Temporal lobes of the brain, 47, 59, 61, 67, 68, 114
Terblanche, Gert, 16
Territorial Imperative, 200
Territoriality, 24, 122, 200, 201, 211, 220, 221
Testosterone, 116–18
Time
  binding of, 65
  left hemisphere and, 77, 182–83
  perception of, 183
  prefrontal cortex and, 63, 65, 70
  sequencing of, 65
  See also Tap dancing
Tobias, Phillip, 20, 31, 41, 45, 51, 131–32, 147
Tools
  australopithecines and tool-use, 18, 19, 171
  chimpanzees and tool-use, 204
  first, 92, 93
  gorillas and, 26
  hominins and, 91
  Homo erectus and, 172
  Homo habilis and, 145
  monkeys and, 56
  Neandertals and, 177
  Olduwan tools, 19, 145
  Paleolithic stone tools, 178
  stone tools, 7, 19, 51, 90, 91, 124, 171, 187
  tool production, 51, 89–91, 124–25, 182
  See also "2001" model
Toth, Nicholas, 187
Toumai ("Hope of Life"). *See* *Sahelanthropus tchadensis*
Transvaal Museum, 19, 27, 28
"Treetop," 216–19
Tugen hills, Kenya, 101
Turkana Boy. *See* KNM WT 15000

Dean Falk is professor of anthropology at Florida State University and honorary professor of human biology at the University of Vienna. Over the last twenty-five years her research has focused on early hominins, brain evolution, comparative neuroanatomy, and cognitive evolution (including language origins). Professor Falk became an elected fellow of the American Association for the Advancement of Science in 2000, and received the Austrian Decoration of Honor for Science and Art First Class in 2003.